VOICES OF CONCERN

VOICES OF CONCERN

Critical Studies in
Church of Christism

Edited by

Robert Meyers

MISSION MESSENGER
139 SIGNAL HILL DRIVE
SAINT LOUIS, MISSOURI 63121

PUBLISHED BY MISSION MESSENGER
SAINT LOUIS, MISSOURI

PRINTED IN THE UNITED STATES OF AMERICA

To the thousands of concerned ones in
the Churches of Christ
whose voices can never be heard we dedicate
these
"Voices of Concern"

TABLE OF CONTENTS

INTRODUCTORY

Any dynamic group expects criticism from the outside, but criticism from within is a shockingly different matter. A man's business acquaintances may chide him without real effect, but the strictures of his wife can be an intolerable thorn in the flesh. It is like this with religious groups. So long as the rebukes come only from beyond the party walls, some degree of reason tempers the response and the opposition is likely to get courteous, if cool, treatment. But when the criticism comes from one's own fellows and near kin, emotions may be harder to control.

Some of us within the Church of Christ segment of the Restoration movement, and some recently out of it, have felt it imperative to analyze its failures. This anthology of essays is a criticism of a religious way of life. It is written by men who have remained within the Church of Christ, or by those who have felt they had to seek wider fellowship but still love dearly the people they left behind.

In such an enterprise malice and vindictiveness have no place. The world has too much of both without our adding more. Each contributor to this book was told that his study of Church of Christ short-comings had, above all else, to be compassionate. It has not been our intention to vent spleen, but to expose an unacknowledged disease in the body of a living thing which we love. We criticize not because criticism is a stimulant without which we cannot be happy, but in hope of improvement of a fine people.

For those Church of Christ readers who will, we hope, read this book, we offer what may be the most important of our prefatory comments. Although several writers here represented have left the Church of Christ segment of Christendom, there is no intent to urge a similar exodus for everyone else. Most sensi-

tive men who depart from a childhood church wish
they might never have had to do so. This book pleads
with the Church of Christ to spare such men the agonies of separation by creating an atmosphere in which
independent minds may feel at home.

One fact seems too clear for anyone to overlook. As
leaders in all churches are increasingly educated, the
tension between party strictures and the free mind will
increase dramatically. Men trained to study analy-
tically and critically will not be content with unyielding
orthodoxy. They will not submit to coercion. If they
are driven out because they will not conform, the result will be intellectual suicide for the churches losing
them. With thoughtful men excluded, the stalwarts left
behind to guard the walls will be only those who have
never dared challenge any tenets of the system, men
who can be "counted upon," men who are safely
"sound" and "loyal." But knowledge cannot be frozen,
nor the quest squelched, nor the adventure stopped
arbitrarily at some point in time or place. Real
disciples are always on the move toward widening
horizons; they cannot walk permanently with a company whose eyes are turned backwards.

Nothing is clearer than that the Church of Christ,
along with many other religious groups of similar pattern, is losing men it cannot afford to lose. Intellect
alone may be of no value to a Christian group, but intellect wedded to the kind of spirit shown by the essay-
ists in this book provides a commodity too rare in this
world to toss away carelessly.

Many in the Church of Christ are completely unaware of how many intelligent, compassionate Christian men and women have departed from them in
search of freedom from dogma. As a lifelong member
of the Church of Christ I know well the tract racks
laden with pamphlets entitled "WHY I LEFT" and
dealing with converts to the Church of Christ from
Methodism, Mormonism, Presbyterianism, and the

like. But I had no idea how many more might be placed there and entitled WHY I LEFT THE CHURCH OF CHRIST. I have been surprised at the number of unusually capable men and women who have quietly slipped away and are now working in other religious establishments. For every one who agreed to express himself in this book, a dozen other equally gifted persons declined for one reason or another.

I can provide an illustration of what I mean. From one small circle of my friends at Freed-Hardeman College, six of the most intelligent and articulate no longer serve in the Church of Christ, although all of them originally trained for the ministry. One of them is an Episcopal priest. None of them are represented in this book. There are hundreds more like them, graduates of our Christian colleges. Those of us who have compiled this book consider that fact significant enough to bring to the attention of our readers. We feel that emphasis on those who left other churches to come to us and complete disregard of our own talent drain is a dangerous distortion. When we know only this side of the story we are blind to facts and there is an ever-present danger of cultivating a superiority complex at the expense of our religious neighbors. If this book does nothing more than to awaken good Church of Christ members to an ominous, steady drain of talented persons, it will be worthwhile.

Since this collection was conceived and carried through on my initiative, I am the proper person to justify it or to suffer for its failure. If I know my motive, it is this: I believe that a great stirring in the Church of Christ betokens the possibility of a more charitable tomorrow. Thousands are restless and dissatisfied with the aridity of exclusivism and authoritarianism. Bright young minds are refusing to be put off with answers that have no more to commend them than the hoary beard of antiquity.

Such people need an articulation of their feeling of
sterility; they need a voice to help speak what they
sense and to help find words for what they feel. And
they need a guide to healthier outlooks. While this collection was in progress, a young woman came into my
church office seeking help. Near hysteria, this daughter of an orthodox Church of Christ minister had
grown dissatisfied with the cold legalisms of her
church, but her love for her father was immense and
beautiful. Torn terribly between the urgent need to
make a change religiously and the desire to remain in
her father's good graces, she was near prostration.
She doubtless spoke truth when she said in agony, "If
I were to change churches my father would die of a
heart attack. I would kill my father!"

If this book can contribute to an atmosphere in
which such agony need no longer occur, it will be valuable. If it can help a father feel that he may well be
delighted if his child leaves the home church so long
as her motive is a passionate desire to find *for herself*
the highest and holiest way of worship, it will be abid-
ingly useful. It goes forth with that sincere hope from
all of us who had a part in it.

A few of those asked to write felt it would do no
good because those who need the essays most would
never read them. And those who do read, they said,
may read with such bias that they will get no profit.
I can only reply that many people helped me find my
way from one plateau to another because they committed what they thought to print. If one young man,
caught up in the agonies of spiritual travail, desperate
and heartsick at the discrepancy between what he sees
and what he has been taught, reads a single one of
these essays and says, "That's it! That's what I've felt
but been unable to say; I see more clearly now the direction my spiritual journey should take," I shall be
repaid for every hour spent.

Some will wonder about the variety of sentiments

expressed here. It is not only unimportant to us that
we do not agree with each other in every detail; it is,
rather, a matter for rejoicing that in these pages men
who accept Jesus as Lord may speak their minds without restrictions. We consider the variety itself a significant part of the lesson this book would teach. Free
minds cannot be predicted. The Spirit of God really
does move at liberty like the invisible air, and it impels
men in various ways. There are writers here who believe in the principle of Restorationism, and men who
do not; men who believe in what is loosely called
Fundamentalism, and men who do not; men who are
restrained and analytical, and men who verge upon
the mystical in their rhapsodies about the guidance of
God's Spirit. The book obviously means to urge no
one way of religious expression, but to plead from such
evidence as is here the need for *unity in diversity.*

This kind of unity would have kept most of the people who left. Few of them were eager to go away.
They went reluctantly after becoming convinced that
they could live only in the atmosphere of freedom.
One of my former college classmates, rejecting an invitation to write, said that the only feeling evoked
from him by consideration of the world he left behind
was sadness. Still another, an Abilene Christian College graduate, said that the emotion-packed years in
which he wrestled with the problem of whether to
separate or not had left him too numb to make a contribution. He feared, too, that "the folk who really
need to read such a book will never have a single look
at it. If some do get the copy, they will be unable to
read the heart of the message."

Perhaps this is too pessimistic. Words spoken in
love and reason can work miraculous changes. The
soil is more favorable than many think. A widespread
unrest and sense of spiritual barrenness prevails
among thinking men in the Churches of Christ. The
hour is propitious for suggesting remedies and for

trusting the divine energy in the seed of truth. With hands that have clasped yours, and long to do so always, all of us who have written now commit this seed into your keeping.

Robert Meyers

LOGAN Fox bears a distinguished name in the Church of Christ. Born in Tokyo in 1922 of American missionary parents, he has attended David Lipscomb high school and college and holds a B.A. from George Pepperdine (1946). He has taught at Pepperdine (1947-48, 1960-63) and at Ibaraki Christian College, a Church of Christ-sponsored school in Japan (1948-60). He has served Churches of Christ as a minister in Aldan, Pa.; in Harvey and Chicago, Ill.; and in San Fernando and Los Angeles, Calif. His wife and five children are presently members with him of the Vermont Avenue Church of Christ in Los Angeles.

Mr. Fox was further educated at the University of Chicago (M.A., 1947) and at the University of Southern California, where he was admitted to doctoral candidacy in 1963. He holds an honorary LL.D. from Pepperdine (1959). He has written and edited a number of books, all in Japanese. Currently he is a certified psychologist in California, in private practice since 1962.

DESTINY OR DISEASE?

By Logan J. Fox

If the unexamined life is not worth living, as
Socrates declared, it is probably equally true that no
unexamined religious movement is of any worth. Be
that as it may, for twenty-three years now (ever since
my first year in college) I have been impelled to seek
to know myself—as a man, as an American, as a Christian, and as a member of the Church of Christ.

Self-knowledge is never easy, but in my experience
nothing has been more difficult than the effort to
understand my relationship to the religious fellowship
in which I was born and reared.

If this were my problem alone, there would be no
point in writing about it. But I have seen and talked
with scores of others entangled in this same web; I
think there must be hundreds of thousands in our fellowship who share this frustration. Perhaps our problem is not unique to this fellowship and something of
the same sort is being faced by countless numbers in
all of the "restorationist" Christian groups.

Some of our people in the Church of Christ have
left it to become members of freer fellowships. Far
larger numbers have lost all interest in active church
life, being unable to give themselves to the partisan
positions typical of so many of our churches but unable
to find relief by identifying with any other groups.
Even more Church of Christ people are merely marking time, I believe, while they hope vaguely that
"things are getting better," although they have no
clear idea what this "getting better" does or should
entail.

For myself, it seems that the freeing of my energies
for other constructive tasks is tied to the solution of
this problem. My religious heritage has at times

seemed to me almost a messianic destiny, and at other times a dread disease. I am coming to feel that it need be neither. As I trace some of the steps I have taken, I shall at the same time describe the Church of Christ I know.

This picture will, of necessity, be very personal. I hope that the people I describe will feel I have been fair to them. They are the only Church of Christ I have known, and I have felt that this personal account might prove more helpful than one more abstract. In thinking back over my experiences I find them dividing into five periods: (1) age of innocence, 1-13 years; (2) sectarian zeal, 14-18 years; (3) the walls crumble, 19-25 years; (4) missionary activity and church politics, 26-40 years; (5) a layman, 41-.

AGE OF INNOCENCE

I discovered myself as a Christian in the home of my parents, missionaries in Japan. We were the only Christians in that part of Japan; everyone else was a "godless heathen" whom we were there to save. Summers we spent at a mountain retreat to which missionaries from all over Japan joyfully went to avoid humid heat and even more oppressive loneliness. We children attended a Union Sunday School and our parents often worshipped with the Union Church. I never wondered what kind of Christian anyone was. It didn't seem to matter.

Being born and reared in the church has had two very important consequences for me. The first is that in a real sense I have been a Christian from the day of my birth. In our brotherhood we teach that people are added to the church only by hearing the gospel, believing it, repenting of sins, and being immersed in water. But while I was not baptized until the age of ten, I was in the church long before that. Sometimes I experienced this as a wonderful privilege; at other times it was an awful responsibility.

The second consequence of my family's Christian commitment is that I did not *choose* the Church of Christ as preferable to some other religious group. I was reared as a Christian and later discovered that my membership in the church was to be experienced in the Church of Christ. All of us who have been thus reared must inevitably experience our church life very differently from those who choose the Church of Christ deliberately as a "way out of denominationalism."

Even before I was baptized I was a missionary. We were taught the Bible daily, we prayed daily, and we tried to convert our Japanese playmates to Christianity. We were taught to trust God and to be obedient to Him, and we learned that God has a special work for Christians to do and that this makes us all special people. About the only Christians I knew until I was ten were missionaries, and they all had this same sense of dedication.

When I was ten our family went to Nashville for two years while my father attended David Lipscomb College. We children attended the Lipscomb elementary school and we really thought that Nashville was Jerusalem and Lipscomb was heaven. What a thrill to be in a place where everyone was a Christian! I want to emphasize this because a failure to understand this rapture would cause my readers to fail to understand the conflict that later developed. As children, among the missionaries and at Lipscomb, we were not conscious of being in the Church of Christ. We were in the church, we were among Christians; that was the sum of it. It was all thrilling, meaningful, satisfying.

While at Lipscomb I responded to the preaching of E. H. Ijams and was baptized. It was there that Frank Pack, then a college student, helped me make my first public talk in the elementary school chapel. It was there, as a child, that I came to know and love the Baxters, the Ijamses, H. Leo Boles, and Hall L. Cal-

houn, as well as younger men like Frank Pack, Norvel
Young, Howard White, and Batsell Barrett Baxter.

Back in Japan for my thirteenth year I was active
in helping with the evangelistic effort. I decided then
that I wanted to be a missionary and when we sailed
in August, 1935 I said to my Japanese friends who
went to the boat with us: "I'll be back!"

Thirteen years later I did go back, but before that I
was to experience both the birth and the death of sectarian zeal.

SECTARIAN ZEAL

My junior high school years were spent in Los
Angeles, experiencing the American public school and
actively participating in church life at the Central
Church of Christ. One year in Fullerton, California
came next, and this in turn led to three years back in
Nashville again at Lipscomb High. These were my
sectarian years and they were dominated by my learning about two things: true morality and the true
church.

At Central Church of Christ I became one of the
leaders in the young people's class. These lively adolescents lived in "sinful" Los Angeles and they both
frightened and attracted me. I found release from my
fear and feeling of inferiority by playing the role of
the preacher. The elders were delighted and fed me
with praise as I "courageously" attacked the sins of
drinking, dancing, movies, and petting. And I, for all
practical purposes, skipped adolescence. I still feel
that the church is wrong to single out adolescent problems as examples of worldliness and lasciviousness. It's
a wonder any of our young people grow up to be
normal. Fortunately, most young people don't take all
this preaching as seriously as I did.

Also at Central I met G. C. Brewer, one of the giants
among Church of Christ preachers. I heard him attack
communism, evolution, and the sectarian spirit he

found among us. I was especially impressed by his explanation of how we might be a separate religious group and still not be a denomination. His logic on this point is a part of the heritage of our people and, while it no longer convinces me, is one of the most valiant and ingenious of efforts to escape our historical dilemma. He would say: "Suppose I have a bunch of cards and I sort them into stacks according to the name of each card. In the course of sorting them I find some with no name on them, so I put these in a stack by themselves. Can't you see that while they are not 'denominated' (bearers of a special name) they will inevitably be separate from those which are denominated?" He would then go on to castigate us for using "Church of Christ" in a denominational sense, insisting that in the New Testament the church had no special name.

As an aside, I must say that while G. C. Brewer's logic no longer convinces me, his spirit still commands my respect. His prayer meetings at Central remain in my memory as high peaks of spiritual experience. As much as any man of his generation he transcended the fetters of "the denomination that isn't a denomination."

While at Fullerton in my fifteenth year, two experiences reinforced the feelings aroused in me by G. C. Brewer's prayer meetings and these feelings, I think, helped keep me from being completely satisfied with the sectarian position I was to learn in Nashville. One of these was meeting and hearing J. N. Armstrong. He preached in a one-week meeting at Fullerton and was much in our home. He made me feel I knew how Elijah or Amos must have appeared. He made me fear God without being afraid of Him, and he incarnated a quality of goodness I had never before seen. The other experience was learning about the book of *Romans* from my father. He has always loved the book and he has insisted that Paul in Romans makes it clear that salvation is a matter of grace, not of law. It took several years for this message of *Romans* to take root in me, but the seeds had been planted.

In the fall of 1938, I returned to Nashville and Lipscomb, to spend three years in high school and two years in college. It was in Nashville that by the age of eighteen I was to become a full-fledged sectarian and where, by the age of twenty, I was to be well on the way out of that same sectarianism. What a place Nashville has in my heart! And how well Nashville represents some of the best and some of the worst elements of the Church of Christ. Ah Jerusalem, Jerusalem!

It is not easy to describe the power of Nashville. What a strange mixture of warm, southern hospitality and frightening capacity for revenge; of piety and sentimental devotion to the Bible coupled with shrewd, ruthless practicality; of fierce, almost paranoid, certainty coupled with fearful rejection of all differing views as "dangerous." In few places is the church so dominated by a few men, yet as I seek now to understand how I was taught that the Church of Christ is the "one and only true church" I find no particular name coming to mind. Rather does this central dogma of our brotherhood so thoroughly permeate the area that its source cannot be discovered. Like the myth of white supremacy, or the sacredness of the Bible, or the existence of God, it is taken for granted and never questioned. One may play at being open-minded; in fact, such play is encouraged to prepare one to be "ready to give an answer to any who asks concerning the hope within us." But one never *really* questions whether we are in truth the true church. To do so is taboo, unthinkable. And the few who seriously question are first laughed off, then gently warned, and finally ruthlessly cut off as dangerous and beyond hope. For three years I absorbed this spirit in which I was immersed and, scarcely realizing what was happening,

came to believe this dogma and to be expert in all the
tricky logic used to defend it.

By eighteen I was an up-and-coming young preacher
thoroughly versed in Harry Rimmer's arguments for
God and the Bible, H. Leo Boles' explanation of how
the Holy Spirit can work only through the Bible, M. C.
Kurfees' arguments against instrumental music, and
Walter Scott's five steps in the plan of salvation. I
could quote the proof texts that showed the church was
established on Pentecost, and I knew all the examples
of conversion and how to read Scott's five steps into
each one, thus improving on Luke who wasn't quite
so careful when he recorded the events in Acts. I
knew the arguments against infant baptism, irregular
keeping of the Lord's Supper, the missionary society,
denominational names, and direct operation of the
Holy Spirit. I could explain how the church started on
Pentecost, grew until the end of the first century,
apostatized and did nothing but sin until Luther sort
of got things going in the right direction, and finally
was restored in its purity by the Campbells. I could
further explain that the intervening years were of no
importance, anyway; that just as wheat discovered in
a recently opened tomb of a pharaoh will grow wheat
after thousands of years if planted today, so the gospel,
the seed of the church, will, if planted today, produce
the church of the first century.

Much like Paul, I outdid my teachers. I wanted to
purify even the pure church in Nashville. When I
preached against worldliness I did not stop with con-
demning drinking, smoking, and dancing. I went on
to condemn tea, coffee, and Coca-Cola.

This period reached its zenith in the summer of 1941
when I did my first local work in Pennsylvania and
held my first protracted meetings in Clay County,
Tennessee. Nashville was proud of me, and though I
had won an academic scholarship to David Lipscomb
College, I was urged to accept a Biblical scholarship

instead. I had become what Nashville believed in and I could preach "our" message from A to Z.

Then I entered college.

THE WALLS CRUMBLE

What an intellectual challenge David Lipscomb College was for me! History reveals many strange events brought about by the inexplicable convergence of men and circumstances, and I cannot but believe that the Lipscomb I attended was providentially prepared for me. Men such as E. H. Ijams, Norman Parks, J. S. McBride, S. P. Pittman, and Robert G. Neil were as refreshingly alive as any men I have ever known. I would not want to embarrass these men by holding them responsible for what happened to me, but I do want to record my gratitude for what they did for a cocky, know-it-all sectarian whom God sent to them for chastening.

As a sectarian boy-preacher two experiences signaled that my position was doomed. On one occasion I was preaching the typical sermon castigating the denominations and was making a particularly urgent plea that all people caught in the web of denominational prejudice should be open-minded. I insisted that they try to put out of their minds all preconceived ideas and read the Bible as if for the first time. At that moment it was almost as if a voice whispered to me, "Have you?" I was so stunned I could hardly go on preaching. I knew I had *never* really questioned my own position and I knew I had no business asking anyone else to be open-minded.

The second experience came after I had finished a particularly aggressive sermon against worldliness. I gave the invitation and challenged the hardened sinners to repent. The song ended without any response and we had the dismissal prayer. Then a little twelve-year-old girl came up to me and with tears streaming down her cheeks told me she had decided never to go to another movie for the rest of her life. I was shocked and cried to myself, "What have you done?"

It was thus with some chinks in my armor that I began to take the steps which in six years led me to the position which I have found convincing now for nearly twenty years. I trust it may be helpful to some if I elaborate on those steps.

1. The first step was the discovery that truth is self-validating and needs no external supports. The idea was planted while I was still in high school by a teacher who one day said of the truths in the Sermon on the Mount, "These statements are not true because they are in the Bible; they are in the Bible because they are true." He went on to suggest that truth is the very nature of the universe and that what is true has always been true and always will be. This struck me then as being very important, but it was not until the following year, when I was in college, that I felt the full force of it. I still remember the night I decided that I did not need to carry truth on my frail shoulders, that it could stand by itself or it wasn't the truth. And so I unloaded the burden I had been carrying and said, "Tonight I will go to sleep and not worry about truth." With what relief and joyful ecstasy I opened my eyes in the morning to find that truth had survived the night without my help! I have never since worried about defending truth. Truth does not need us, we need it. We do not support it, it supports us. It is ours to accept truth, to obey it, and to proclaim it. And if we discover that something we had thought true is not true, we have lost nothing but error and are then closer to truth. I cannot exaggerate the importance this has had for me, and I can think of nothing that I would with more earnestness commend to my brethren than this attitude.

2. My next step was the realization that immersion in water is not a *sine qua non* for the regeneration of man. We as a people have consistently claimed that we

do not believe in baptismal regeneration, but as a matter of fact our position comes down to this because we have never been willing to recognize as Christians the unimmersed. There has been no surer way to be branded as "unsound" than to suggest that we ought to fellowship Christians who have never been immersed. To my mind, there is nothing which so blocks the spiritual growth of our people as this position. Just as the Jews misunderstood and misused the covenant-sign of circumcision, so we have taken the covenant-sign of baptism and distorted its beauty and power in our effort to prove its absolute necessity.

As mentioned earlier, I had grown up in Japan thinking of other denominational people as Christians. I now began to feel our inconsistency in singing the hymns and using the Bible reference works of people we considered "out of Christ." But it was hearing E. Stanley Jones and reading his books which finally clarified the problem for me. It all boiled down to one simple fact: if God sent His Holy Spirit to live and work in a man who was not immersed, who was I to refuse to recognize him? And since the evidence of the presence of the Spirit is the fruit of the Spirit, then it is undeniable that regeneration is not always correlated with immersion.

I now believe that baptism plays much the same part as the exchange of vows in marriage. It is a profound covenant given by God and used by God for our salvation. People have been known to be married without a ceremony, but happy are those who, when asked if they are married, can say, "Yes, we were married on such and such a day." It is possible, also, that one might be born again and filled with the Spirit without being baptized, but happy is he who can with gratitude and confidence point to the day he was baptized.

3. Even more of an issue for our people has been the conviction that the Bible is verbally inspired. Rethinking this question was my next step. Most helpful

to me was Harry Emerson Fosdick's old book, *The Modern Use of the Bible.* Reading such men as Fosdick, Sockman, Jones, and others, I came to realize that rather than making the Bible live, the verbal inspiration theory was killing the message of the Bible. I saw that while we virtually worshipped the Bible, we weren't really getting its message. Much as the Pharisees who "searched the scriptures" but failed to see how Jesus fulfilled them, we were experts in manipulating proof texts but failed to let the Spirit teach us. I saw that while we insisted that every verse in the Bible is inspired, we really took the position for practical purposes. In other words, we used verbal inspiration to give divine authority to the doctrinal position which we carefully extracted from (or read into) the Bible. I saw that while we claimed "every scripture is inspired of God" we used perhaps ten per cent of the Bible and conveniently let the rest go. Next to our position on baptism, I am convinced that our view of the Bible is the biggest barrier to spiritual growth among us.

4. Accepting the Bible as literature made me conscious of the importance of history. I came to see that the Bible really bears witness to God's activity in history, and that if we are to know Him we must become sensitive to what He is teaching us in the historical arena. I learned to love history and realized that historical questions must be answered by historical methods rather than by revelation.

This meant for me the discovery of the church's history and of our place in it. I realized that we had either ignored history or twisted it to suit our special purposes. I came to see the Restoration Movement as a *historical movement* and to evaluate it from the historical point of view.

Years later in Japan, a fine Japanese scholar who had learned something of our movement gave this pointed critique: "You folks have to make up your

minds about history. First you take it seriously, seeing the development of the church from Pentecost until
the end of the first century, then you ignore history for
seventeen hundred years, then you take it seriously
again as you see the achievements of your restoration
movement." Of course, he was painfully correct. We
must make up our minds about history.

5. The next step was the psychological. After Lipscomb I attended Pepperdine College in Los Angeles
and was delightfully introduced to psychology. For
me this meant learning that there are reasons for behavior, and that all human behavior can be studied
systematically, including religious behavior. What a
thrill and relief it was to discover my kinship with
other people. My problems and conflicts were not
unique and I had been feeling guilty for many things
which were perfectly normal.

But most of all, the study of mental hygiene gave me
a broader, more realistic understanding of morality
and ethics. I came to see that *holiness* and *wholeness*
are not only linguistically but essentially related, that
the unholy is exaggeration of the partial. To be saved
is to be made whole, and Christ is Lord because when
we put Him at the center of our lives everything else
falls into a harmonious whole.

6. Soon after discovering psychological man, I discovered man. It may seem strange to say this, but in
reality I had been very much isolated from the general
culture both in Japan and in America. The church had
been my whole world.

It all came to a head one night when I saw the movie,
A Tree Grows in Brooklyn. In the story there is a
conscientious, good wife; a lovable, irresponsible,
drinking husband; a wayward, warm, impetuous sister
of the wife; and a little girl who lived by her heart.
And I loved them all. I realized that people can't be
divided into good and bad, right and wrong. I couldn't
blame the good wife for scolding the husband and for

trying to keep her wayward sister away from her daughter, but I could also understand why the daughter loved her father and her aunt. I left the theater and walked the dark streets of Los Angeles with a heart bursting with love and hot tears scalding my cheeks. I felt as if I had just joined the human race, and I felt as if I knew Jesus for the first time. With what stark clarity did I know then that it is not right to feel self-righteous and isolate ourselves so terribly from the people Jesus loved. We have been wrong to cut ourselves off from the world in our efforts to be pure. It has kept us from being the salt of the earth.

7. Also at Pepperdine I learned the discipline of philosophy. Studying with such men as E. V. Pullias, Ralph Wilburn, and Russell Squire I learned to be afraid of no question and I discovered how difficult it is to study any question with real thoroughness.

We as a people have been wary of philosophy, especially the philosophy of religion. But two values of the philosophical approach should, I think, command our interest: *perspective* and *tentativeness*.

Perspective comes from having a map. Certainly, studying a map is no substitute for actually living in the places marked on the map, but real experience is greatly enriched when we know something of where we are in relation to other places. As I see it, philosophy is simply our effort to construct the best map of human experience that we can. If we would discipline ourselves more with history and philosophy, we would be able to see ourselves and our beliefs in clearer perspective.

Tentativeness in the positions we take is absolutely necessary for real growth in understanding. Unless we can learn to investigate sympathetically new ideas while withholding ultimate commitment, we shall find ourselves fixated to inadequate positions which make all growth impossible. What I miss most of all in such papers as our brotherhood publications (e.g., *The Gos-*

pel Advocate and *The Firm Foundation*) is a friend-
liness to tentative positions. How I long for a free
forum among us where ideas can be advanced, tested,
and then either pursued or withdrawn, depending on
how they stand up.

8. From Pepperdine I went to the University of
Chicago, and there I faced Darwinian evolution and
Watsonian behaviorism. For me this was really coming
to grips with scientific hypotheses and learning to deal
fairly with them, whatever the consequences might be.
It was there I heard the scientist's paraphrase of Job,
"Scientific method is my master, and I will trust it
though it slay every cherished idea I have held." I
must confess that this attitude laid a firm claim on my
mind, though my heart was reluctant to follow.

I now feel that any hypothesis is a tool and is to be
judged by its usefulness. Such hypotheses as evolution
and behaviorism are to be neither accepted nor rejected
on the basis of emotion, but must be appraised critically
on the basis of their usefulness in organizing and explaining observed facts. To the extent that any hypothesis is useful, we will use it; where any hypothesis
fails to fit the facts, we will look for a more adequate
one.

As for our faith, it must live in the midst of a world
where we question, observe, and analyze any and all
facts that come to our attention. Faith has nothing to
fear from science or philosophy, and a faith that is not
protected from the best academic research will be puri-
fied and strengthened. At Chicago I learned something
of the strengths and weaknesses of science, and I
learned that God is not afraid of anything man might
discover.

9. It was also at Chicago that a whole new world of
service was opened up for me—that of counseling and
psychotherapy. Studying with Carl R. Rogers, the
founder of non-directive or client-centered counseling,
I learned a new definition of love. All of my life I had

struggled with what seemed to me the inconsistency
of love's being commanded. How can one *love* in
obedience to a *command?* But in learning to be a
counselor, I found an answer that has satisfied me.
The counselor learns to *accept* the client, whatever the
client's behavior or feelings. This involves neither approval nor disapproval, but is a deep respect for the
person and worth of the client. This, to me, is love,
and this is something we can do in obedience to the will
of God.

This concept of acceptance makes real for me the
meaning of divine grace and forgiveness, and I can
better understand the transforming, redemptive power
unleashed through Jesus. I am now convinced that
the church is failing in its mission of healing because
we have failed to heed Jesus' words, "Judge not." We
have relied on the power of social disapproval in trying to change people's behavior, rather than relying on
the power of acceptance or love. In this, we have
shown that we trust the power of the world more than
we trust the spiritual power of love and holiness.

10. Last of all came the step of ecumenicity. Again
it was in Chicago, the home of the *Christian Century.*
Reading this most stimulating of religious journals,
and hearing Charles Clayton Morrison speak, I became convinced that in the ecumenical movement not
only is the spirit of Jesus very much alive, but so also
is the spirit of Thomas and Alexander Campbell.
Nothing is more incongruous than the attitude of the
Church of Christ toward this effort at Christian
unity! Of all the things which we have hammered
away at, none has been more attacked than the sin of
division. We have been the great advocate of *one
church.* Now when this plea is taken seriously by the
Christian world and sincere efforts are put forth to
achieve unity, we have attacked the effort as dangerous, compromising, and sinful!

Granted that the ecumenical movement mirrors

within its efforts all the failings of worldwide Christianity, it remains also true that it reflects the most earnest hope and fervent dedication of the best minds and spirits within the churches. We should rejoice in the effort of the ecumenical movement, we should participate with other Christians of good will in seeking ways to realize Jesus' prayer for unity.

With these ten steps over a period of six years, I was no longer a partisan member of the Church of Christ. All during these years I knew I had a decision to make. Should I leave the fellowship in which I had been born and reared, or should I somehow find a way to work on within it?

MISSIONARY ACTIVITY AND CHURCH POLITICS

Many of us have struggled with the question: What should I do when I find myself in serious disagreement with the position occupied by most members of the religious group to which I belong? The most obvious answer is, of course, to get out. Many have done this, and many of us who have not have been told that we ought to.

I have found the idea of leaving the group very tempting. Why not be associated with people whose views are nearer my own? To remain with people who find one's views offensive is to be either continually involved in controversy and disturbance or to be vulnerable to the accusation that one's silence proves one either a coward or a dishonest fifth columnist. Why, in spite of this, did I choose to remain within this fellowship? My decision was based on three very deep feelings:

First, my idea of the church is that it is not a voluntary association of people so much as a body into which we are born by the will and activity of God. Therefore we do not join or leave the church by choice. I can fail to fulfill my destiny as a member of God's people, but I cannot lay aside my responsibility.

Second, I grant that one may choose to worship and serve in a particular fellowship because of opportunities for personal growth or greater usefulness. But personal convenience is too shallow a basis for one's religious commitment. The unity of the church will never be achieved by people of like interests and convictions banding together and calling themselves the church. The church *is* one, and it is made up of all of God's people. We do not choose our brethren; they are given to us by God. Once I thought members of the Church of Christ were the only Christians. Now I stay with them because I cannot deny that they *are* Christians (not the only Christians, not Christians only, but Christians), and I have no business withdrawing myself from any Christians, especially those among whom God has put me.

Third, I have felt that if I *am* right and my brethren are wrong, then instead of leaving them I should share with them what I believe. I know that this sounds proud, but each of us, it seems to me, has no alternative to this position. If I do not think I am right, I should change. If I do think so, I should not—indeed, cannot—change, and I should labor to convict others.

While I was still a student at Lipscomb, one of my teachers talked with me about my feelings. He asked me if I were interested in leadership. I said that I was. He then said that if a locomotive is to pull a train, it must do it gradually so as not to break the coupling. By being concerned only with one's personal growth, he suggested, one may, like an uncoupled locomotive, go racing down the track, but the group will be left behind. This made sense to me, and with the energy and idealism of youth I decided to commit myself to responsible participation in the Church of Christ.

For me this meant returning as a missionary to Japan where the end of Japanese militarism had opened up unprecedented opportunities for Christian missionaries. I was especially thrilled with the possibility of sharing in the creation of a Christian school.

From March, 1948, to March, 1960—for these twelve years the work in Ibaraki, Japan was my life. Here was a chance to be constructive, to work within the framework of the brotherhood, to build on the foundation in Japan laid by my father and others, and to make a contribution to the Christianizing of Japan.

The first challenge we met was the question: Is Ibaraki Christian College going to be in the main stream of the Church of Christ? Much of the pre-war work of the Church of Christ in Japan was done by missionaries sent out by brethren in Louisville, Kentucky, who were of the pre-millennial persuasion. So we were asked how I.C.C. was going to stand on this issue. Pre-millennialism had never been an issue in Japan, and most of us young missionaries did not want to make it an issue in our work. But we finally decided that if we were going to ask the larger brotherhood for support, we should take a position that would engender confidence. Thus we took a stand on this issue and committed I.C.C. to the main stream of the brotherhood and ourselves to the tortuous path of church politics. I'm sure we couldn't have done it unless we had had the help of E. W. McMillan and the Union Avenue Church of Christ in Memphis, Tennessee. These brethren, to us, represented the very best of the central movement in the Church of Christ, and we decided to walk with them. I still do not regret this decision and believe yet that E. W. McMillan and Union Avenue represent the most constructive elements in the Church of Christ. If one must be political in the church, one could do no better than to stand with men such as these.

The second challenge we faced was the radical differences we discovered among those of us who worked together to start Ibaraki Christian College. Three of us were from Harding College in Arkansas and three from Pepperdine, and every time we turned around, it seemed, we were in a debate with one another. But after four years a strange and wonderful fellowship was achieved which was so unique in our experience that we still call it "the spirit of Ibaraki." It is difficult to explain, but essentially it was the discovery that we could be different and still work together. Perhaps it is what Campbell had in mind when he said, "In faith, unity; in opinion, liberty; in all things, love." We discovered that while our explanations of the Bible differed impossibly, our proclamation of the gospel was very similar. Most of all, we found that it was good to be together, to play, to sing, even to argue. We found that we loved one another and that this love had nothing to do with the philosophy, or even the doctrine, held by each. And so we experienced the emergence of an atmosphere of love and freedom in which differing convictions did not need to be suppressed.

The third challenge we faced was that of being really non-sectarian. On the mission field we cannot escape the painful truth that "an unbelieving world is the price of a divided Christendom." It was my hope that while we confessed our roots in the Restoration movement and worked responsibly within the main stream of the Church of Christ, we could still be representatives in Japan of the whole Christian church. Up to a point we were able to do this in two ways: first, by stressing the great central truths of Christianity like faith in God, Christ's atonement, and the Biblical view of life; and second, by working primarily in areas where no Christian work of any kind had been done before so that we were the only spokesmen for Christianity. But, inevitably, the question of our attitude toward other Christian groups became an issue. As far as possible, I wanted to work with them, let them share in the teaching program at I.C.C., and present a solid Christian front to a seeking Japan. Ultimately this became the reef on which my excursion into church politics made shipwreck.

Because of our day-to-day contact with one another, those of us who worked together in Ibaraki learned to live with the tensions generated by our differences. But by 1956, the criticism levelled against us by missionaries in Tokyo, together with the concern expressed by leading brethren from America who visited our work, forced us to back off from the policy of wider fellowship. And it was then that I began to see the limits that would be placed on our work because of our involvement with the main stream of the brotherhood. I carried out a policy of expedience until our return to America in 1960, but in 1962, when we considered going back to resume leadership, I found myself unable to agree to stay within the imposed limits. I had the feeling that after fifteen years of trying to pull the train I had not made it move much. And if I were to pull it at all, I'd have to pull it in a direction I could not conscientiously go. So I resigned from my church ministry, quit the faculty of Pepperdine College, and brought to an end my effort to achieve spiritual ends by political means.

A LAYMAN'S VIEW OF HIS PLACE IN THE CHURCH OF CHRIST

It is still my decision to remain within the framework of the Church of Christ. This should not be taken as a judgment upon those who have made, or will make, other decisions. I do feel, however, that I should try to state for myself and for others the way I now view this movement of which I am, in the providence of God, a part.

1. A historical movement. The most obvious answer to the question, "What is the Church of Christ?" is one of the least often seen in the writings of our people. The Church of Christ is a historical movement. It is one branch of the Restoration movement, a nineteenth century reform movement in America associated

largely with the names of Thomas and Alexander Campbell. The original movement was conceived as being a part of Protestantism and must be classed with other "free church" movements. One branch of this movement likes to think of itself as being the main Campbellian stream while others are "digressive." It is my judgment, however, that the Disciples are the more rightful heirs of Campbell, while we in the Church of Christ are more the children of David Lipscomb, H. Leo Boles, and other post-Civil War leaders of the church in the South.

Three issues were important in the development of this branch of the Restoration movement that thinks of itself exclusively as "the Church of Christ" while studiously calling itself "churches of Christ." The first is that we have taken a negative attitude toward art and culture, as typified by our opposition to instrumental music in the worship. The second is that we have taken a negative attitude toward education and scholarship, as typified by our opposition to a critical study of the scriptures. And the third is that we have taken a negative attitude toward effective organization of the church, as typified by our opposition to the missionary society. All three of these issues make it plain why we are often called "antis."

On the positive side we have continued to profess our dedication to the unity of all Christians, although obviously we cannot be very serious about this. We have stressed simplicity of worship, which we have achieved to an admirable degree. We have stood for a study of the Bible, and this, too, has been a genuine interest which has produced a kind of Biblically informed people.

Our biggest problem, I think, is our stand on immersion. Our hearts and minds tell us that people baptized by sprinkling are Christians, as witness our use of their hymns in our worship, our use of their reference materials in our study of the Bible, and our use of their sermon books in the preparation of our sermons. But our doctrinal logic tells us that they *cannot* be Christians because they have not been immersed. So we must continue to refuse any fellowship or recognition to other Christian groups, and this is killing our soul.

2. Does the "restoration plea" have sufficient vitality for Christian commitment? This is a pressing question that all of us must face, but especially the young among us. I would answer both *yes* and *no*.

As a *movement* among Christians, I think there is a place for the Restoration plea. It bears witness to some important issues and can, if it is properly handled, make a real contribution to the total church. But to claim that we are *The Church*, the exclusive body of Jesus Christ, is unthinkable. We cannot commit ourselves to ourselves, and we cannot urge others to do so. By the mercy of God we are Christians, but we are Christians of a particular persuasion and a particular history. In other words, all our protestations to the contrary notwithstanding, *we are a denomination.* We should confess it and join all other denominational Christians in asking God's forgiveness and His guidance.

3. What can a "loyal opposition" among us do? These four things, I would suggest: First, we can be free. Freedom is not someone's gift, nor is it something we need permission for. We must not complain that we are not free. Christ has set us free and it is ours to act freely. Responsible ecclesiastical leaders have very limited freedom. Instead of judging them and calling them names, those of us who are not burdened with such leadership must exercise our freedom, for ourselves and for them. Second, we can confess what we really believe. Albert Schweitzer wrote, "Nothing is better than the truth." In Romans 10, Paul said that we must not only believe in the heart but confess with the mouth. God helping us, let us determine

to speak and write our minds. We may be right or we may be wrong, but we can do no other than to confess what we believe. There is a crisis of faith among our people. Our pulpits are filled with men who do not believe what they preach and who dare not preach what they believe.

Third, we can act rather than react. Too many of us have childishly blamed others for a situation which is not their fault. Some may have chosen to be expedient and to reap the reward of popularity at the price of painful conflict. If we do not choose to be expedient, we make the choice freely and without bitterness, and we shall reap the reward of peace of mind at the price of popularity. Those who choose one course need not blame and judge those who take the other. God will judge us all and may He have mercy on all of us!

Finally, we can be what we are. Increasingly I have come to feel that the only real decision any of us has is Hamlet's "to be or not to be." In other words, we don't decide *what* we will be but only *whether* to be what we actually are. For myself, this is at the heart of my present strivings. I am a member of the Church of Christ, so I must be that. I am not in the main stream of this movement, so I shall not pretend to be. I am a Christian, a part of the whole great movement in western civilization that goes back to Jesus and the Jewish people, so I will sink my roots deep into this heritage and know my kinship with all other Christians. I am a human being, a man, so I will cherish my human soul and love all men as fellow members of my race. It is my intent to be all that I am, and I feel that this is not to be accomplished by giving up any part of my heritage or by leaving my people.

4. What is to become of this movement? God only knows, and it probably really doesn't matter in any ultimate sense. Certainly I have no compulsion any longer to try to "save it" or to "destroy it." God will judge and God will dispose.

It seems to me, generally speaking, that we are going down the road the Southern Baptists have traveled, but about fifty years behind them. We are, like them, increasingly liberal in practical matters like Bible school methods, but like them, we are changing very little doctrinally.

I see a renewal of the "lay ministry" among us. Of course, we have never recognized the distinction between clergy and laity, but in the twentieth century we definitely developed a clergy. Now there are an increasing number of men who are preaching while they earn their living doing "secular" work. I am pleased with this tendency and predict that there will be an increase in it. In a church without effective organization, such as ours, this is probably the only way we can have a reasonably free pulpit.

CONCLUDING STATEMENT

I add this final word in an effort to give perspective. As I think back over the issues that have been such great concerns for me, I realize that many of them are of little importance when viewed in the light of the pressing problems of our day. The world totters on the brink of an atomic holocaust. America is torn by racial strife. Countless individuals struggle to find meaning for lives threatened by despair. Of what possible significance can be the conflicts of one small religious group?

I can say only that these issues *have* been most pressing concerns for me, and that I have found it possible to turn my attention to what now seems more important only as I have solved for myself some of the religious problems I inherited. It is easy for one not involved in such a heritage to say, "Why don't you forget about such petty problems?" For me, the only way out was to work through the problems and the foregoing essay records that long endeavor.

My prayer for myself and for all concerned Christians is that we may be given the wisdom and courage to focus our minds on the great central truths which Jesus taught and embodied, leaving partisan strife to die in the deserts where it was born.

J. P. SANDERS was born in Nashville, Tennessee in 1917. His father was a Church of Christ minister and the family, on both sides, are members of that church. Mr. Sanders attended the Austin, Texas high school for the blind, graduating as valedictorian in 1936. He graduated *summa cum laude* from Abilene Christian College in 1940, with a major in English and Bible. He earned an M.A. at Vanderbilt in 1941, and a B.D. from Vanderbilt's School of Religion in 1943, where he won the Founder's Medal for scholarship. He studied at Yale in 1943-44.

Mr. Sanders served Churches of Christ in Covington, Kentucky (1944-47) and Cincinnati, Ohio (1947-50). In the Ohio area he preached in most of the Churches of Christ in the Great Lakes region and served the *Christian Leader* as associate editor. From 1950 to 1954 he served the Kilburn Avenue Church in Rockford, Illinois, where he also organized and directed a camp for under-privileged children.

In 1954, Mr. Sanders accepted a call to the First Christian Church in Anaconda, Montana, remaining until 1959. He went next to the First Christian Church in Missoula, Montana, and remained there until June, 1964. He moved to the Fruitridge Christian Church in Sacramento, California, in 1964. His strong concern for social justice keeps him involved in many service areas. He works now with the Sacramento Peace Center, is on the board of the city's Society for the Blind, and labors with the Social Action Commission of the Sacramento Area Council of Churches.

THE FAILURES OF FUNDAMENTALISM

By J. P. Sanders

When faith dies, its remains are embalmed into a creed. After fire goes out, only ashes are left as a reminder of the warmth and glow. When the spirit flees, the letter stays.

This alternation is discernible in literature, art, politics, and religion in what we know as *convention and revolt*. When a creative and dynamic spirit appears, it finds the old forms and conventions inadequate for its use. It revolts against them in order to express itself in its own way. Its new forms are fluid, experimental, subservient to the spirit that struggles to express itself. In time, however, even this revolt is captured by the system-makers who proceed to turn the revolt into a new and rigid convention. After a while, a new rebel arises to break through this convention and form his own medium. New wine can never be contained by old wine skins but must be forever finding new ones. Each new skin in turn becomes old.

A Shelley finds the literary conventions of his day brittle and confining for his free spirit. He rebels and shocks contemporaries with radical innovations. The critics who followed him, however, accepted his new forms and made them into another orthodoxy. In religion there is a built-in tension between convention and revolt. It is not always described in these terms but is more often described as conflict between letter and spirit, between law and grace, between works and faith. To put it in personal terms, the alternation of convention and revolt can be seen as the perpetual struggle between priest and prophet.

Micah, the revolutionary prophet, attacked the priests head-on when he asked religion's basic question: "With what shall I come before the Lord?"

Micah wanted to know if (as the priests were saying) he could come to the Lord with burnt-offerings and calves a year old—that is, would outward ceremonies and works of obedience bring him to God? If he brought thousands of rams and ten thousands of rivers of oil—would the multitude of the works bring him to God? This was a clear taunting of the priests and their system of external works and doctrinal orthodoxy. In contrast, Micah made the startling challenge: "What does the Lord require of you but to do justice, to love mercy, and to walk humbly with your God?"

Space does not permit me to explicate this tension as seen in the writings of Hosea, Isaiah, Amos, Jeremiah, and some of the late psalmists. All of them, in their own way, challenged the same orthodoxy and with the same revolutionary insights.

Twice Jesus quoted Hosea's succinct attack on the priests: "I desire mercy, and not sacrifice." He used it to summarize his own battles with the Pharisees. He told them to go and learn what Hosea meant. His hearers were proud students of the Scriptures who were surely familiar with this saying from their prophet. Jesus seems to be saying that they had so conventionalized the rebel that they could no longer comprehend what he was really saying. Thus the priest, though well-versed in the letter of the law is unable to lay hold of the spirit of the law which is its true meaning. It was their misunderstanding of the prophets that let them decorate the tombs of the prophets while they themselves were unprophetic and would have killed the prophets if they had lived at the same time with them. The Daughters of the American Revolution are perhaps the last ones to comprehend that revolution because they themselves are so unrevolutionary. The Pharisees had conventionalized the prophets' revolt and made their heresy into an orthodoxy. What the prophets had cried out in the power of the spirit, the Pharisees had formalized into the letter. Faith had become a creed, the fire ashes. The dynamite of the prophets could now be handled with safety.

It was this battle for the prophetic faith which brought Jesus to his death. Defenders of the priestly orthodoxy would not let him live. He showed them that their own prophets, Elijah and Elisha, did not share their racist views. His statement that "the sabbath was made for man, not man for the sabbath," was itself enough to mark him as a dangerous radical who was distressingly "free" in handling Scripture and its requirements.

Paul's conversion, in my understanding, was not so much the conversion from one religion to another as it was the conversion from priestly to prophetic faith. He said he was brought up in the "strictest sect" of the Pharisees. He evidently was unhappy in it quite early and was tempted to rebel, for he "kicked against the goad." He was wretched under that strict system, for he found in it only condemnation. If Paul had been brought up in the prophetic tradition instead of the priestly, his subsequent life would doubtless have been much different. Needless to say, in that event Christianity itself would be much different. What Paul found in Jesus Christ was what Jesus himself had found in the prophetic stream of Judaism. When he wrote that "the letter kills, but the Spirit gives life," he was probably speaking out of his own harrowing experience of changing from the priest to the prophet.

Paul soon found that even Christians, called to the prophetic faith, could fall back to the priestly way without leaving their formal relationship with the Christian church. Christians can make a convention in their turn out of the Christian revolution. Paul found it necessary to remind his Christian friends that "circumcision is nothing, and uncircumcision is nothing, but faith working through love." This was precisely the same point Jesus had made about the sabbath's being for man, not man for the sabbath. Paul's battle with the Judaizing teachers in Galatia was the same as Jesus' battle with the Pharisees, or the battle of the eighth century prophets with the priests of their time.

FUNDAMENTALISM AND THE PRIESTLY TRADITION

The Protestant Reformation was the revolt of the prophetic spirit of the sixteenth century against the conventionalized religion of the priestly medieval church. Luther's stress on faith within as opposed to outward works, on individual conscience as opposed to dogmatic orthodoxy, on the freedom of the man in Christ—all this was but a re-phrasing of the old prophetic language. Again, it was the struggle of the spirit against the letter.

In our day, this prophetic Protestant revolt has been conventionalized into a new orthodoxy and rigid creed. This modern priestly form of Protestantism goes by the name of Fundamentalism.

As we have seen, the words and phrases used in the battle change from age to age, but the basic issues remain the same. Fundamentalism has the four inevitable marks of the priestly tradition in all ages, and in our time we have chosen to term these issues as follows: Scriptural literalism, legalism, sectarianism, and social irrelevance. I should like to discuss these marks in order and demonstrate how they are the essentials of any Fundamentalist—or of any other priestly system.

SCRIPTURAL LITERALISM

The priest, in seeking a system of faith which can be the unquestioned basis for conformity within the sect, may find authority for the system either through an infallible church or an infallible Scriptural interpretation. If he chooses the latter, the interpretation must be literal, since close attention to the *spirit* of the writing is individualistic and leads to heterodoxy. The jot and the tittle become supremely important, for the system as a whole depends upon them.

In his conviction that he can discover through the letter what the early church was and taught, the priestly type is persuaded that he can "restore" that early church by duplicating it detail for detail in our time. Restorationism is the effort to catch an historical process at one moment of its evolution and to fossilize it at that point for eternal duplication. Literal interpretation, at the most, can hope to resurrect only the corpse from the past; the experimental, fluid, and dynamic life is too elusive for such capture. The early church was not itself a rigid structure; the development of it, as seen through New Testament letters, shows this clearly. To talk about "restoring" the early church requires that we designate *which* early church—for example, the one of Corinthians, or the one of the pastoral letters.

It seems to me that literalism, with its consequent efforts at restoration, fails to take into account the most elementary findings of modern Biblical scholarship. The Scriptures were obviously not written to be complete descriptions of anything, or blueprints. Paul, for instance, wrote letters as they were needed and addressed himself to the specific problems before him. He did not self-consciously write Scripture. He did not try to portray in detail what the church was; his readers already knew. We do not even have all the letters he wrote, and what he said that has now been lost may be most vital to any type of literal interpretation. Trying to piece together a coherent picture of the early church from these miscellaneous fragments is like following a truck loaded with a pre-fab, hoping that we can rebuild the house from the few pieces that chance to drop off.

There have been so many glosses, additions, and editorial changes in the process of time that we have no way of knowing exactly what the original text was. From what we have, we get glimpses—little more.

One detail will suffice here. Acts 20: 7 says that "on the first day of the week, when we were gathered to break bread . . ." From this passing reference, some restorationists have tried to develop a pattern as to frequency of celebrating the Lord's Supper.

All that this verse says, however, is that on that particular day of the week that particular group in that place met to break bread—whether it was the Lord's Supper or a common meal is not even made clear. We do not know whether this group always met on that day, or if it did we do not know that other groups did; certainly we do not know whether it was a common or universal practice. The fragmentary nature of the Scriptural record makes any such conjecture vain.

Restoration, it seems to me, is not only futile but also undesirable. Why should the church of the twentieth century want to be like the one of the first? That church became what it was in order to meet its needs and exigencies; to attempt to follow its exact form today is to deny the urgency we ought to feel for meeting the needs and exigencies of our own day.

We can read the New Testament and find the spirit of Christ at work. We can see men "compelled by Love," going forth to call men to God through Christ, and into fellowship with each other. But to assert that we have discovered the pattern of what that church was is to assert more than we can prove and more than we need to assert. The spirit of that early church can still give us life, but trying to live by its letter— which we cannot even discern fully—is lethal indeed.

LEGALISM

We have seen that the priest seeks an exact system of faith which can be the basis for the sect, and he seeks it through the authority of the church or the authority of literal Biblical interpretations. This system is a code of requirements, or what is often called "the plan of salvation."

Legalism sees sin as a violation of the written code. The code may or may not have relevance to man's need; it may be simply arbitrary requirements revealed by God. Man's disobedience to these rules becomes an affront to God.

The Pharisees loved the sabbath but saw little in it except its legal value as a rule to be kept. Jesus called on them to see the real meaning of the sabbath— it is made for man. These people were scandalized when Jesus pointed out that one of their heroes, David, had illegally eaten the sacred bread when he was a hungry fugitive. Man's need had precedence over legal requirements and taboos.

Paul, under legalism, was wretched because he was honest enough with himself to know that he could not fulfill any law which God would give. The fault, he said, was not in the law but in his own fleshly weakness. He went on to say that not only *his* flesh, but *no* flesh, could be justified by law. Under legalism he had to fulfill the law to be justified, but he could not fulfill it, so that the law was to him constant death and condemnation. In Christ he found freedom from legalism through a new basis for salvation: his relationship to God through inward faith. Now, as a son, he worked harder than he had as a slave—not to fulfill legal requirements, but in response to the love that had set him free.

The dilemma which Paul posed remains legalism's dilemma. How can imperfect man be saved through the keeping of a perfect law? Some solve this dilemma for themselves by reducing the law's requirements to a keepable minimum. Since man cannot measure up to the law, then cut the law to his size.

Some, for example, put great emphasis on baptism as "essential to salvation." They do not usually put the same emphasis on forgiving enemies as "essential to salvation"—though Jesus said more about this than about baptism. Some will make a test of fellowship on church polity but will not make a test on the weightier matters of justice, mercy, and faith. In short, legalism, in its efforts to find justification by works of the law, eliminates the more difficult requirements in order that it might establish a law that can be kept.

Since legalism holds sin to be a legal violation, it holds salvation to be a legal payment. Man as a sinner must do certain things required of him for forgiveness. This is like paying a grocery bill or any other legal obligation—so much for so much. If the grocer agrees to discount the bill and will settle for five cents on the dollar, still this is a legal transaction and a means of achieving debt-free status by meeting the required payments.

Prophetic religion would insist that salvation is not through a "plan" at all, but through a relationship; not through meeting requirements, but through love. Good works are a response to God's love, not a means of earning it. When love is there, there is a seeking to know God's will for his family; this means an involvement with the social problems of the day. Jeremiah blistered the priests in besieged Jerusalem for offering the people a false hope through legalism. The priests were saying that the city could not be captured because it had God's temple and because its people were obedient at the altar with their ceremonies. Jeremiah said that the truth was that "if you thoroughly amend your ways and doings, if you thoroughly execute justice between a man and his neighbor, if you oppress not the sojourner, the fatherless, and the widow, and shed not innocent blood in this place neither walk after other gods to your own hurt: then will I cause you to dwell in this place . . . " The people, following their priests, were trusting in their scrupulous obedience to outward forms of religious practice and were ignoring the real will of God, which is for the relief and help of his people. Jeremiah called on the people, as Micah did, to seek God through social justice to his people, rather than through obedience to meaningless legal requirements.

Legalism begins with a God who is Judge, loving his law and wanting it kept; prophetic faith begins with God who is Father, loving his children and wanting justice and mercy for them.

SECTARIANISM

Priestly religion seeks to establish a legal system or code for salvation through literal interpretation of Scripture. The code so arrived at must be accepted in detail by all who would be of the "in-group." Agreement on this legal code becomes the touchstone of belonging to the group. Those who differ are of the "out-group." The in-group, by definition, becomes a sect, and its accepted interpretation becomes its creed, whether written or unwritten.

Restoration and its "plea" became such a creed for the sect which separated itself from other Christians on this basis. This view of the church is the same as that held by the medieval Catholic Church—the only difference being that restorationism marks the church by its "true doctrine" while Catholicism marked it by the "true priesthood." In both cases the church is seen as a definite organization, exclusivist, infallible.

In the early days of the restoration movement, it was held that restoration of the early church pattern was the only means for uniting Christians. Unity and restoration were part of the same plea. It was thought that if the Biblical pattern could be presented, right-thinking people would all agree on it and unity would follow.

However, time and experience have convinced us that there is no one pattern that is convincing to all right-thinking people. Historical criticism has shown that with the process that produced the Scriptures it is impossible for any coherent pattern to be found. Thus, far from being a basis for unity today, pattern-ism or restoration may become a sure and certain bar-rier to unity and has, as a matter of fact, resulted in more divisions. Any pattern we propose becomes di-visive, marking those who reject it as the "non-church," and those who accept it as "the church," that is, a sect.

A group may advertise itself as being non-sectarian, when the very claim is in itself sectarian. By this claim, it marks itself as being different from other groups, unique in having some special truth that keeps it from being a sect. A group may say that it has no creed, while its very "creedlessness" is its test for ex-clusion, or its creed. If an unimmersed Christian should seek to enter that church, he might well find the sect's creed on immersion barring his way.

Paul told the Romans that "the kingdom of God is not eating and drinking, but righteousness, peace, and joy in the Holy Spirit." Evidently some of them were literalists and legalists, exalting petty details into required doctrine which all must accept. Paul told them to center on the real matters of the faith. He urged them to get rid of the legalism and sectarianism that caused them to quarrel and divide over the mi-nutiae.

We have not yet seen a sect built on justice, mercy, faith, peace, and righteousness. Such great concerns produce something greater in fellowship than a sect.

SOCIAL IRRELEVANCE

The sect, by the nature of its life, is introspective. It has mirrors where windows ought to be. Its con-cern is for its own housekeeping problems—how to maintain the orthodoxy of the sect, and how to bring others to it. It must constantly define and redefine its terms so as to guard against creeping heterodoxy. In this introspection, it loses significant relationship to the world around it. The sect is not only separated from other sects but is also cut off from the mainstream of secular life. Being absorbed in its own institutional purity, it becomes irrelevant to the social concerns of the world.

Since the sect seeks to live by a document of two thousand years ago, which it interprets with great literalness, its look is also primarily retrospective. It lives in the backwater of life, talking of old questions and ancient issues but unable to come to grips with the contemporary urgencies. The early church was vital and dynamic, turning its world upside down, because it was valiantly dealing with the problems of its day. To try to live by a literal imitation of that church and its solutions is to be called from the living present to the dead past.

In a world like ours, filled with revolutionary change and challenge, the church must find through faith the insight and courage to minister as the early church ministered—but not by the same letter. A world with increasingly crushing problems of exploding populations, urbanization, automation, racial tension, emerging nations, armaments escalation, the constant threat of nuclear disaster, mounting discontent of the world's poor in the presence of over-abundance—in all this the church must have something more to offer than dry-as-dust irrelevances about the form of baptism, frequency of the Supper, and church polity. While the world is topsy-turvy in its search for new and meaningful value and understanding, the church cannot sit it out, arguing about the details of its own housekeeping chores. The church must be in the world to minister to it, and to give its life as a ransom for many.

When Paul was brought before Gallio for trial, his Jewish accusers babbled and quibbled about hair-splitting differences of their literal interpretations. Gallio, a pagan but a judge concerned for justice, became disgusted and said: "If this were a matter of right or wrong, I would deal with you. But since it is a question of words and names in your own law, see to it yourselves. I am not minded to judge in such matters." He *drove* them from the judgment seat. Here is the sad spectacle of a pagan man driving religious men away in indignation, not because they were too challenging and demanding, but because they were too trivial, talking nonsense to a man concerned about more vital things.

In his parable of the good Samaritan, Jesus did not have to include a priest, but he did. The priest was pious, orthodox, meticulous about proper details of doctrine and practice in his temple functions, but he passed by his neighbor's need. His religion was of the temple, not of the road or marketplace. The one Jesus approved in the parable was the heretic, the despised Samaritan, who doubtless worshipped at the wrong temple in Samaria and who followed corrupted rituals at an illegitimate altar. Jesus' contrast between the priest and the Samaritan was not the contrast of race, for we do not know the race of the man who needed their help. He was contrasting priestly religion—the religion of the altar, the legalistic, literalistic, sectarian religion of the Pharisees—with the prophetic religion that is relevant to the bleeding of needy men.

When Jesus talked of separating sheep from goats, he said not a word about sound doctrine, the true sect, or any of the other priestly conditions. On the contrary, he talked about social needs: feeding the hungry, clothing the naked, ministering to the thirsty, the sick, imprisoned, and strangers. Jesus held that separation comes at the point of a man's involvement with his brother's need and his willingness to sacrifice to release him from misery. He further said that when we minister to men we minister to him. Micah had asked how we shall come to the Lord. Jesus said that we come to him through ministering to suffering. This is not far from Micah's own answer: "to do justice, to love kindness, and to walk humbly with thy God."

The twenty-third chapter of Matthew contains parts of the bluntest and most scathing prophetic denunciation of priestly religion to be found anywhere in literature. There Jesus scored the Pharisees because they would carefully "tithe mint, anise, and cummin, and leave undone the *weightier* matters of the law: justice, and mercy, and faith." The conflict between priest and prophet is always here: which is more important, tithing and the other housekeeping chores of the sect, or justice in the marketplace, mercy towards the oppressed, and inward faith toward God?

One-tenth of our brethren in the United States are humiliated from morning until night every day of their lives simply because they are darker than most of us. Their cries for justice have gone unheeded, even by the church which should have been most concerned for this brother beside the road. The cry and demand has been taken into our streets. Still the nation resists, and still the church hesitates to take an unequivocal stand for their rights as men. Could anything be more priestly than for us to continue to baptize, commune, tithe and the rest, while our brethren and their children are daily humiliated? Shall we continue to call the people to solemn assemblies, to religious feasts, to prayers, and hymns, or shall we with Amos say that all these externals are no delight to the Lord but that we must let "justice roll down like waters, and righteousness as a mighty stream"?

Let justice roll down like waters for the colored people of the United States and of South Africa and everywhere else. Let justice roll down for the two billions who are hungry from birth until death, while we, the minority, kill ourselves with fatness. Let justice roll down for the hungry who need bread instead of our bombs. Let justice roll down like waters, that His kingdom may come, that His will may be done on the earth even as it is in heaven.

LAURIE HIBBETT was born in Alexandria, Virginia, the fourth generation of English settlers whose religion was Episcopal with a sprinkling of Quakers. When her father married a Tennessee girl, he agreed to bring his children up in his wife's Church of Christ faith. Mrs. Hibbett was still an infant when her father died and her mother moved to Nashville; from that time forward her history was Church of Christ. She married a graduate of a Church of Christ college; maternal grandfathers on each side were elders.

Although Mrs. Hibbett is now Episcopalian, she says, "I would no more repudiate my Church of Christ sources than would St. Paul his Hebrew culture. Though with St. Paul I found it necessary to press on, forgetting the things of the past, I remain deeply attached to this regional phenomenon and these are the people I claim as most fully my own." Mrs. Hibbett is the author of a charming, widely-read short story entitled, "Fruit in His Season."

A TIME TO SPEAK

By Laurie L. Hibbett

For everything there is a season, and a time for
every matter under heaven . . . (Ecclesiastes)

The woman was seated alone in a pew near the
center of the big Gothic church. The lights had not yet
come on and except for herself the church was empty.
She was there early in order to think about an essay
she was preparing on a serious subject. Why was she,
a born and bred member of the Church of Christ,
seated here now as an Episcopalian? This was the
question she was attempting to answer for herself
and her friends.

When she thought of putting her reasons on paper,
it seemed to her that there were no words to deal with
her former church as gently as the isolation of its
members deserved.

"Perhaps all I could say to them would be, 'God loves
you.' But I would have to add, 'Reach out to Him,
above your leaders who plant themselves so squarely
between you and God, and who say to you, 'Accept our
teaching or reject the Christ.' "

"I would have to add, 'This is not where the choice
lies, really. You may reject Church of Christ teaching
and still find God through Christ.' " It was her hope
that someone as troubled by the Church of Christ as
she had been would read her words and take heart.

She knelt on the prayer stool. Turning to a passage
in the prayer book she read silently:

Almighty God unto whom all hearts are open, all
desires known, and from whom no secrets are hid,
cleanse the thoughts of our hearts by the inspiration of
thy Holy Spirit, that we may perfectly love thee and
worthily magnify thy holy Name; through Christ our
Lord. Amen.

She rose from her knees and sat motionless in the perfect stillness. Above her the vaulted ceiling arched like the hull of an inverted ark. She looked forward to this time of quietness before the service began. It was here, in facing the cross, that she could come to terms with the reality of suffering and, accepting, find mysterious release. Here the cross was the focal point of both the teaching and the architecture of the church.

She closed her eyes and in memory returned to a Church of Christ auditorium. She saw herself as a child, a young woman, a mother, silently absorbing and appraising a philosophy of God, man, and salvation, as sermon after sermon rolled down from the pulpit and into her heart. These churches, too, followed a pattern of design based on their doctrine. As in the Episcopal Church, architecture and teaching were closely coordinated. But in the Church of Christ there was no sign of a cross. There was no time for meditation.

"I had no right to impose on them an unnatural quiet they did not want," she thought. "But my own nature called for a sanctuary, and I had to find it."

She knew there were others in the Church of Christ who would have preferred meditation to small talk before the service. She felt they were needlessly deprived of the visible symbol of the cross as well as of the meaning of the cross in the Christian faith. She saw them as a people who cannot admit the cross into their buildings or into their hearts, for to be confronted by the cross would be to lose all sense of earned salvation.

So the baptistery, instead, looms high in the Church of Christ building—as in its teachings. The cross features only an incident in the life of Him who, as they teach, made baptism the chief condition of salvation. Reconciliation, therefore, is not a gift, fully effected by Jesus on the cross. It is a reward, earned by man through obedience in baptism.

In the Church of Christ auditorium had she looked to left or right of the pulpit, her eye would have met a score board with postings of statistics. Straight ahead in dead center would be a stage where later a preacher would star as sole performer. He would flex his closed Bible at the congregation. He would say which verse is requisite to salvation, which is not. His sermon would be the core of the service. Beneath the stage, at the very foot of the preacher, would lie the body and blood of our Lord. She groaned inwardly and covered her face with her hands.

Lord, have mercy upon us.
Christ, have mercy upon us.

She opened her eyes to survey her present surroundings, where to look ahead was to face the cross. There was no escaping it. Here she looked *up* to the Lord's table. It was higher and nearer the cross than the minister's stand. His position to the side reminded both him and the congregation of his subservient role to these two holy mysteries, the cross and the sacraments.

She thought the place of the minister in the Church of Christ was overdone. The space given his pulpit, the time given his sermon, the songs picked to underscore his theme—all these geared the service to one man and his mood. It was too heavy a burden for him, too passive a role for the congregation. "Perhaps I won't mention this," she thought; "there is so much else."

She might begin by explaining the error of the name, Church of Christ.

"Church of Christ," I shall have to tell them, "is a misnomer when used exclusively, as this church uses it. Church of Christ is the generic term for all Christian churches of all ages. It belongs equally to all denominations and has always been understood to mean the whole state of Christ's church. As such it is neither

identifying nor realistic when applied to a specific
regional phenomenon within Christendom."

Because of this misunderstanding of its own name,
the Church of Christ lacks true identification even
among its own members. The Church of Christ person
must ask the Church of Christ stranger the age-old
question, long admitted by more realistic denominations: "Which branch?" The Church of Christ (the
denomination) within the true Church of Christ (the
whole of Christendom) has lesser Churches of Christ
within it. Ad infinitum. *Which branch* is still as
reasonable a question now as when Alexander Campbell started his movement to make the question obsolete.

But why should the question be obsolete? Paradoxically, the man most typically regional may be most
universal. The greatest Christian of all, St. Paul, belonged to a sect and said so. "I am a Pharisee," he
said in *Acts* 23: 6, although he belonged even then to
the Church of Christ. Nor was Jesus superman but
typical man. Son of Man, he liked to call himself, to
show how typical. He was connected with a region
(Galilee), with a race (the Jews), and with a time
(under Pontius Pilate). He was not called Cosmo-
politan but Nazarene, an unpretentious local name he
never denied.

"I am a Southern woman, with an Episcopal father
and a Church of Christ mother, one as regional as the
other. My theology, such as it is, has been colored by
these facts. How could I believe that the denomination, the Church of Christ, transcends history, persons, external influences, errors of interpretation or
translation of the Bible, and the limitations of human
understanding?"

She thought now with deep compassion and respect
of her forefathers crossing the mountains from North
Carolina into Tennessee, where every man with his
Bible might establish his own church. That many did

was a practical necessity. God does not leave Himself
without witnesses in any generation. Any ordained
churchman who smiles at the theology of these settlers
may well be asked, "Where were you?"

But although she revered her Church of Christ an-
cestors, she knew they were not all of Christendom,
then or now. She thought all churches might be viewed
with more tolerance by one another if they could see
each other as a temporary craft, rising and falling on
waves of historic necessity, as a sort of ark to carry
us through the flood until the waters recede and we
step out on firmer ground. The visible church is always a frail makeshift to bring us to shore. It is not
always pleasant in the ark. We are varied and often
incompatible creatures who live within. We stay there
because it is worse outside. Death is there.

"If they had called themselves simple Campbellites
and had admitted their place in time, it would have
helped," she thought. "For they are neither the beginning nor the end of Christ's Church."

So much for the name. There are other matters.
There are serious doctrinal errors.

Again she turned to the Prayer Book and read silently, this time from Psalm 133:

*If thou, Lord, wilt be extreme to mark what is done
amiss, O, Lord, who may abide it?* Foretelling the law
of grace, the psalmist asks a rhetorical question.

She would have to say something about the Church
of Christ and grace, that uniquely Christian word. To
her mother church, grace was a dangerous word, a
word to be used only when it could be carefully explained away. To mention grace was to follow with a
warning of the inherent pitfall of trusting grace fully.
Salvation by works, not by grace, was (and is) the
teaching of her mother church.

Therefore, as a teenager, it was with astonishment
that she had read one day in the Bible, "For by grace

you have been saved through faith; and this is not your own doing, it is the gift of God—not because of works, lest any man should boast." Holding the open Bible in her hand and pointing to the chapter and verse in the manner of her people, she said to her mother, "This knocks our theory into a cocked hat." She said it in sorrow, for there is no satisfaction in discovering that you and your people before you have built your faith on an erroneous opinion.

Perhaps more people are reading the Bible nowadays, she mused, for in recent years the word grace crops up oftener in Church of Christ sermons. Grace had been uncovered by someone who had pointed out the word just as she had pointed it out. It was there. So the preachers were saying, "Grace is a good word, but it means grace to be baptized in order to be saved by the graciousness of God in granting baptism as the means of salvation." Which is nonsense. Grace means grace. But she knew well that for the people of her girlhood, this notion of a free gift of God was incomprehensible. Some puritanical harshness in the nature of these Scotch-Irish church fathers said to their God, as they said to the world, "I will accept nothing I have not earned."

"It's magnificent," she thought, "but it is not Christian."

In similar fashion, she reflected, they have dealt falsely with the Holy Spirit and have said, "The Holy Spirit means the Bible." Here again she saw a trace of rugged individualism in characters who refused to be "carried to the skies on flowery beds of ease," an attitude which they feared was encouraged by emphasis on the Spirit.

"And here I must tread lightly," she said, slipping again to her knees. "For the Holy Spirit is the Holy Spirit, and I am not worthy so much as to say the name, much less to explain it." She began to pray again:

O, God, who didst teach the heart of thy faithful peo-
ple by sending them the light of thy Holy Spirit, Grant
us by the same Spirit to have a right judgment in all
things and evermore to rejoice in his Holy comfort;
through the merits of Christ Jesus, our Saviour, who
liveth and reigneth with thee, in the unity of the same
spirit, one God, world without end. Amen.

She rose to a sitting position again and thought
about the Church of Christ and its relationship to the
Holy Spirit. "I could not say that they have a false
concept of the Holy Spirit. They have almost no concept of it at all."

Campbell and other fathers of the Church of Christ
had seen in frontier revivals too much of the mass
hysteria said to be caused by the Spirit. They wanted
none of this sensationalism. Like most reformers, they
tended to over-correct. The result was that the Spirit
was not included in the body of dogma of the Church of
Christ. The nearest concession made by the group was
to admit that the Spirit had dictated the Bible. In
effect, they asked this question: do you follow the
Bible along the picked path of Church of Christ teaching, omitting this verse as unessential, exalting this
verse as requisite to salvation? If the answer was yes,
then one could assume the Spirit was leading him.

"They have cut the heart out of the Christian religion," she thought, "when they stripped it of grace
and the Holy Spirit."

What is left?

This brought her to the center of the problem, she
felt. The Church of Christ, whatever else it may have
discarded or ignored, has the Bible. This simple affir-
mation probably constitutes the group's chief problem.
Here supposed strength turns out to be actual weakness. "This fact will come to light whether I say it or
not," she thought. "For more of their people will read
the Bible for themselves as the educational advantages

of the group increase with new prosperity. They will see how preposterous this unqualified claim is."

It pleases the Church of Christ, she knew, to say to the world that it stands on the Bible alone, against modernism and atheism, and that herein lies the crux of its quarrel with the rest of the Christian and secular world. But there are many other Bible churches, and they also stand on the Bible alone. One would suppose, in reading Church of Christ literature, that this church has much in common with other evangelical, conservative Christians. Yet the truth is that the Church of Christ allies itself to no such groups, nor permits any of them to link themselves with it. Churches which do not accept the Church of Christ as final authority on interpretation of the Bible meet an insurmountable wall. This is not a Bible church against a non-Bible world; this is a church which claims to love the Bible but determinedly avoids such parts of the Bible as it does not stress in its circumscribed doctrine of selected scriptures.

Because of its claim to stand on the Bible alone, the Church of Christ will not face the fact that it has, in common with other churches, a body of dogma based partly on scriptures, partly on church authority. In each new generation the young preacher must go through the motions of assembling from scriptures the exact doctrine of the preceding generation. If he discovers new truths in the Bible, he is quickly branded as unsound. *He does not have to depart from the Bible to acquire this stigma. He has only to pick unfamiliar verses within the Bible.* So unless his Bible reading is superficial, he is soon at odds with his brotherhood. The group wants no prophets bent on pouring new wine into old skins. The brighter the rising star of the student, the earlier his meteoric fall. The leap of faith from the Church of Christ as Saviour to Jesus Christ as Saviour is a hazardous one. With blind faith in the Church of Christ shattered, many young men give up Christianity altogether.

She turned to the back of her prayer book.

Item 6. Holy Scriptures containeth all things necessary to salvation; so that whatsoever is not read therein nor may be proved thereby is not to be required of any man . . . that it should be thought requisite to salvation.

This is, in essence, the belief of all Protestant churches, and no church has a monopoly on the idea of Bible authority. However, most churches are frank to say that church authority also plays a part. The church itself as a corporate body has implied power to take action or set precedent that may not be proved by the Bible. This is done as often in the Church of Christ as in other churches and the Church of Christ has, as time and money have allowed, added whatever innovations as have seemed necessary for the general welfare. No one would think of taking them to task for this, but the group should admit that it does act from time to time on church authority, not on Bible authority alone. To call itself a Bible-only church makes it appear deluded to those who study the Bible.

Further deceiving itself, the group advertises itself as bound to stay within the written word. Not only does it fail to do this, but its people are not free to go about unrestricted even *within* the written word. Its members may speak where the Bible speaks only if the Church of Christ speaks to the subject.

For example, the Church of Christ rules out such scriptural practices as the ministry of healing, the holy kiss, the washing of feet, mutual edification or the priesthood of all believers, the selling of all things and holding them in common, and the laying on of hands with which the book of *Acts* is replete. None of these items apply today, the Church of Christ states flatly. Yet all may be proved by the Bible.

The Church of Christ by its constituted authority has a right to ignore these passages. I defend this right. But its members would be happier if they understood that Church of Christ policy is determined by church authority, not scriptural authority alone. Let the leaders openly announce the church dogma, explain that certain scriptures are disparaged by preference of the group and others emphasized for the same reason. Let them reveal the hidden hierarchy which determines such matters, and then take their place modestly, realistically, with the ranks of Christendom. Many of their followers could then breathe a sigh of relief at being released from the embarrassment of defending an untenable position. One could then respect their denomination as a lately come but welcome part of Christ's church.

Grace, the Holy Spirit, hierarchy. These are frightening words to the Church of Christ. There is a word of even stronger taboo among its members, however. This is the word "creed." It is denied by the group that they have a creed. Actually, they have a rigid creed known to all of them. They find unaccountable satisfaction in the fact that their creed is not *written*.

"Is a creed any less a creed because it is not written?" she recalled asking an aged seer in the Church of Christ. He gave her a long look but did not answer. These people are timid, wily, cautious of traps. They have the natural cunning of the person who seeks to trap others and is therefore always alert to being trapped himself. To those who do not know them, they appear both suspicious and crafty. Actually, they are frightened. (I know. I was there. I was frightened.) She pictured them as a flock of timid birds that must be lured with crumbs toward the rest of Christendom. One false move could startle them away. Yet she did not wish to trap them nor to hurt them. She was unarmed. It was she who was vulnerable to them because of her love for them. Her only wish for them was that they might be released from the trap of their own making.

She wished that they might learn to pray with other Christians. Turning to one of her favorite prayers, she read:

Almighty God, whose most dear Son went not up to joy but first he suffered pain and entered not into glory before he was crucified, mercifully grant that we walking in the way of the cross may find it none other than the way of life and peace, through the same thy Son, Jesus Christ, our Lord. Amen.

In the Church of Christ such written prayers, however comforting, are suspect, regardless of their truth. At the communion service in the Episcopal Church the minister would say, "And now as our Saviour Christ hath taught us, we are bold to say . . ." And then in unison the congregation would begin, "Our Father, who art in heaven." Early Christians could be identified by claiming God as their Father. It took courage in those times of persecution for a convert to admit the Christian relationship in public assembly. "Bold to say" was therefore appropriate.

In the Church of Christ, however, the Lord's Prayer itself is forbidden. A member of the church may compose his own prayer on the spot, leading the congregation through phrases of sometimes doubtful theology, but when it comes to the Lord's Prayer, the group will not join in. A technicality precludes it. "Thy kingdom come" is a forbidden petition. Christ's kingdom has already come, they teach. It is the Church of Christ. His kingdom is here in this specific form as the only kingdom, now or ever. The Lord's Prayer is not said in the Church of Christ.

She was bold to say it now, her long-mute tongue finding joy in release: "Our Father, who art in heaven. . . . Thy kingdom come."

"How can I welcome into Christendom a people who

refuse to join in the Lord's Prayer with other Christians?" she asked silently in the dim stillness.

And now a chill spread through the building and enveloped her. Her heart grew cold as the disturbing truth rose into her consciousness. "Their doctrine breeds tragedy," she whispered.

For this woman, leaving the church of her childhood was not a rebellion against imagined restrictions nor a newly acquired taste for a more intellectual group. There was something deeper, something which made the Church of Christ theory intolerable to what was best in her nature. She had found through cumulative experience that rigid notions of sound doctrine can be dangerous to homes and even sanity, and this she could not reconcile with the gospel of Christ, which is good news, not bad. To understand this, one must know that the Church of Christ has an order of priority in which church doctrine always takes precedence over ethics, morals, common sense or common weal. Because of its claim to a perfect and unalterable plan of salvation, it may stand adamantly against the common good of the community.

She thought of a young girl, a charge of the state, who had been shuttled from one foster home to another. The one stable factor in her life had been a continuing association with the Methodist Church. She was placed in a Church of Christ home where the family promptly made a concerted effort to disillusion her about her Methodist background and to break her connection with the Methodists. This family believed what every orthodox Church of Christ minister teaches, *that any Church of Christ congregation under any circumstances is preferable to any other church, and that proselyting is a divine duty at whatever cost to the spirit of the convert.* This may be disastrous when the victim is a child with few words but strong emotional ties to another group. The girl asked to be

placed in another home and this was done, but all cases
do not turn out so well.

There are lighter cases of rigid doctrine in operation against ethics. "But I will not let the essay de-
volve into comedy," she promised.

Two Church of Christ women discussed a noted
swindler:

"What did he do with all that money?"

"He gave it to the Lord."

"If I had been his lawyer," she thought, "I would
have built his defense on the grounds that in the church
which produced him, money is the spiritual status
symbol. Men are under pressure to make money, in
order to give money, in order to prove by money that
they love God, and that He loves them. The heroes of
faith in this culture tend to be financiers. Whatever
shadow of suspicion falls on sharp business practice
is covered by the doctrinal verity to which they subscribe: 'He gave it to the Lord.' "

There are sadder cases, involving more than money.
She remembered the young husband who left his wife
and small children destitute because, as his mother ex-
cused it, the wife would not go to church with her
husband. Church-going may even take precedence over
family support. And she recalled that none of the
husband's church friends whom she encountered felt
that his action was unjustified.

How many such cases could she remember? The
world would not contain them. There are good people
in the Church of Christ who deplore the wrongs done
in the name of dogma and the Lord. But the attitude
too frequent among them is that the more one silently
endures these absurdities, the more pleased God is
with the forbearance. Jesus was not so tolerant. His
cleansing of the temple was the act of a man outraged
at injustice. He snatched the nearest thing at hand
and went to work on reforms. Because primary obedience is to the church, righteous indignation—that

most purifying of emotions—is stifled in the Church of Christ. Blind loyalty is to the church, not to justice; to the church, not to morality; to the church, not to simple everyday *goodness*.

Needless to say, family relations suffer. The hearts of the sons are turned against the fathers and the hearts of the fathers against the sons. Religion becomes the divider instead of the healer of the breach. Here, in the name of religion, husband and wife are at odds in an eternal triangle—men, women, and God— in which God set against man has placed woman at the base of the triangle. The marital relationship is summed up in Church of Christ doctrine by St. Paul's, "Wives, be in subjection." Property rights, personal rights, rights connected with the rearing of children— the wife has none if the husband decides to make a test case of this scripture. The dangers of this doctrine for the emotionally unstable man are plain.

A woman who tries to explain the Bible in the Church of Christ is in the unfortunate position of substantiating (by her very desire to explain) the charges being made against her kind. Plainly she is not fully subjected or she would not be possessed with the idea that she has something to say. So the more she says, the blacker it looks for her case.

She had wanted to say that St. Paul's "subjection" is used in juxtaposition with Christ's crucifixion. "As the church is subject to Christ, so let wives also be subject in everything to their husbands," and "this is a great mystery and I take it to mean Christ and the Church" (*Eph.* 5:23). The subjection of which St. Paul speaks is elicited by the boundless love of the husband, as Christ loves the Church. Thus it is the husband who sets the tone of marriage since he represents Christ in the relationship. The wife's responsibility is to respond lovingly to his sacrifice. She is subject to him because he is crucified for her. If he is not the type of Christ, if his role is not saviour through sacrifice, then the wife's subjection to him is neither required nor commendable. The Christian woman worships the Christ image in her husband. If it is not there, she may be worshipping Satan. "Strong words," she thought, "but the Bible is strong meat for those who believe it."

Her mind turned to the Church of Christ practice of public confession by one person before the assembled congregation. Lacking any adequate scriptural precedent, the custom stemmed loosely from a verse ("confessing your faults one to another") which suggested person-to-person relationships in private talks, not person-to-audience. The Church of Christ family never knows when a moving sermon may trigger a march to the front of the church by some unstable member who will confess what is often his own grievance thinly disguised as his error. Surprising family situations are disclosed in public, but solutions remain as remote as before.

"I could give a dozen examples of harm done by this practice," she thought. She began to sort them in her mind for typical cases, but as each dreadful circumstance was relived she discarded it as too painful to repeat. Yet these sad histories had been recounted in public assembly to a curious congregation. She was glad to be in a church where there is only general confession by the congregation in unison. No opportunity is offered in general confession for the exhibitionist to compound his crime by exploiting it in public confession.

The church was filling now. Usually with her own prayers said, she tried to join her silent prayer to that of whatever person came in and knelt to pray. Would they have found strength for their separate tasks for the week in the services she recalled from young womanhood? Many who have sat through those services have found them strangely unnerving.

"I can't afford the demoralization," a young friend

had confided to her about the Sunday service in his church. But he had kept on going. If he attends any religious service now it is in the institution to which he is confined. He was brighter than the group, but he was loving, and out of loyalty and pity for his parents he would not leave the Church of Christ and break their hearts. He has been forced to pretend to an ignorance he does not have. An inexorable toll is demanded of the spirit that buries its talent. But the church which advertised its visiting evangelist as "A Teacher From God," (I knew him; he was actually from Texas) demands modesty of its lay members, and the brilliant one is called proud if he does not hide his light beneath a bushel. My young friend is innocent, but those who preached to him are not.

An angel stared down at her from the stained-glass window as she half turned towards the light. Stern-faced but beautiful, he was a thoroughly masculine angel. In his hand was an arrow-straight dart of light. Beneath was inscribed, from Isaiah, "I will make justice the line, and righteousness the plummet."

"I will warn them," she said to the angel. "They must stop this dreadful business of substituting a limited system for the limitless Son of God. They must step down and let the people see God, who is worthy to be loved not only with heart and soul but with strength and mind."

Is God tyrant or father? Do our minds threaten Him as if He fears our growing knowledge may usurp His power? Or do our minds delight him, as the mind of the child delights the father in whose image the child is made?

"God is not interested in your opinion," the Church of Christ preacher had said to her when she was a young girl, years ago. And she, left alone with God, had said to Him, "Of course you are! Why would you number the hairs on my head if what goes on inside does not concern you?"

Shortly after that she had written a letter to an unknown Church of Christ preacher who had left his denomination for another brotherhood. In his reply he had written about God as the seeker of the lost sheep, as the father racing out to meet the son, as the offerer of the supreme gift, as the placating one, not the one to be placated. He had written:

"The sheep is found through God's initiative and is returned with rejoicing—redemption through love. God's way of changing our hearts and lives is through overwhelming demonstration of love and concern, not through threats and intimidations. We love Him because He first loved us. 'Love compels us,' said Paul about his own life. The cross leaves us without excuse; we have no answer for a love like that."

Her happiness at hearing her view of God confirmed, she resolved to begin her search for deliverance, not only for herself but for her people. There was no hurry. She stayed on for many years, waiting for an indication that she had God's permission to leave the church to which He, in His wisdom, had assigned her at her birth. At last, in the fulness of time, the Church of Christ slipped off her shoulders as a worn cape drops when the last thread breaks. It had not warmed her for years. She scarcely noticed when it fell away.

"May someone in the Church of Christ who needs such a message as my friend wrote to my need in those dark days find in his words the blessing I found and continue to find," she prayed quietly.

The service was beginning. The minister stood on a low step before the congregation and gave the call to worship:

The hour cometh and now is when the true worshippers shall worship the Father in spirit and in truth: for the Father seeketh such to worship him.

"Thank you," she said in her heart to God. "Thank you for seeking us. Thank you for deliverance."

Whatever the original estrangement between man and God, the Grand Apology had been offered. Whatever our personal estrangement, He is there waiting to make amends. He is there in such profound reality that the knowledge is almost more joy than we can bear. There would never be ways enough to show her gratitude, but she would begin by writing the essay as best she could.

Help me to write. Bless the one who reads, as I was blessed by what I read. For the sake of Him who saw Thee as Thou art, and who taught us boldly to say, with Him, Our Father. Amen.

NORMAN L. PARKS is professor of political science and head of
the department of social science at Middle Tennessee State
University. He was educated at David Lipscomb College, Abilene
Christian College (B.A.), Peabody College (M.A.), and Vanderbilt University (Ph.D.).

Prior to his present position, Mr. Parks taught for eleven years
at Vanderbilt and Peabody, and served for a time as senior editorial writer on the Nashville Tennessean. He was dean of
David Lipscomb College for eight years, and also taught at
Freed-Hardeman College and Oklahoma Christian College.

Although he has preached and taught often in Churches of
Christ, Mr. Parks considers himself anything but a professional
pulpiteer. Of his experiences in this field, he writes:

"I have spoken in many churches and on occasion still do, but
because of a lack of the pulpit stance and orthodox sermon
technique it has not been hard to preserve my non-professional
purity. At MTSU I conducted for a number of years a 'labora-
tory' in fellowship by sponsoring a student magazine called *The
Campus Christian*. The editor came from a premillennial
church, the assistant editor from a Disciples church, and the
staff from other segments of the Church of Christ. It was remarkable how well they worked and worshipped together. Such
experiences may sometimes tempt us to say, 'If there were only
some way to protect the young from the old.' "

THY ECCLESIA COME!

By Norman L. Parks

In a world of national states the problem of citizenship may be truly insoluble for a person like the late Mrs. Schwimmer of Supreme Court fame who had "only a cosmic sense of belonging to mankind." In a religious world of sects and denominations there is perhaps something of an inevitable alienation for those who have only a cosmic sense of belonging to Christ.

This appears to be particularly true within the confines of the Campbell-Stone Reformation movement, where fragmentation has reached a crisis stage. One may deeply desire to be a "disciple at large," but the degree of his acceptance by this or that fragment will depend on his acquiescence in its prescribed parochial loyalties.[1] The theory of congregational independence will in no way protect a congregation from proscription if it extends full fraternity to any prominent disciple branded as unorthodox by that faction's ruling hierarchy.

Though never claiming less than discipleship-at-large, this author has spent his active religious life within the parochial confines of that now badly fragmented wing of the American Reformation denominated "Church of Christ." Within this time he has seen its leadership abandon the main goals of the Campbell-Stone movement—unity of all Christians and the reforming of religion by purging it of hierarchy, clergy, institutional machinery, *collegia de*

---

[1] Preachers are keenly aware of the tests which they must pass, for example, before they can appear on the Church Council ("lectureship") programs sponsored by Church of Christ colleges. Trafficking in reputations is an important business of the lectureship managers. The vigilance of these guardians of orthodoxy ranges far and wide, as the author was recently reminded. A young instructor at David Lipscomb College told him in 1965, "I became deeply prejudiced against you as a freshman because Dr. ——— held you up in class as an example of dangerous liberalism." It had been 23 years since this writer had taught at that college!

propaganda de fide, non-Biblical terminology, and all post-Biblical dogma, ritual, and trappings which are made measures of orthodoxy. Indeed, he has seen this group develop the very accretions and perspectives which Campbell and Stone attacked and so widen the gap between itself and "that ancient sect first called Christians at Antioch."

Viewed sociologically, the Church of Christ is far advanced on the sect-denomination continuum, though there is a spread among its major segments. The Church of Christ (one-cup, one-book, one-assembly) is closest to the sect pole. In its emphasis on lay leadership, lay teaching, informal services, and its sense of hostility to the "world," this group is closest to the pioneer spirit of the preceding century. It would probably have a strong appeal to the underprivileged urban masses if its evangelism were directed at the urban slums. The Church of Christ (premillennial) is also closer to the sect pole, though developing colleges and a clergy. However, it is distinguished by its marked pietism, its sense of the presence of the Holy Spirit, and its consciousness of a broader fellowship. Both the Church of Christ (institutional) and the Church of Christ (anti-institutional) are near the de-nominational pole and may be considered together.

The Church of Christ colleges freely describe themselves as "church related" in educational circles, and they follow clearly identified denominational goals.[2] The faculty of the oldest college must formally commit themselves to follow the canons of faith prescribed by the board of directors. These colleges talk in terms of campaign goals of $10,000,000 and $25,000,000. They maintain seminary departments and some invent degrees which match, alphabetically at least, those of

---

[2] The reader is invited to examine the brilliant analysis of the miscarriage of Christian education by Robert Meyers, "Church of Christ Colleges: Is Anything Wrong?" **Restoration Review,** Fall, 1960, and the reflections of Alexander Campbell on colleges to propagate religion in **The Christian Baptist.**

Protestant seminaries. One college bulletin with a prescience unmatched in prophecy actually pinpointed the number of God's redeemed at slightly in excess of two millions! The church press boasts that the Church of Christ is now the ninth largest in America and "the fastest growing." As a middle class denomination, sociologically speaking, its clergy is well paid, gross income of $8,000 to $15,000 not being uncommon. Far from being a sacrificial vocation, its ministry offers some of limited education and ability more than they could command in secular work. Some of the larger churches round out their professional staffs with associate or assistant "ministers" and "directors of education."[3] The church long ago dropped its frontier-inspired hostility to imposing church edifices ("decorated like a theatre to gratify the pride of life," as Campbell described them), and makes efforts to put buildings in the "best" part of town.

Like the larger denominations the Church of Christ has given preeminence to the professional "pulpit." Its occupant is the one man known to all within and without the congregation. Advertising features his face, his name, his sermon subjects. The service is built around him, what precedes his front-center sermon being preliminary and what follows being anticlimactic. In the author's home city laymen are less likely to fill the Church of Christ pulpit than those of other Protestant churches. When the "regular" minister is absent, nothing is more certain than that another pastor will take his place.

To at least as great an extent as most of the leading denominations, the Church of Christ (institutional) has rejected the "Christ against culture" concept of 1

---

[3] The development of a professional pastoral office has been carried out under the term "minister." An English transliteration from the Latin Vulgate translation of the Greek original, the term actually meant "slave" and was used to describe the relationship between man and God of those who were "bought with a price." In no instance did it indicate office or the relationship of a preacher to a church. The absurdity of "assistant slave" needs no comment.

John in the economic sphere and has come to terms
with the world. Capitalism is viewed as a part of God's
law and the business order as the fruition of the divine scheme. The successful businessman, provided he
is not niggardly with his money, is emerging as the
layman hero of the church and the logical candidate
for deacon or elder. The board of elders itself is patterned after the corporate board of directors. Nowhere
has "the Protestant ethic" enjoyed a higher endorse-
ment. The social radicalism of the nineteenth century
pioneer and redneck has been replaced by a deep-dyed
economic and social conservatism which is hostile to
social reform, welfare programs, state intervention in
the economy, labor unions, racial integration, disturb-
ers of the status quo, and "those who have turned the
world upside down" (Acts 17: 6).[4]

The eagerness of the church colleges in seeking federal grants[5] and loans reflects the shallowness of the
commitment to the principle of separation of church
and state. The stream of right-wing political propaganda from the executive offices of certain of these
colleges drapes the robe of religion with a contemporary form of Social Darwinism and is an eloquent
testimony to the fact that the Church of Christ has
made its peace with the world.

With respect to government, its members seek high
office, its congressional representatives being conspic-
uously in the neanderthal wing of politics. Abandon-
ing its pacifism, the church gives status to its ranking

---

[4] See unpublished manuscript by Rex Turner, president of Alabama Christian College, entitled, "The Attitude of a Christian in the Midst of a Race
Crisis." The Christian, says Mr. Turner, must never cause "excitement" or
support change in a society. "The present trend on the part of a segment
of gospel preachers and leaders to crusade for the cause of desegregation
is contrary to the true spirit of Christianity." However, there is little doubt
that the Chistian colleges will open their doors to Negroes in order to receive federal grants and loans. Such is the power of mammon when Christianity itself is unable to effect the result.

[5] One such college, which mimeographed its own biology textbook in order
to eliminate the word evolution from the science vocabulary, has received a
federal grant in excess of $400,000 to erect a science building. Another
college, known widely for its private enterprise emphasis and its constant
criticism of "Socialistic" spending, has received a federal grant for over
$340,000.

military. Socially, it has made adjustments in keeping
with its economic ethic. Dancing may still be occasionally identified as "reveling" in sermons, but the
minister, to prevent the young people from attending
the high school junior-senior "prom," may preside over
a late-late skating party featuring hand-holding part-
ners performing to music.

The Church of Christ appears then as a lower middle
class phenomenon "on the make" at its socio-economic
level. In the author's own area it includes the congress-
man, the university president, the county judge, the
city mayor, the sheriff, bank executives, bar leaders,
medicos and dentists, and sundry business executives.
Approximately 20 per cent of the local university's
5,000 students come from Church of Christ homes. In
general, the church does not compete at the upper
middle class level, its economic ceiling being second
level "organization men," smaller business tycoons,
and junior oil millionaires. Nor is it active at the "un-
washed throng" level, leaving the lower urban classes
and slum warrens to the Pentecostals and Jehovah's
Witnesses. In summary, the Church of Christ's behavior as a sociological group reflects the expected
pattern of religion interacting with social factors
(breakup of older communities, urbanization, indus-
trialization, impersonalization of society) as the group
moves along the continuum toward mature denominationalism. This interaction centers around the drives
and frustrations of men within the social stratum in
which the church largely functions and the means of
dealing with them. In a society in social and economic
flux, religion itself is in a constant process of change,
and in this fact lies part of the crisis which has en-
gulfed the Church of Christ.

Though the church meets most of the sociological
criteria of a mature denomination, it still remains at
the sect stage doctrinally, as reflected in the priority
given to doctrinal affairs at the expense of ethical

principle. There is a powerful instrument of solidarity and cohesion in the boast, "We have the truth," when aimed against other religious groups. Doctrinally it is on a continuous military footing. Its militant state of mind allows little room for love or accommodation and none for unity in diversity. Since it is no longer at war with the secular economic world and infrequently effects confrontation with its denominational rivals, it tends to turn its sectarian hostilities inward and is presently devouring its energies in internecine conflict.[6]

In a second respect, the church remains at the sect stage in its claim of "literal" adherence to Biblical command, example, and "necessary inference." In this area it has tended toward bibliolatry. This adherence follows the sect pattern of careful selectivity of Scriptures to support the party's position. It is interesting to see which examples are binding as examples, and which are not. Examples which are *not* considered examples make up a long list: foot washing, observing the Lord's Supper on Saturday night (assuming Acts 20 refers to the Lord's Supper), speaking with tongues in public or private, observing the love feast, solos and group singing in assembly, anointing and prayers for the sick by the elders, the teaching function carried on in the main by the elders, deaconesses as well as deacons, religious head-coverings (not fancy hats) and uncut hair for females, wearing of jewelry, and congregational participation in decision-making on the Antioch and Jerusalem model. Anyone insisting upon the Biblical pattern in these matters would quickly be termed a troublemaker and would sooner or later be excommunicated.

---

[6] A phenomenon of more than passing significance is the attraction which its pulpit has for the charismatic leader with authoritarian and aggressive characteristics. Aggression which would not be tolerated in other situations may find complete sanction in the pulpit. These psychological types vent their hostilities and find verbal outlet for deep-seated aggressions in "skin-'em-alive" attacks on persons and groups. They are often adept at exploiting the neurotic guilt and fears of their hearers who have accepted a system of meritorious salvation, bringing them temporary relief and attaching them to their personal following.

But other criteria less clear or certain than some of the above are made the standards for establishing the claim of the Church of Christ to uniqueness: the Lord's Supper every Sunday (and Sunday only), mass singing only and without an instrument, the "right name," the "laying by in store" every Sunday, the "right" baptism where validity is best ascertained by the "soundness" of the baptizer, and the right "organization" of the church under a plurality of elders and deacons.

In its emphasis on the external observance of certain doctrinal formalities and in taking for granted or ignoring the really fundamental questions of religion, the Church of Christ is "majoring in minors." The emergence of "the lonely crowd"; the impersonalization and institutionalization of business, education, religion, and government; the involvement of man in far-off places and crises beyond his personal reach, and the decline of "community" have turned men to religion for answers. But one may search literature and sermons of the Church of Christ in vain for concern with such questions as: what is the meaning of life? how does the individual cope with the sense of meaninglessness, with frustration, with suffering? how can one really know God? how does one learn to love, and how does one learn to teach others to love? how do the just live by faith? how can a deeper understanding of the grace of God be won? can the Christian live a life free from fear? how is the Christian free from law, from sin, from death? how does freedom accord with necessity? how can we better meet man's need for fellowship?

While an ever increasing number of its younger generation find themselves increasingly concerned with issues like those above, the Church of Christ poses as the most fundamental question of all the "right church" issue—a matter that is inherently institutional and denominational. The criteria which it advances to

identify the "one true church" among the many claim-
ants are those which distinguish an organization rather
than a people or a way of life. Those who are involved
with the deeper issues of life are seeing these criteria
as peripheral.[7]

Let us consider the criterion of "name"—that the
true church is the one with the right name. The very
term "church" is unBiblical, substituted for the Greek
ecclesia (assembly) by ancients who were involved in
creating a power structure within the Christian religion. The *ecclesia* of Christ has no name. It is as
absurd to emphasize the name of the assembly of
Christ as to emphasize the name of the sun. Paul's
warning to Corinth shows that the "of Christ" cry can
be as denominational as the "of Luther." With respect
to the hard legalism read into the criterion of baptism
for the remission of sins, reflection will suggest that
baptism is an individual expression of faith in Christ,
while remission of sins is God's role, not man's motive.

And the legalist's case for the Lord's Supper every
Sunday and Sunday only is shadowy. It was first
observed on a weekday evening, and Christ's omission
of a prescribed time or frequency for its observance
suggests his concern for the spirit of it. It is by no
means certain that Acts 20:7 refers to the Lord's
Supper, but if it does, the occasion was Saturday night.
No day is more of a "holy day" than any other day in
the Christian life, and the making of the first day of
the week into a holy day has no more Biblical basis
than Christmas or Easter.

Completely without authoritative substance is the
"lay by in store" command based on 1 Cor. 16:1 and
making weekly church contribution a required act of
worship. The incident referred to was a means of dealing with a particular problem in the early life of the

---

[7] One young college student remarked to the author recently that "you go
to church and you hear the same old things, just doctrinal rocks being rolled
around, and what is said is not really relevant to your needs and concerns,
and then finally you stop going and you don't feel very guilty about it."

more variety

church. A congregation composed of artisans and wage earners operating on a week by week economic schedule were instructed, "Every first day of the week each of you is to put aside (at home) and keep by him a sum in proportion to his gains so that there may be no collecting when I come." This had nothing to do with a church treasury and it was not an "item of worship." As a law applied to Christians with monthly or seasonal income, it is absurd. Instances of giving in the New Testament always related the giver and the gift to a specific purpose—a fundamental characteristic of alms—and never to an impersonal treasury for undefined ends or to a group worship act on a holy day.

The legalistic case for congregational singing without a musical instrument is at best negative—silence of the New Testament on the subject. Here again the emphasis is qualitative, as in other aspects of worship. It is remarkable that the legalists stop short of their own logic in refusing to accept solos ("if a man hath a song") or group singing ("speaking one to another").

The criterion of "the divinely patterned" organization stated in absolutes leaves too much unanswered. It assumes that the church, instead of having organization as a means, *is* an organization completely subject to the authoritative rule of elders and deacons (junior executives) responsible only to God. If every church is scripturally required to have a select few to "rule" it, why is the Bible not clear in explaining how these men became authorities? Why is the suggestion that they be elected by the congregation for a term of one or two years greeted with horror? What is the scriptural basis for a self-perpetuating board of elders and deacons? If the modern church must have deacons, but not deaconesses, why does the New Testament fail to mention a single function they discharge (the explanation that they are "servants" is not valid, since all Christians are also servants)? If elders are pastors, why do they not do the job instead of hiring a professional shepherd? Why is not the popular election of "the seven" by the Jerusalem church regarded as a working example for the church to effect organization? Why does the Church of Christ utilize a prejudiced translation, designed to support the episcopal system, to establish the right of elders to "rule"? How much of a "divine pattern" exists in a plurality of elders but a single "minister"?

Alexander Campbell described the church in its activities as "radically and essentially" democratic; a fraternity of equals, such as Paul pictures in 2 Cor. 8:14, can be nothing else. Removal of authority and responsibility from the members and their concentration in the hands of an elite is as dangerous to the welfare of a church as it is to a state. People alienated from decision-making lose initiative, creativity, and obligation. The pews become passive, the services ritualistic, religion professionalized, and influence weak. When elders spend $10,000 of church money on a single enterprise without advice or consent of the members, hire a preacher without so much as a "by your leave," and assert the power of ultimate decision as to what members may believe, what they may read, whom they may hear, and who may lead the prayers or voice a sentiment, the result is a dictatorship in defiance of the whole nature of the Christian society. However "good" individual elders may be personally, the whole system is wrong.

This analysis has proceeded far enough to indicate that the Church of Christ has chosen to rest its identity on some doubtful, peripheral, or erroneous criteria while neglecting weightier matters. It has nothing fundamental to lose in holding that though the frequency and time of the Lord's Supper is moot, its observance each Sunday is an appropriate response of those who wish to remember Christ. There is no loss in conceding that while there is no "law" on the church treasury, weekly collections represent a practical way for members to consolidate their giving for specific purposes, provided this practice does not substitute for private alms giving. There would be no loss in granting that there is no merit *per se* in singing with or without an instrument, but there is no limit to the power, richness, depth, and spirituality of a capella singing when developed by hard practice, mastery of music, and individual specialization. There would be no loss in agreeing that while there is always a place for leadership (in contrast to "ruling"), the power of any group is magnified by full participation in decision-making. There would be no loss—except the loss of the cocoon of legalism which has been spun around the entire church.

The redefinition of its identity in non-legalistic concepts will be necessary before the Church of Christ can communicate in the larger assembly of God. The steady attrition that accompanies the increasing education of its members cannot be stopped until the disgracefully mediocre scholarship and shallow legalism of its present pulpit, press, and seminary leadership is modified by a deeper spirituality, a greater magnanimity, and sounder learning. Actually such a process is under way. Beneath the surface there is a vast unrest, indeed, in the very citadels of orthodoxy—the colleges —as well as elsewhere, demanding a religion of grace and a gospel of good news to replace the hardshell legalism of the core church. In 1965 a college located in the heartland of "orthodoxy" lost a half dozen of its abler young men for this reason, and it will lose others, either by resignation or purge.

It is ironic that though the American Reformation was a revolt against Calvinism, the Church of Christ is today one of the most Calvinistic bodies in the Protestant arc. In spirit it has gone all the way back to Geneva to produce a modern version of *The Institutes of the Christian Religion*. Its code is constantly revised to include new laws on the millennium, biology, institutionalization, fellowship, capitalism, Biblical scholarship, or whatever is the issue of the moment. Legalism and authoritarianism reduce Christianity to a system of law and a salvation by merit, authoritatively proclaimed and enforced. Such a religion presents the God-man relationship in dichotomies of creator-creature, wrath-fear, command-submission, and authority-conformity instead of I-thou, friend-friend, redeemer-redeemed, father-son. Its authoritarian God is jealous of his rights and angered when denied propitiation by money, time, service, and ritualistic observance. His will is stated in laws, and to break one of them is to suffer guilt for all. He forgives, but only when directly asked, and watchfully totals all of man's debits and credits.

Such a view of religion produces two extremes. One is the self-righteous, judgmental, and aggressive person who lives up to the "law." The other is the insecure, neurotic, fear-ridden, and guilt-laden individual who, try as he may, is overwhelmed by the possibility that he has not been right enough or done enough to win salvation. For both types the lesson of Romans remains unrevealed. Between the extremes are others, who, for sanity of mind and to escape the plight into which legalism thrusts its victims, find an answer in reducing the laws to formalities within their reach. Others manage in spite of the law approach to find meaning in a religion of grace and faith. These are the people who see the Christian assembly as a community of seekers, who desire to promote fraternity, dialogue, and love, and who would welcome the exploration of the "freedom that is in Christ Jesus." Needless to say, they are preservers of its candlestick.

Efforts to enforce conformity reflect the degree of authoritarianism in the Church of Christ. The free man questions, tries, tests. He acknowledges no authority to which he does not freely consent as internalized truth. He is subject to no control above his own conscience. He does not obey because it is commanded, but because it is the way of truth and wisdom. The free life is also the faith life—faith in the determinable elements of life as well as in its spontaneity, freshness, and potential. The free man defines authority as the *right to acceptance* which is inherent in truth, fact, reality. He is not free to believe or practice anything else, because it would be injurious or self-defeating. To him the only conformity that is healthful is the conforming of thought, feeling, and action to truth—to the true reality outside of self. Authoritarianism, in contrast, emphasizes externalized power, superordination and subordination, superiority and inferiority, rule and submission. It finds lodgment in father-dominated families, class-structured societies, anti-democratic governments, and legalistic religions. It has psychological roots in individual personality: overly-felt need for security, which may be temporarily satisfied by either submission or domination; fear of self-direction and preference for obedience to outside authority; tendency to conform compulsively to the orthodox; preference for "order" and discipline over freedom and spontaneity in human relations; satisfaction derived from identifying with a superior "authority"; emotional rigidity and limited imagination; excessive concern with group acceptance; abnormal loyalty to the in-group; insecurity in the presence of out-groups; attraction to the cult of personality—the WHO rather than the WHAT or the WIIY; the tendency to look on "those in authority" with reverence and loyalty; acceptance of an inferior status for women.

The authoritarian view of the social order is revealed in an essay by a Christian college president on the segregation issue:

True enough, slavery is unlawful in the United States. The fine principle involved in the master-slave relationship, however, obtains today in both social and civic relationships of a like nature as it did in Paul's day. The fine principle involved in the master-servant relationship, [sic] obtains in such as the employer-employee relationship, the literate-illiterate social relationship, and the privileged-underprivileged social relationship. The system of jurisprudence often refers to the master-servant doctrine. . . .[8]

Certain evils inevitably flow from an authoritarian religion: (1) a passive, submissive membership lacking in imagination and creativity; (2) aggressive, power-hungry leaders who sublimate their own insecurity by speaking as oracles and demanding acceptance; (3) loss of freedom of inquiry and freedom of speech; (4) little identification with God as love; (5) centralization of decision-making in a handful of "authorities"; (6) growth of coldness, formalism, and ritualism; (7) the use of scholarship to preserve the status quo, thus stopping progress; (8) conflict between rival "authorities," producing factions and splits; (9) increased pressure for conformity in opinion; (1) growth of suppressed anxiety and guilt in the membership; (11) rejection of the idea that a congregation is a democracy or brotherhood of equals; (12) tendency of the leaders to hold the ability of the general membership in low esteem, making it necessary for the authorities to decide for them so as to avoid "mistakes"; (13) concentration of control of the church property and funds in the hands of a few; (14) an "etatist" rather than an instrumentalist view of the church, holding the church to be an organism superior to and, in a sense, separate from the individual and for

---

[8] The confusion of the values of a dominant Southern social class with the principles of Christianity in this statement by Rex Turner reflects the middle class ideology of the Church of Christ. Communism is frequently attacked from the pulpit, but democracy is bluntly rejected, particularly in the religious society. The author has heard the right to work emphasized, but never the right of workers to bargain collectively for the price of their labor. He has heard socialism attacked, but never private monopoly. He has heard capitalism praised, but never a word about the tension between the profit motive as self-aggrandizement and Christ's "deny yourself."

the good of which the individual can be sacrificed; (15) interpersonal relations definable in terms of "brother's keeper" rather than "brother's brother"; (16) insistence that "the" faith is a finished system completely known to the authorities, beyond re-examination, and capable of being authoritatively defined and enforced.

A power structure is an inevitable part of a legalistic religion. Not since Puritan days has as much power gravitated into the hands of the ministers as in the contemporary Church of Christ. This post-Biblical officer has gathered in his own hands the teaching function which originally belonged to the elders. In the typical church he is at the center of the decision-making process. Excommunication bulls are prepared by him. Supervisory functions fall to him. The church bulletin is his voice. He speaks ex cathedra for the church. He influences the choice of personnel for the "Crusade for Christ" and the "Youth for Christ" revivals. He attends the annual council at the nearest church college to help firm up the party line and make contacts for future engagements, and in this capacity serves as the main link between the brotherhood power structure and the congregational power structure.

The latter is made up of the self-perpetuating board of elders and deacons who "rule," control the treasury ($50,000 a year spells considerable power), grant recognition to complaisant members, and "silence" the "dangerous" ones. The elimination of the mass of members from any significant role in what the congregation is to do or how its money is to be spent is unquestionably a major landmark in the development of the Church of Christ into an authoritarian denomination. The total elimination of women from the business meeting reflects the conviction that they, like children, are "subordinate." A highly educated woman member, with a personal income in excess of most men in the congregation, may make banking and commercial decisions of major importance during the

week, meeting men on the basis of equality, but be
deemed entirely unfit to pass on the business of the
church. However, with the growth of the power system, the mass of male members has, in effect, fallen
into the same state of inferiority.

Viewed either sociologically or scripturally, the
Church of Christ is not the church of Christ. Its members, in a sense, are neither "Christians only" nor "the
only Christians." Its fragmentation cancels out the
first proposition.[9] The arrogance of the second dis-
plays an attitude wholly contrary to the genius of
Christianity. The author believes that there are great
numbers of noble, dedicated Christians in the Church
of Christ. He has no desire to be alienated from them.
As children of God they are in his family and should
share with all the others his fellowship. Any difference in opinion or understanding of religious truth
should never be a barrier. But indifference alone
could lead the author to ignore or gloss over the denominationalism, authoritarianism, corroding legalism,
or depressing institutionalization of power in the
Church of Christ.

There is the plaint that one must not criticize the
church lest its "image" be hurt before the world. The
acid language of *Galatians* should be answer enough
to this rationalization. It is not the image of the church
but its essence that counts. If the Church of Christ is
not capable of self-examination, there is no hope for it.
If it cannot accept unity in diversity, there is no place
for it. If it cannot deal with differences and new concepts by dialogue, there is no progress in it. If it cannot preach "good news" instead of legalistic "bad
news," there is no need for it. If it cannot replace law
with love, there is no redemption in it. If it cannot

[9] No clearer example of this can be offered than a recent incident in
Murfreesboro. When a group given to the "anti-institutional" persuasion proposed to start a congregation on one side of the university campus, the
"minister" of the "institutional" Church of Christ located on the adjoining
side of the campus urged the zoning board to block the proposal. His argument was that "We do not fellowship this group."

promote the Christian ethics which will reconcile rather than alienate people, there is no vitality in it.

A fellowship of reconciliation is still its possible future. The author has never encouraged any frustrated Christian to abandon the group for a wider fellowship. He does not believe one must be surrendered for the other. Nor can he think of a more urgent service than to work for the reign of God to come more fully to the Church of Christ. The difficulties and ostracisms for those who stand for fellowship and reconciliation that will bridge differences and allow for each man his own exploration in the realm of faith may well increase before the tide recedes. For those who can hold fast, this may be a kind of saving suffering which Kierkegaard saw as a part of the process of "becoming" a Christian.

The goal is well worth the perseverance: an *ecclesia* which embraces the imperatives of truth while rejecting the law-obeying concept; which is a society of love and trust, not of command and obedience, for this is the will of God; which avoids judgment and promotes free interpersonal relationships; which can hold fellowship with imperfect men without "endorsing" their imperfections; which views religion as a way of life, with no distinction between the secular and the religious; which holds the church to be people living in confraternity rather than an institution; which accepts the necessity that a Christian society must have organized effort, but views organization merely as a means; which rejects the domination-subordination dichotomy in favor of an order of equality in which the only primacy is that which flows from a superior example and a richer experience. With such a consummation in mind we can still pray, "Thy ecclesia come!"

THOMAS P. HARDEMAN ministered to Churches of Christ for seventeen years and taught in Church of Christ Bible colleges for six years before leaving to serve the Unitarian-Universalist Church as lecturer and teacher for three years. He is at present deeply involved in the varied social welfare programs of his home state, Florida.

Specializing in Biblical studies at David Lipscomb College (Nashville) and Freed-Hardeman College (Henderson, Tennessee), Mr. Hardeman completed his B.S. at Murray State in Kentucky (1947). He went on to the University of Illinois, where he earned his M.A. in 1949 and his Ph.D. in 1956, both in philosophy. He has taught philosophy and religion courses at Florida Christian College (1949-52 and 1955-58), at the University of Illinois (1953-54), and at the University of Tampa (1955-61).

Concentrating on social services in recent years, he has been Project Director for the Community Service Foundation in Florida (1962-64) and is presently its vice president. He is a member of many philosophical and social welfare organizations and has served as an officer in most. He has conducted many radio and television programs based on his twin interests and continues to be busy as speaker and writer. He was consultant to the OEO Task Force for the Community Action Program in Florida in 1964.

Born in Graves County, Kentucky in 1925, Mr. Hardeman is married and the father of four children.

WHY?

By Thomas P. Hardeman

For what the birth of the masses?
Or why the lives of the few?
To what run the paths of the greatest?
Whither it leads, what they do?

For what the breath that is given?
Or whence the power to fly?
For what all the glories of heaven?
Is every answer a lie?

Man born to die is a question,
Ever and always to seek
Not the mysteries of God high above him,
But the mission of man who is weak.
Is it pain? Is it joy? It is neither—
Not regret nor false bliss can repay,
But the good that man does to another
Is the end of his life every day.

(Pat Hardeman, 1946)

After two years each at David Lipscomb and Freed-Hardeman, what an experience it was to confront Emerson and the professor who taught him to me. Properly schooled to combat evil, I helped secure the professor's censure for calling "sacred truths" into question. It was poetic justice that my own similar questioning led me fifteen years later through the same fires he suffered.

The professor was more easily disposed of than was Emerson, who lingered inside, caused much disquietude, and eventually outweighed earlier influences. The poem above, so indebted to Emerson, was born in Murray, Kentucky after many days and nights of youthful, enthusiastic questioning of my place in the scheme of things. It also represented the first serious grappling with two basic thrusts in my life—"the mysteries of

God high above him," and "the mission of man who is weak."

I remember so well the immediate reaction of parents and friends to these lines. "Why do you say it is *not* man's mission to seek the mysteries of God?" they inquired. So deeply was it ingrained in me to be "sound" that I said something like, "Well, there are many mysteries not revealed to man in the Bible. We must deal with what is revealed." But I had not meant that when I wrote the poem. Humanism, flowing from sources deep within me (in streams dammed up subsequently by many years of obsession with conceptualizing and rationalizing those very "mysteries" rejected in the poem), wrote the lines.

My graduation address at Lipscomb High School had been entitled, "The Value of Service." Although it received the compliments of the brethren at Lipscomb, it is basically a humanistic document, heavy in its emphasis on man's duty to his fellow man. Subsequently, this concern for service to others sometimes led my preaching to dwell on those practical evidences of religion which Jesus loved to stress. I shall never forget the poignancy of the occasion when one minister disposed of such a sermon by snorting, "Why, Brother X (a church cooperation partisan) could have said every word you did." He dismissed all that Jesus said! Why? Because Brother X could have said the same!

Eventually, however, I became the protagonist and apologist. Because debaters are so highly regarded in the Church of Christ, a fluent young man can easily have his head turned by praise of his cleverness in debate. Pride in the skill of forensic effort quickly dominates any effort to weigh fairly one's own position. However, the remorseless requirements of logic itself forced me to reconsider each of "our" major tenets. I was undone by the honesty of the very methods I used. I knew that propositions seeking to capture the essence of the conceptual system inherent in the verbal in-

spiration view of the Bible simply had to be consistent.
The truism that if two propositions contradict, one
must be false, led to my reassessment of many widely
accepted views. For example, if we are truly "silent
where the Bible is silent," what justification could there
be for adding to the simple description of disciples
meeting on the first day of the week to break bread the
dictum that Christians must do it every Sunday, but
never on any other day?

Debating was my undoing, or, rather, the undoing of
my earlier creed. Men like Frank Pack and E. H. Ijams
early kindled an interest in philosophy, leading eventually to my graduate major in that subject. I wrote to a
friend that I was planning to major in philosophy
"in order to contrast man's views on right and wrong
with God's truth on the subject." This helps explain
why my years of graduate study in philosophy, filled
as they were with preaching and debating, never really
allowed the great thinkers of the ages to combat my
creed directly. I studied them to use them in combat.
This continued until one momentous night when my
favorite professor and I clashed in a friendly but deeply
probing debate on the foundation of the Christian
faith, the bodily resurrection of Jesus. Literate and
skilled, this professor led me into an examination of the
very concept of evidence for "supernatural" events. My
brethren wrote high praise of my efforts, but Sara
and I questioned the basic presuppositions of my arguments.

Having no definitive criteria for determining the
supernaturalness of historical events, how could I be
so sure that a given event was supernatural? I
wondered, and I wonder, despite the arguments of
A. E. Taylor, C. S. Lewis, *et alia*.

My creed was shaking on its foundations. Perhaps
with a different field of graduate study for the previous
years I would have backed away from such painful
reappraisals and silenced my doubts. This may be

sufficient cause for the warnings frequently uttered against "our" preachers becoming immersed in philosophy. Still, the training from childhood, the host of friends and relatives, the many tasks I had planned, the books I had written and would write—all these conspired to delay my departure and extend painfully my inner struggle. One does not cast off the commitment of faith and family as lightly as he sheds a coat for an hour. I shall list below some of the issues (minor by contrast with the major struggle just mentioned) involved in the dissolution of my "Church of Christ Faith."

My early and adult manhood can be divided into several periods with labels easily obtainable from those who went through similar experiences. The Lipscomb years, for example, were concerned with piety and evangelism. The Freed-Hardeman years concentrated on a doctrinal soundness based on selected "pioneers," on McGarvey, and on moral correctness consisting mainly of conformity with "brotherhood" rules of conduct. The post-Freed-Hardeman years at Murray State introduced me to part of the real world, in contrast to the monastic kind of life in the Freed-Hardeman complex (a type of life so unreal in its abhorrence of the outside world of "infidels" that the head of the school could jestingly call them "in-for-hells," and refer to sectarians as "insects").

At Murray State there were pagans, preachers, priests, and all sorts of people whom I set out to save by vanquishing them in argument. This interest diminished in direct proportion to my immersion in the delightful studies of political science, literature, and philosophy. Here I met Emerson, Plato, Aristotle, and a line of intriguing authors from St. Augustine to the more recent empiricists and rationalists. Here was Kant with whom I really did not struggle till postgraduate years. Here was Mellon, the English professor, with whom I did struggle immediately. (Straight from Freed-Hardeman and filled with authoritarian attitudes, I secured his demotion on grounds that his liberal views had a bad influence on students; it eases my conscience slightly to know that seeds he planted bore fruit later in my life and vindicated him completely in my own memories).

Most importantly, at Murray State, I met Sara, that beautiful Irish Catholic girl whose religious upbringing was so abhorrent, challenging, frustrating and, ultimately, deserving of warmest admiration, that I loved her at once, ridiculously rebaptized her, joyfully married her, and have been blessed by her and our four children beyond description. Together we have loved, fought, and struggled for life's meaning and purpose. Sara must have loved me far more than I knew.

Ironically, the reputation I gained as defender of the faith by attacking my English professor won me an invitation to a church near the University of Illinois, where I could preach while doing graduate work in philosophy. Those first years, during which I earned my Master's Degree, were my most partisan and argumentative years. The church wanted to reach the University with its message and our method was across-the-board attacks on everything from Disciples to Darwinism. The philosophy I was being taught was neatly compartmentalized, often utilized for my sectarian purposes, but was not contemplated. I had yet to learn that philosophy yields up its secrets only to men with time and will to contemplate.

Next came the call to Florida Christian College. Before my decision was final there was bitter infighting among friends and relatives as to whether I should join the family forces at Freed-Hardeman (my father hoped I would not), or go with the new administration to Florida. For the next three years I talked so much, either in preaching, debating, or overload teaching tasks, that I had little time for more than routine studies. Still, through all this, I found time to edit a

paper and write articles, mostly in apologetics, and to
do an exhaustive study of Freemasonry to determine
with complete authority that "a Christian" simply
could not be a Mason. How "sound" we were! During
this time the college, with minor exceptions, moved to
the right to join the *Gospel Guardian* forces in anti-
church-cooperation (meaning no-contribution-from-
church-treasury-to-causes-lacking-specific-apostolic-ex-
ample).

The Florida Christian College years (1949-52) came
to an end after a beautiful midsummer night when
Sara joined me for a weekend in Atlanta after two
months' separation because of my evangelistic work.
We talked things over carefully and decided to go back
to the University of Illinois where I could complete a
doctoral program in philosophy. The same church I
had served earlier now had a new building near the
campus and wanted me to return.

What exciting years followed! The study of philosophy and ancient history, learning to read several new
languages, working in the new medium of television,
more writing, establishing and teaching in the Mc-
Garvey Chair of Philosophy of Religion, debating and
endless preaching. During this time Sara managed to
sing, to play in the symphony, to pursue her college
degree, to have a baby, and to help me immensely in
everything I did.

But unanswered questions persisted.

I shall never forget the shock of having challenged
my philosophy professor to name a better account of
creation than the first chapter of *Genesis*, only to have
him reply: "The first chapter of *Genesis* with the first
and fourth days reversed." All of Milligan's *Scheme
of Redemption*, with its sober description of a "lumi-
niferous ether" activated on the fourth day, plus all of
Rimmer's instances of light independent of the sun,
seemed weak by comparison—and still do.

I returned to Florida Christian College in 1955, but

this time with a difference. My contract was with two schools, FCC and the University of Tampa. The contract was symbolic of the widening schism in my own interests; it foreshadowed the break that had finally to come. Teaching philosophy at the University of Tampa half the week, teaching philosophy and apologetics at FCC the other half, and preaching in Jacksonville on weekends to a church whose leadership was just breaking away from FCC, was quite a life. The church in Jacksonville was "soft," Tampa University was "worldly," and to cap it all, my Ph.D. in philosophy had made me suspect at FCC.

By the year 1957, I loved the world. Whether loving the world in the "Demas" sense, or in the spirit of John 3: 16 (as I believed), my involvement with the world outside the "Church of Christ" was so complete that I moved in the fall, by mutual agreement with FCC, to exclusive teaching at Tampa University. A simply incredible church quarrel led to the formation of a new congregation of which I became minister. This church met first in my home because the split with the other church occurred just after my being put to bed for six weeks with what was believed to be a heart attack. When I was able to preach again, another building was ready. But I was not the same. Those weeks in bed, which I had intended to spend in reading, were spent instead in thinking and rethinking.

My felt obligation to the world was very real and somehow I had to solve the problem of whether this obligation could be discharged through the "Church of Christ." Within a year after getting up it was apparent to me that it could not.

It is certainly of little significance to anyone else, but for the sake of those who have asked me, I wish I were acute enough in self-analysis to say just how much the frustration of my felt obligation had to do with my questioning the whole of traditional theism. At any rate, the doubts became overwhelming.

In order to fulfill several desires, I became minister of a Unitarian Fellowship. Here my questioning was welcomed and heartily shared, though the degree of social commitment of the members was disappointing to me. In every sermon I made serious effort to explore ethical and religious alternatives in a way I never could before. These years were happy and fruitful, even when filled with the controversy that a vocal liberal invariably encountered in a southern city. My wife and I were pleased to note our children's growth in independence of thought and feeling in those character-forming years. Stimuli for this independence came both from the Liberal Religious Youth of the Unitarian Fellowship, and from their participation with their parents in the defense of several causes we felt to be involved in our obligation to society.

Looking back over the skirmishes of those years. I see how the spirit and tactics of my earlier religious debates were now employed in such causes as promoting internationalism (especially the U. N.) against the isolationists of our community, upholding constitutional rights by work *for* the American Civil Liberties Union and *against* the John Birchers and assorted reactionaries. What I had yet to learn was the way communities can be moved by working with, rather than against, their leaders. This came to me gradually in the throes of constant controversy. The art of political compromise is not easily learned by a staunch idealist. But it can be learned.

In 1957 my public defense of the United Nations against the American coalition of Patriotic Societies, headed by an arch segregationist gubernatorial candidate, led to a weekly TV program, "Your United Nations." During the two years or more that I did this show, I was in a running battle with the Birch forces that were ultimately to pressure the Tampa University administration into denying me tenure, and eventually banning me from the campus. The contro-

versy spread over many states and resulted in my
basic decision not to go North, but to stay right here
in the South where I felt an obligation regardless of
the particular work I might have to do to earn a
living.

Separation from the University coincided with my
decision to leave the ministry. Something new
emerged—a human being without title of preacher or
professor, just a citizen with a family to feed and to
enjoy. The problem of feeding was solved admirably
by an immediate offer from a wonderful Rabbi who
asked me to join his real estate firm. No one was ever
kinder or more generous than he was to me. The new
world of business was fascinating, hard, intensely
competitive, and profitable. Working day and night
to sell property, I was allowed several weeks off to run
for political office—really the best way to learn politics.
I have never regretted running or losing, though it is
terribly expensive.

Then it happened. The real beginning of a new
career. Community Service Foundation, searching for
a Project Director, offered the position to me. Their
work had been mainly in beginning self-help programs
for underprivileged southern Negroes. I had been involved in enough causes, I thought, so I visited the
President to get the job for a friend. He turned down
the friend, and I turned him down again. But I could
not put it out of my mind. I sat alone through the night
in a hotel room wrestling with the decision. After all,
I had for the first time in my life a job whose rewards
were directly proportioned to the kind of ability and
energy used in it. Finally, I made the choice for this
new work—this new kind of ministry. Sara calls it
"doing the Lord's work." And how we have worked!
Starting and coordinating for a year an after-school
and Saturday enrichment program that enrolls over
2,500 Negro children (now an official program of the
school system); training several VISTA groups for

their work in the War on Poverty; setting up a state-
wide program to benefit the wretched migrant farm
laborers in Florida—and so on, and on—doing the
Lord's work.

I have no recommendations as to what course others
should follow who may be troubled as I was. I know
only that I am experiencing a fulfillment of the old
idealisms, uncluttered now by quarrels over dogma or
ritual. I no longer feel the need to prove the rightness
of these actions. Time, experience, and the judgment of
God and men will do that. But, knowing how many
have wondered, I made the promise in this essay that
I would list some of the barriers to my remaining in
the Church of Christ. Here they are:

The only-true-church issue. I once reviewed a book,
Christianity Rightly So Called, in which the author
had defined the essentials of true Christianity in such
terms as to include Christians in all conservative denominations. This list of essentials was too broad, I
argued. The Bible, not conservative Protestant
churches, defines the essentials.

But that argument cuts equally well against the
"Church of Christ." Which branch of this post-Camp-
bell body is the true church: the anti-Sunday School
branch? the Nashville branch? No one has written anything like a "scriptural" justification for the view that
all these comprise the true "Church of Christ" and that
some number of them are "erring brethren." Nor does
it seem likely. Still, that view prevails—or did among
many "church members" several years ago. The movement begun by Jesus has had a complex and checkered
history. It now strikes me as pure presumption for any
man to try to say where the "true" church stops and
"false" ones begin, although God knows I have been
guilty of it often enough.

The binding of apostolic examples. The "true
church" issue is vitally connected with the question of
"binding apostolic examples." Early I learned that the

binding obligations of "true" Christians are (a) direct commands, (b) apostolic examples, and (c) necessary inferences. The commands did not bother me too much except for certain ones like the holy kiss and the injunction to anoint the sick with oil, both of which (along with several others) my church conveniently dismissed. More recently, as part of the cooperation controversy, I was bothered by the "Do good to all men" imperative addressed to the Galatian churches but interpreted with all sorts of restrictions by anti-cooperation brethren.

The apostolic examples, however, were troublesome. Not until my 15th year as a minister, after attending innumerable lectureships, did I hear a young speaker at the Florida Christian College lectureship say in a discussion of how to justify the binding of examples: "We begin by assuming that Acts 20: 7 is binding, and all others we bind are derived from that assumption." How true that is! How little anyone said against it. How many have privately admitted it and expressed the hope that somehow, somewhere, somebody would find justification for what "we" had bound on the "church" for so long. Could it be, for example, that esteeming "one day above another" really is for the individual conscience to decide?

The necessary inference position is even worse. The trivial instances usually adduced do not really support the practical requirements of "our" positions. For instance, is it really a "necessary inference" that because Paul commanded collections to be taken on the first day of the week he also included communion in that command and limited *it* to the first day? Logicians would be highly dubious of the "necessity" of this inference. An inference is "necessary" only if, by asserting the premises and denying the conclusion, one is involved in self-contradiction. In this case, that does not happen.

The Communion. As I preached repeatedly on this

subject, a question began to burn in me: if one combines the scriptural account of "the living bread," which is Christ's flesh, with the accounts of the last supper, are not the differences in representation, consubstantiation, and transubstantiation at least *trivia* and at most *different* ways of commemorating Christ's sacrifice? The charge of cannibalism often made against transubstantiation on the grounds that a communicant actually eats flesh rests on a crude ignorance of the doctrine. If Christ is "present" in some way in the bread and/or wine, he is remembered and his sacrifice becomes more meaningful. Whatever others may think, my own hope is to see Protestants and Catholics taking communion together—each interpreting Christ's "presence" as his perspective dictates.

Casuistical Morals. I was indoctrinated at an early age against drinking, gambling, dancing, "mixed" swimming, Sunday (and at some periods *all*) movies, and women's (and at times *all*) smoking. I was disturbed when occasionally I allowed the facts of Biblical remarks on dancing to upset my church's dogma against it. The trouble really began when our eight-year-old daughter was bitterly denounced, along with her parents, for enrolling with neighborhood girls in a ballet class. Nothing seemed amiss in her behavior. No scripture or moral principles I could find made it suspect.

Then our love of activity with our children caused us to subscribe to family rates at the local community swimming pool next door to Florida Christian College. What was a delightful family experience became a scandal when pictured by the puritanical. Again, no scriptural or moral principles condemned our action.

Along with the controversies touched off by what we knew to be innocent behavior went an intensive study of Christian ethics and morals in the light of a fresh examination of the New Testament. The results were revolutionary. Paul had asked, "Why should I be judged by another man's conscience?" Yet this same chapter was used in the Church of Christ to argue the necessity of being judged by any and everyone's conscience. Paul's assertion that "nothing is of itself unclean" had been forgotten in a puritanical assault on everything that somebody did not like.

Truly disturbing to us was that good friends in "The Church" agreed with us privately, but implored us not to do the things in question "lest you destroy your effectiveness in The Church." The rightness of the actions when done in moderation and with respect for the rights of others implied to us the freedom to do them. It still does. If "The Church" would not tolerate us when we were doing something right, then the necessity of our tolerating "The Church" became questionable.

The Church of Christ seems unwilling to allow individual members to use their own consciences in deciding whether to dance, drink or gamble in moderation. The dogmatism in these matters stems, it seems to me, from the assumption that God has spoken in clear sentences and that he has given infallible understanding of His will. In reality each person, especially ministers and elders, becomes a miniature Pope, with *ex cathedra* utterances on any matter that either God or the "pioneers" has vouchsafed to him. Safeguarding the system of doctrine becomes much more important than reflecting Christ's regard for people and their needs.

POSTSCRIPT

My aversion to traditional theism has somewhat abated. I am intensely interested in and excited by the fresh ecumenical winds blowing across today's churches. May they not diminish! Let us hope that when Christians finally get together they do not ignore those Jewish thinkers who are finding new appreciation for the person and work of Jesus. A warm cooperation among all segments of our Judeo-Christian tradition in the interest of helping solve humanity's pressing problems would be most significant. Before such a moral force, aided by the good people of Eastern and African traditions, perhaps even the age-old spectres of war and peace, poverty and plenty, justice and injustice, could be banished. That would truly be the real millennium.

CARL L. ETTER graduated from Abilene Christian College in 1922, and did graduate work in religion at the University of Michigan and the University of Southern California while preaching for Churches of Christ in Detroit and Los Angeles. He went to Japan in 1928, intending to spend his life as a missionary. When his sponsoring Church of Christ declined to support him while he learned the language, he became a teacher in one of Japan's government universities and supported himself for four years. Upon leaving the university, he offered again to do missionary work, but the sponsoring church felt incapable of supporting him because of the depression in the United States.

Mr. Etter was offered scholarships at the University of Edinburgh and at the School of Religion in Berkeley, California, but he returned to southern California. After continued studies at the University of Southern California he began work with the Los Angeles city schools as supervisor of guidance and rehabilitation for physically limited students. He considers the chance to help some 25,000 handicapped students become vocationally adjusted a "compensating experience for one who was dedicated to the ministry and to missionary work in the Church of Christ."

Before leaving the Church of Christ, Mr. Etter declined invitations to serve as minister for churches in California, Michigan, Tennessee, and Texas, and to become president of two different Church of Christ colleges. He earned the Ph.D. degree in 1953 from the University of Hokkaido. His doctoral dissertation on the animistic religion of the aboriginal tribes of Japan was published as a book, entitled *Ainu Folklore*.

IN SEARCH OF FREEDOM

By Carl L. Etter

EDITOR'S NOTE: When Carl and Grayce Etter left the Church of Christ in 1945 many of their friends were dismayed. The following explanation of their move appeared in the *West Coast Christian* in that year. Mr. Etter has added recent comments in a postscript at the end of this essay.

Since the *West Coast Christian* carried an announcement of our affiliation with the Congregational Church, a number of friends have written to us expressing regrets. These kind letters have been appreciated and we are preparing a brief statement for the information of these interested friends.

The shock which these good people have received from our move is quite understandable. We are members of Church of Christ families which have been identified with the church for several generations. We are former students of Christian colleges, and I served as head of the Religion Department in one of them. In days gone by I have had opportunities to serve those schools as dean and also as president, and have occupied Church of Christ pulpits from Detroit to Los Angeles. For four years we were in Japan where I taught in the Hokkaido Imperial University and assisted in establishing the first Church of Christ mission in the northern islands of Japan.

Therefore, our religious change has not been made in ignorance of the Church of Christ and its teachings. Neither has it been made in haste, nor in anger, but out of deep conviction—a conviction that has grown over a period of many years of university training, prayer, and thoughtful consideration. Our reasons for this change are legion, but we shall list only a few of them in this statement.

First, we do not subscribe to the belief that the Church of Christ, as it is so labeled, includes all the true Christians. To become identified with another religious group is no evidence that one is not a member of the Church of Christ in its true and universal sense.

Second, the teaching of the Church of Christ is based upon a superficial interpretation of the Bible and is fundamentally in error. This is true with reference to the nature of God, Christ, the Bible, the Church, man's mission in the world, and many other issues having both theological and social implications.

Third, the teaching of the Church of Christ is inconsistent and contradicts the announced slogans of the so-called Restoration Movement. The Church of Christ proposes to speak where the Bible speaks and keep silent where it is silent. It does neither.

Fourth, the Church of Christ claims to have no creed except Christ, but it has over twenty unwritten creeds to one of which one must subscribe in order to have fellowship with that particular wing of the church with which one chooses to become identified. Some of the letters which we have received, including letters from ministers known to be "sound in the faith," point out that the Church of Christ is becoming increasingly interested in heresy hunting. How do these heresy hunters determine when they have found a victim? They hear his speech, or read his writings, and weigh what they hear or read against the teaching in the unwritten creed or creeds which they have adopted as their standard. Christ was wise enough to stay out of the writing field, but He was finally apprehended by heresy hunters of His day and condemned on the basis of hearsay. The hearsay was inaccurate, as it always is, but His devotion to truth was strong enough to lead Him to His cross rather than recant and subscribe to the unwritten creed of those He knew to be in error. Had He done otherwise He would have died in oblivion, and probably would have lost His own soul as did the heresy hunters who nailed Him to His cross.

Fifth, the Church of Christ claims to have all the truth, but, in fact, is groping in darkness. It absolutely forbids new light to enter, and perpetuates its own inadequate insights by refusing to hear those who have persisted in their quest for truth. The founder of the Christian religion met the same type of religionists in His day and told them it was a case of the blind leading the blind.

Sixth, the Church of Christ makes great capital of its abilities properly to divide the word of God, but the system used is without scriptural sanction and has the net result of rejecting large portions of the Bible on the grounds that it was written to another people or a different age. The historical apppproach to Bible study restores every verse of the Scriptures and makes the entire Bible throb with intense interest to the modern student.

Seventh, the educational program of the Church of Christ is unwilling to trust the youth of the church with the facts of life and religion. It exposes its youth to a smattering of superficialities and when they go on for more advanced learning they are often left in a state of frenetic confusion. Some of them drop by the wayside, a few go on to new convictions, and others apathetically fall in line with public opinion in the church, ratifying and perpetuating the existing order. Our souls are stirred by mixed emotions when intelligent, highly-educated ministers say, "We know these to be the facts, but our people are not yet ready to receive them. We must go slowly and lead them gradually." We would be the last to betray these ministers. We fully recognize their desire to remain with the people whom they love better than their own souls, but we feel that a deeper loyalty to Christ should inspire them to take up their crosses and follow Him who said,

"Ye shall know the truth, and the truth shall make you free."

Eighth, the leaders of the Church of Christ have placed it in an embarrassing position by continual warfare upon science and the scientific attitude. This fight against science is based upon fear that it will destroy faith in the pet shibboleths of the church. It does. Some of the most cherished doctrines of the church of Christ burst like irridescent bubbles when exposed to the searchlight of the scientific approach in religion. The Apostle Paul was using scientific terminology when he said, "Prove all things; hold fast that which is good." Real science does not drive one away from true religion. Dr. Millikan is an ardent Congregationalist, and other scientists are also devout Christians. The scientific approach to religion should have a salutary effect in driving out much of the superstition and fear which has haunted religion through the centuries, and will help the Church to retain in its leadership many good men who otherwise would be lost.

Ninth, the message of the Church of Christ is negative in much of its teaching, and offers no constructive program to take the place of that which it condemns. With reference to many of its "thou shalt nots," it could well afford to "eliminate the negative and accentuate the positive."

Tenth, the Church of Christ has such great faith in the correctness of its position that it has developed a smugness that borders on that holier-than-thou attitude so well illustrated by certain religious sects who received the most scathing rebukes of Christ in His day.

Eleventh, the Church of Christ preaches undenominational Christianity, but in reality is the most denominational of all denominations. It is neither Protestant nor Catholic, but a group of small, warring sects which are little denominations within a denomination.

Twelfth, the Church of Christ preaches unity and practices division more paradoxically than any church

with which we are familiar. The greatest need in this
war-torn world is united effort on the part of Christian
peoples around the earth. In our opinion the Church of
Christ will not espouse such a cause, but will continue
to tear itself to pieces over minor issues while the world
burns.

Thirteenth, the Church of Christ refuses to cooperate
with its religious neighbors in movements that are
designed to make the world a better place in which to
live, but compasses land and sea in quest of proselytes
on the basis that it has a more certain pattern for
reaching heaven. Jesus told the proselyters of His day
that their converts became two-fold more the children
of hell; we may well ask ourselves if we are not helping
history to repeat itself at this point.

Fourteenth, the Church of Christ, in many places, is
trying to carry water on both shoulders by appearing to
be liberal to the world and strictly orthodox to its own
brotherhood. In one case the Church's position on undenominational Christianity was deliberately made to
appear as a broad-gauged liberal Christianity which
was wide open to peoples of all religious faiths. Certain
of our Christian colleges have found this to be a good
way to gain prestige with the educational leaders of the
community.

Fifteenth, the Church of Christ claims to be allied
with the religious fundamentalists, but its position is
more accurately described by the term incidentalist.
The merest incidental in the daily experience of New
Testament characters is magnified into a matter of
great importance and around it is built an article of
faith for the unwritten creed.

Even a matter which was so incidental that neither
Christ nor the Apostles referred to it in any way is
included in the creed on the basis that the New Testament is not only inclusive but exclusive in its teaching.
Instrumental music is an incidental which falls in this
category. The modern hymnal and many other things

might well be condemned on the same basis. The incidentalists in Christ's day placed religious significance on the incidental of washing hands; and it is strange that the Church has not done the same for the washing of feet, because they have a New Testament example for that custom.

The Jews and Samaritans considered the place of worship an incidental of great importance, but Jesus pointed out to them that the place of worship is a mere incidental and focused their attention upon the more important fact that God is a spiritual being and "seeketh such to worship him." Those same religionists crucified Christ because He discredited other incidentals in their religion and pointed them to the "weightier matters of the law." From the viewpoint of His adversaries He was a modernist in His day, but in reality He emphasized fundamentals and they magnified incidentals. Incidentalism should not be mistaken for fundamentalism.

Sixteenth, the Church of Christ has its eyes on the past and is more concerned with "old paths," than in directing people to paths they can follow successfully in our modern age. Although we wear the habiliments of civilization, some of us have not advanced far from the primitive tribal faith in the witch doctor. Our gullibility and non-scientific approach to the concepts of our forebears have prevented us from getting a true perspective of the world in which we live.

For example, in order to preserve preconceived and inherited theories of Biblical inspiration and interpretation, we vilify God before our youth by identifying Him with the wars of the Jews and the slaughter of ancient races while we do and say little to outlaw war and relieve race tensions in our own day. We pay great tribute to the inspired prophets of old and attribute marvelous things to the New Testament period of inspiration, but oppose as unscriptural innovations everything that might add beauty and inspiration in the religious experiences of our own children. These are only a few products of this backward look in religion as practiced in the Churches of Christ.

Seventeenth, the Church of Christ does not encourage growth and has a set policy which opposes change. No institution, including the church, can hope to survive in this changing world unless it encourages constant reappraisal of things as they are and stimulates hope that leads to action for their betterment. This does not mean that eternal verities are to be kept in constant flux, but it does suggest that these lasting values must constantly be reoriented in a changing world, just as Jesus did for religion in His day. Any other policy leads to an enduring social stratification based on birth, race, religion, or wealth—whether inherited or otherwise acquired.

Eighteenth, the Church of Christ has no place in its fellowship for one who does not conform fully to the status quo. Even though we cast him out of our ecclesiastical circle, we expect him to remain with us and expose his children to our unfair attacks. Every man, woman, and child needs a sense of security and a feeling of belonging. It has been my observation for many years that the Church of Christ withdraws these essential requirements of the human spirit from those who manifest a tendency to do independent thinking. This is a subtle type of force. A more democratic institution appeals to reason rather than force to secure its end.

Nineteenth, the Church of Christ has a double standard for judging persons who are accused of violating what the church considers to be New Testament teaching. Those who transgress the moral code are dealt with on one basis and those who depart from the Church's theological position are dealt with on a different basis. Here is an illustration of how two leaders were handled: one man was reported liberal in his point of view, the other was convicted of immoral conduct. The liberal was cast out and forced to seek another fellowship, even though he loved the church with every fibre of his being. The man who had violated the moral law was exalted to the most honored positions in the church. This illustration could be multiplied tenfold.

Twentieth, there are many indications that the Church of Christ is showing signs of decadence and that it is running a marathon race with catastrophe. It is true that certain shifts in our population are causing increased membership in some sections of the country, but there is little manifest interest by those from without. Of greater significance is the fact that many members of the church are discontented, discouraged, and starving for spiritual uplift which does not, and cannot, radiate from a church whose message is basically negative, argumentative, belligerent, and antagonistic.

Having been denied in the Church of Christ a wholehearted fellowship in which we could raise our family, we have sought the fellowship of the Congregationalists, not because they are perfect nor because they have all the truth. But they encourage scholarship, are in harmony with modern religious thought, practice tolerance within and without their fellowship, earnestly seek and accept new truth, have a rare faculty for discerning fundamentals, do not disproportionately emphasize incidentals, weigh all related facts in their interpretation of the Bible and religion, have neither a written nor unwritten creed, have a constructive and modern educational program for youth, encourage intellectual honesty, take cognizance of the present and look toward the future, cooperate fully with every good cause, encourage growth, are not opposed to change, allow for individual differences in spiritual growth, and fellowship those who have attained different levels of religious thinking in their development.

If we ever come to feel differently we shall be frank

to say so, and shall be as sincere then as we are now in the stand we are taking. In the meantime, we are still your friends and shall continue to love you as we always have.

POSTSCRIPT, 1965

My wife and I have, in our hearts, great and abiding sentiments about the church of our childhood and always rejoice in every report of its achievements and progress. It is heartening to know that an increasing number of its leaders are assuming an open-minded attitude toward the facts of modern scholarship in religion. My wife and I enjoy the friendship of many Church of Christ members, even though we are no longer affiliated with that fellowship.

It is my feeling that the Restoration Movement was motivated by conditions in the religious world which were oppressive and in need of reform. I was impressed anew with this on a recent eight months trip around the world during which my wife and I visited thirty-two countries. The shrines and temples in Oriental countries, the monuments and pyramids of Egypt, the colossus of St. Peter's and the fabulous cathedrals of Europe are all monuments to the slavery of the poor, illiterate masses and to departures from the simple foundations of all world religions, including Christianity.

I believe that the attempt to restore the simplicity of the New Testament church was a worthy cause and that the Church of Christ stood in the vanguard of a movement which could have resulted in great good had later leaders in the movement not succumbed to narrow, authoritarian dogmatism which turned it into one of the most denominational sects of our modern age.

EDITOR'S NOTE: Many years ago the *Gospel Advocate* published an undated pamphlet in which G. C. Brewer reviews the reasons given for their departure from the Church of Christ by both Mr. Etter and Mr. Reedy, whose essay appears elsewhere in this collection. Mr. Brewer admits that "no two young people in our times have been held in higher esteem than Carl and Grayce Etter" and praises their "fine personalities, their zeal and their faith." He then considers their arguments in order, referring to them as "the educated Reedy and the spoiled-child Etter," as "a disgruntled and a renegade preacher," as "this blind, blatant Modernist," as "apostates," and declares that "Verily the Etters and Reedies like Judas went to their own place!" The pamphlet can be purchased from the *Gospel Advocate* for $1.

ROY KEY is now senior minister of the First Christian Church (Disciples of Christ) in Ames, Iowa. He has had many years of close ties with Church of Christ pulpits and schools. He is a graduate of David Lipscomb College and George Pepperdine College and has taught at Dasher Bible School in Valdosta, Georgia. He has served Churches of Christ as a minister at several places in the Los Angeles, California, area, including two years at Fillmore and one year at the Sichel Street congregation. He preached for three years on Long Island and for ten years in Chicago (approximately five years each at Harvey and West Suburban Church of Christ in Berkeley).

The holder of many scholastic and personal honors (among them the presidency of the Pepperdine student body), Mr. Key has an M.A. from Pepperdine, a B.D. from Drake University School (1962), and has attended Union Theological Seminary, McCormick Theological Seminary, and Chicago Lutheran Theological Seminary, during his sojourn in New York and Chicago.

While at Drake University, Mr. Key preached for the Lohrville Christian Church and taught a freshman course in introduction to the Bible at Simpson College in Indianola, Iowa. Following his graduation from Drake, he spent a year as associate minister for University Christian Church, Des Moines, Iowa, moving in July, 1963, to his present position.

A LETTER TO DADDY AND MOTHER

By Roy Key

FOREWORD

I am glad to say a word about my decision in 1960 to enter the fellowship of the Christian Church (Disciples of Christ). Since it was made out of great agony of spirit and through long months of struggle in prayer, there are no simple statements that can convey the meaning of the experience. Therefore, rather than write an essay now about what took place four years ago, I have chosen to bare my most intimate thoughts and share with you a letter which I wrote to my parents.

It is with reservations that I permit publication of so personal a correspondence. Though many will read with compassion and understanding, I fear that some will stare with scorn. But I know of nothing I could say now that would speak to the real reasons for my decision more clearly than this letter home. I wrote it broken in spirit, with the realization that had I been a better Christian I might have been able to pay a starker penalty. Some pages I wrote barely able to see the paper before me and, at times, literally on my knees.

Because my heart aches for the estrangements among us; because I know that God is at work through the cross to bind up our wounds and make us whole; and because I want to make every effort I can to help heal our rift rather than widen it, I consent to the publication of this letter, with the prayer that our Lord's petition for oneness may be more fully answered.

*　　*　　*　　*

Dear Mother Sue and Daddy,

Crises come to us individually and as families. Some of them are terribly painful, but all of them are guided by God for good, if we permit. Together we have weathered many a storm, but one is coming now which is unusually fierce. I shall try to tell you how it has risen. But that is a long story, and I want to start at the beginning.

When we were children at home, times were hard; but even when the rain didn't come and the cotton was stunted and the corn burned, we were not anxious. We were sure that our parents could take care of everything. Since we believed that you loved us, we were secure in your care.

God must have given us parents that we might learn love and obedience, learn better how to think of Him and find security in Him. Afterward when life brings change, disappointment, disapproval, and finally death, we may face them all in the knowledge of a Father's concern.

You made it possible for your children to find in God a Father who understands, cares, forgives, and empowers. Often, in trying to picture our security in His love, I have said, "If my Daddy or my Mother were God, I would not be afraid."

Undoubtedly, our family relation helped to reveal the personal kinship of love as the highest tie possible. It is as high as the heavens above the legal relation— that of one citizen to another, or of the criminal before the judge. The stedfast love existing between husband and wife, or children and parents, is not in deadly peril of crumbling at each moment.

It was a long, long time, though, before I came to see that this intimate, personal, family relation exists between us and God.

The road was long and torturous as it led me to the happy realization that we stand or fall before God not on the basis of code-keeping, but on the basis of loving trust. It was long and torturous because we were taught at church and through our religious papers that the Gospel of Christ is another *law* in the same sense as the Law of Moses. We were taught that we stood condemned or accepted before God on the basis of a complete keeping of that law. So you see, though I was secure in the belief of your love, I was far from sure about my relation to God.

Many a time I dreamed of the Judgment Day, but never did I dream that I was saved. Always I was lost. Still do I remember those nightmares and how happy I was to wake up, finding that you had already covered the distance between our beds and were there in the dark reassuring me. Yet I could not believe that if I died before morning God would take me home with Him. Perhaps I knew that I didn't deserve His salvation. While I didn't deserve your love either, I knew it was there, anyway. That was the difference.

How could I be so sure of my relation to you and so uncertain of my relation to God? I think it must have been because you both knew your love of us better than you knew God's love for you. Our relation at home was one thing, our relation to God something entirely different. You, too, had been taught that the law is supreme and that its slightest infraction endangers the soul. Our family, and many of our brethren, were born and bred in this atmosphere of dark and suffocating fear.

While I was still at home, I began to puzzle over the lack of assurance in the hearts of our people generally, as contrasted with the glad certainty in the hearts of New Testament Christians. Our brethren seemed to know *what* they believed, but they never smiled confidently and declared, "I know *whom* I have believed and am persuaded that He is able to keep that which I have committed unto Him against that day" (2 Timothy 1:12). It was all quite strange for people who kept insisting, "We are New Testament Christians."

One day as I read an editorial from the *Gospel Advocate* on "The Gift of the Holy Spirit," I was shocked and deeply troubled, for I could see at that age that our leading brother had failed to come to grips with the Scriptures. I kept asking myself, "Do our brethren not know all the truth? Is it possible that other religious teachers and preachers could know more about some things?"

Such painful questions I tried to repress, attempting to find security in maintaining that our brethren knew *almost* all the truth, at least all that was really vital. Deep down inside, though, I feared that our hearts were less sure than our tongues.

At Lipscomb and Pepperdine I studied hard to find what it was that early Christians had and we had missed. I enrolled in some Bible courses not required and audited still others, aside from my private study. Not that I was unsure about "The Church of Christ" and what it stood for, but because I was groping for a surer personal grasp of God. I saw brethren full of anxiety, and I felt that I couldn't help them as I ought until I had won victory over that same paralyzing fear.

More and more I studied the books of Romans and Galatians, for in them I caught gleams of light in the dark. Fresh air right from the windows of heaven seemed to blow in my face. I would catch my breath, wondering if we really had a Gospel as good as Paul seemed to say. It was too good to be true.

Nightmares came no more. My dreams were haunted with glory. As Paul described the "righteousness" which God gives to the man who has none of his own but does have "faith in Jesus Christ," my heart thrilled as it never thrilled before. Here was one who had *not* done the necessary work required by the law (I knew this one to be myself), but he *had* believed in Christ. Here was my certainty. Though unworthy of God's

gift of redeeming love, I knew that my whole trust was
in Christ Jesus as Savior and Lord.

What did Paul say of this one? He quoted David's
pronouncement of blessing upon the man to whom God
reckons righteousness apart from works:

Blessed are those whose iniquities are forgiven, and
whose sins are covered;

blessed is the man against whom the Lord will not
reckon his sin. (Romans 4: 6-8)

My heart almost burst with joy. My eyes and soul
spilled over in gratitude. To think that I was really
accepted not on the basis of my perfect obedience to
law, but through faith in Jesus Christ—the thought
was incredibly glorious!

At the moment I was not concerned about arguments
over "faith versus works." I needed no reminder that
true faith lures a man to work far beyond all legal demands. I was seeking no easy way to pardon, a way
devoid of effort. Gladly I would have worked till I
dropped dead, if only I could be sure of God's loving
acceptance. Now I had it as His gracious Gift in
Christ.

On the basis of being perfectly *right* in understanding and life I knew myself lost. Now, however, I knew
of a man (the believer in Christ) to whom God would
not reckon his sins. Here was a standing with God that
did not depend on one's perfection. I found peace in the
midst of my imperfection. I knew that faith was far
more than believing the facts of the Gospel. I could
never have peace through that kind of faith. I knew
that it was commitment in trust to Christ as Savior
and a full reliance upon Him, without stopping to hold
up a single trait or deed of self.

Many, many truths had to be related to this central
one that "in Christ" "through faith" we stand in right
relation to God. I had to study the Scriptural relation
of repentance to faith, of baptism, of grace, of works,
of the Holy Spirit, of growth in Christlikeness. But in

all I could see that God deals with us as persons, not puppets, as sons-in-love and not sons-in-law.

My groping for God was really His grasping of me. How clear it became. The Almighty wants a Family. He offers Himself to us as Father. The Gift is Himself—in loving companionship. He cannot force Himself upon us. No amount of works on our part or marking through sins in some celestial ledger on His part will give to us *Himself*. Love can neither be purchased at the supermart nor created by juggling the entries in the account books of our lives. Our family was not so created, and neither is God's.

As I learned more *about* God it became crystal clear that what brought peace and the deep enriching of life was not mere information. The word "Father" was familiar enough. Only now it became more than a word. It was a window, a window in the Throneroom of the Almighty. I could see Him who ruled the world as "my Father." It was He who had come near in Jesus holding out His hands, grasping ours in His own and refusing to let go, taking us all the way to Calvary and there in the blaze of His Cross illumining the depth of our selfish, fearful pride and the height of His selfless, transfiguring love.

The joy of knowing Him who sees us as we are and accepts us anyway is a heady wine that bursts all the wineskins of words and spills through our souls. I wish desperately that there were some way of saying it so that you would have to understand. I not only want to know that God's Gift to us in Christ is Himself in loving friendship, but I want you to know the Gift is yours, as well as mine. May the Spirit of the living Christ breathe through these pitifully inadequate words something of His own Presence.

Please, let me labor this point, for it is a labor of love. You gave us many things at home: something to eat and wear, an opportunity to go to school, an extra something when it could be squeezed into the budget.

But these were not your greatest gifts. Greatest of all was yourselves. Not just your protection or information about you, but you we received.

If all that I knew of you was that you were responsible for my birth, that you are older and much wiser than I, and that I must honor you, as a family we would be non-existent. What really made the home was to know you, Mother Sue and Daddy. O, this was much, much more than having enough information to write a book about you, even as you know how much greater the joy to be *with* those you love than to hear *from* them.

How would you feel if your children never thought that it was possible to know you personally? What if they thought faithfulness meant studying feverishly the accounts of your movements, memorizing your letters and making a legal code out of them by which to order their lives? What if they were scared to death that a mistake would cause you to cut them off forever? Would this make you supremely happy or break your heart?

What pains me terribly is that we generally in Churches of Christ are breaking God's heart while striving feverishly to be right, absolutely right. We should try to be right, but when we think that our relation to God is based on that rightness, we live under the constant threat of doom. We are not infallible. We blunder. If God will seize such error to damn us, then we are damned, for we are sinners.

To avoid despair we must shout loudly (until we believe ourselves, whether or not anyone else believes us) that we are right on the things that really count. We can take the easier things: immersion, weekly communion, "Church of Christ" name, and contend that these are the things that make us true Christians. Even if we don't love God or our brothers as we ought, we have kept the greater commandments. If we insist loudly enough, we generate a type of assurance, but

the very shouting and stamping of our feet reveal that
we are yet anxious and insecure deep inside.

Among many of our brethren the sense of God's
acceptance is based upon everybody's else's rejection.
Where people disagree, somebody is wrong. People who
are wrong cannot be saved. Therefore, it is not merely
pride and arrogance that make us shout frantically
that we are right. Whatever security of soul we have is
at stake. We *must* be right. We cannot afford to admit
otherwise. If we are wrong, we are utterly lost.

This view makes it necessary to fight fiercely those
who disagree with us. Not simply because we love
them nor because we love the Kingdom, but because our
soul-security trembles in the balance. Only in the insistence that we are right and all other groups wrong are
we able to find sufficient assurance of God's acceptance
to make life bearable. We must cling to it at all costs.

Should we consider the possibility that people in the
"denominations" may be saved, our very faith would
be shaken. How startling a revelation is this! It shows
that our faith is grounded wrong. It is not really faith
in Christ as God's redeeming sacrifice for us. It is faith
in our *rightness* and everybody else's *wrongness*. Of
others like us Jesus once said, "They trusted in themselves that they were righteous and set all others at
nought" (Luke 18: 9).

We have come to illustrate in devastating fashion
what is meant by "*self*-righteousness." It does little
good for us to be deeply offended when outsiders say
so. Our denial is far from convincing. It has become
impossible for us to smite our breasts and cry, "God, be
merciful to me a sinner!" for that confession would
put us on the level of other sinners. Nothing that we
have, or are, or know, would give us any advantage.
We simply cannot afford such humiliation, and it proves
beyond doubt that we really are "self-righteous."

When one realizes that God accepts him, not because
he is good or smart (better and smarter than others),

but while he is a sinner, he wants to sing of the mercy of God. He wants others to know of such a Savior. He finds that he has a security in Christ that does not rest upon the damnation of those with whom he disagrees.

For nearly twenty years I have seen that "The Church of Christ" is not the whole family of God. It can be only a part. All those everywhere who have been "born over from above" are in the family. Jesus said, "He that believeth and is baptized shall be saved" (Mark 16: 16). There are millions aside from us who have done just this. How on earth can we assert, "We are "*The* Church of Christ,' " excluding these whom Jesus declares "saved?"

We must deny Jesus' words or grant that all baptized believers are in "the Church." Some brethren will admit it but refuse to recognize them as brethren by contending that they are "in error." Self-righteousness prompts us to say, "We are the true Christians *not* in error." When our own Brotherhood is split some twenty-odd ways, we are obviously "in error." None of us has hope apart from God's over-flowing mercy. We all have the privilege of prayer and forgiveness. "In Christ" there is continual cleansing. I know not why we should declare that in Christ is continual cleansing for us alone.

The thought seems to be that as individuals we sin constantly, but *as a group* we are perfect, "without error." We fool no one else, and we hardly fool ourselves, for we then hasten to add, "We are without *doctrinal* error." When we have run out of breath asserting our doctrinal purity, our divisions stand there mocking us.

The Church of God on earth is always "in error," morally and intellectually. We ever stand under judgment because of sin. But also through faith we stand under God's mercy. If we decide we do not need to stand under His mercy, but can now rest on our own perfection, we are "fallen away from grace," (Galatians 5:4). If we knew what it meant to be saved by grace, we could catch a glimpse of God's greater Family.

A long bitter road has led us to believe that God forgives every kind of error but "doctrinal" error. What makes us think that He forgives stinginess, lust, character assassination, worldliness, laziness—everything but instrumental music in worship? Such shallowness of heart and head is not born of the New Testament nor of the Restoration Fathers. It is the bitter end of a sectarian spirit that thrives on division and ministers to pride. It destroys us spiritually.

I doubt that we come to see God's larger Family by pointing out how good and right people in other churches are. Judged by Christ's perfect love and obedience they are all lost. *And so are we!* It is by seeing how we are put right, *though unrighteous,* that we come to see how other unrighteous souls are also "through faith" "reckoned righteous." At least, so it came to me.

When I realized that faith is personal rather than creedal, I could say, "I do not know how right or wrong my brethren are on attitudes or doctrinal points, but I do know that I am trusting Jesus Christ as Savior. My relation to Him is personal and not legal." I could see my weakness and His power, my folly and His wisdom. I was gloriously free from the law's condemnation, but Love was there binding me to Him in a glad servitude that I would not escape if I could.

Similarly, I knew that others who laid themselves at Jesus' feet for mercy, as I had done, were as truly saved as I. If He did not "reckon" my sins, He would not reckon theirs. Since both are imperfect, neither of us can afford to boast. This doesn't mean that we can't teach one another, point out the other's faults, if we discern them. If the same Spirit dwells in us both, then He is patiently trying to lead both to the light and mercifully covering our failures.

Because our family has been one where we have attempted to be understanding and forgiving, I am counting on you to glimpse what God is trying to do with His Family and how He feels about His children. He is not trying to send them all to hell, anymore than you are watching jealously to find some reason to sever all relations with your children. Surely, we break His heart when some of His children will not even recognize others in the same Family.

Here is the bend in the road for me—I cannot go on acting as if we are the only Christians, refusing fellowship to others because my "Church of Christ" brethren will not allow it. I cannot continue the kind of church life that rends the Father's Family and breaks His heart. I must protest. Whether it does little good, much good, or no good, I must be faithful to the right as God gives me to see the right.

I wish that I could widen my fellowship without being cut off by those in Churches of Christ. No one can possibly know how much I care for these people, how much I have suffered with them and by them, nor how much more I would try to take, if it would help. But as Paul once had to turn the larger part of his ministry away from those he loved most dearly, I must turn, too. I do it not without months and years of wrestling with my own soul and with God.

Several months back I wrote concerning my health and the killing pressure under which I have worked for years. I do not wish to flee any Divinely-appointed task, but I don't believe that God wants me at this time to sacrifice either my life or my sanity in what seems a fruitless endeavor. Believing also that He does not want me to give up the ministry completely, I must do the best that I know to do, trusting in His guidance.

How much I hope that you can understand. How much I would like to make you proud of me. But I

surely will only make you ashamed, unless you can
understand what I am saying.

There is no easy way for God to take us, break up
the old cemented patterns of thought and lead us into
new paths, even when they lead to freedom and peace.
I am sure, Mother Sue and Daddy, that when you left
the Baptist Church before most of your children were
born, you did not find it easy to do. You had family
and friends to consider. You did it because you had to
do it, because you believed God wished it and that
Scripture led to it. Now we must be as faithful as you
were. It is excruciatingly hard for us, but we wish
that it might be easier for you.

The awareness of your pain is a knife-thrust in my
own heart. It seems a tragedy to come to the place
where one must bow his head in his arms and weep
because he cannot spare a cross to those whom he loves.
But I cannot lay a heavier one upon my Lord. In all
His compassion, He still turns on us with blazing eye
if we let those whom we love better than life itself come
before Him.

I have tried harder than ever before to come back
across the miles and the years to let you walk with me
down to the bend of the road where I now stand. If you
can look up and see with me, I shall fall on my knees
in gratitude to God. If you cannot, I must hold you a
moment and walk on, praying God to keep His promise
of strength to us all, trusting some day that He will re-
move your cross and mine and make the dark things
plain.

Above the storm is God's bow of promise, His covenant of grace with us. He promises to receive us and to
hold us "in Christ," all of us who will really accept
Him. We must trust Him to do just that. He has also
promised to hear our prayers when we come to Him in
faith. Though I have prayed for a long time about this
decision, one day I went down on my knees and didn't
come up until I had it out. I had to come to the place

where I could say "Thy will be done," and mean it. I
ask you to do that now. I am claiming God's promise
in this matter. I am asking you to join me in it. He
will not fail.

With all my love and devotion,

Roy

RALPH V. GRAHAM served Churches of Christ as minister for almost a quarter of a century before leaving in May of 1964 to begin work with the First Christian Church (Disciples of Christ) in Colorado City, Texas.

Baptized in Abilene, Texas in 1939 by Louis Nowlin, Mr. Graham entered Abilene Christian College in that year and graduated with honors in 1944. During his undergraduate years he preached at Tuscola, Texas, at North Park in Abilene, and at Pryor, Oklahoma.

In 1944, Mr. Graham entered Princeton Theological Seminary. During several years of study he preached for the Trenton, New Jersey Church of Christ. He graduated from Princeton in 1949. A year's work with the Flushing, New York Church of Christ followed, after which the Graham family moved to Collingswood, New Jersey in 1952.

During twelve years as minister at Collingswood, Mr. Graham attended Temple Graduate School of Theology, where he received his S.T.M., completed all residence requirements for the S.T.D., and completed twelve hours of graduate study in Guidance at Teacher's College, Temple University.

WHY I LEFT THE
"CHURCHES OF CHRIST"

By Ralph V. Graham

In 1964, after twenty-five years of active membership in the Church of Christ, I said farewell to that
particular segment of Christendom and began work
with a Disciples of Christ congregation in Texas. The
months since then have brought the joy of new friends,
great challenges, much more freedom, and an opportunity to work toward what I consider more authentic
goals.

What I have to say about leaving the Churches of
Christ will not be intentionally impertinent, arrogant,
or self-righteous. I intend to express my views and
judgments clearly, with conviction, and for constructive ends. I have no desire to justify myself, to prove
something to anyone, or to engage in any bitter exchange. What I have, rather, is a word of explanation
to those who have asked, "Why?"

In addition, I feel that such a statement is required
of a friend to friends and brethren who mean much to
him. My prayer is that no one will want to disfellow-
ship me for the step I have taken, that the greatest
possible number will understand it, and that the greatest possible number will consider seriously my criticisms, which I intend to be constructive. I think all of
us should ask ourselves, "What should I believe?"
"How can I live in harmony with my faith?" and
"What do I dare to hope?" When we find adequate
answers, we should follow where they lead. I write
with the hope that what I say will be helpful to someone.

Looking back, I can see clearly how my studies,
working experiences, and association with believers of

different denominations led me gradually into a deeper
and broader Christian commitment than the restricted
liberty afforded me in the Churches of Christ. Being
quite outspoken in my preaching, talk, and writings, I
found the restrictions placed on my freedom of expression intolerably frustrating. I and my congregation became subjected to a West Berlin-type of isolation
because of my views.

In addition to this growing estrangement imposed
from without, I found also that I had come to be in
complete disagreement with the aim, views, message,
method, and attitudes which characterize the Churches
of Christ. I had concluded that in all these areas the
"position" of the Churches of Christ was incorrect
theologically, philosophically, and psychologically, or, to
be quite practical, unscriptural, irrational, and unhealthy. Under the circumstances, I did not have adequate moral support, opportunity to express and
practice what I believed to be the total will of Christ, or
freedom enough to work for the realization of what I
considered to be essentially Christian goals.

In leaving the Churches of Christ I realize I have
widened the distance separating me from my brethren
in that denomination. The opportunity for dialogue has
been diminished. In leaving, however, I did not leave
the fellowship of the body of Christ. I am conscious of
a wider fellowship than many members of the Churches
of Christ feel. I am aware that my departure was the
occasion for some to feel disappointment, some grief,
and some satisfaction for being right in their anticipa-
tions. But I feel no satisfaction in others' disappoint-
ments and griefs. I have no feelings of rancor,
bitterness, or animosity. I do not wish to lose a single
friend nor to dissolve the bond of fellowship I have
with anyone in Christ.

I remember with pleasure a great deal of freedom
in the Collingswood congregation. No one mistreated
me or compelled me to leave. I walked away free, and I

am free now. And I feel that no one should ever be compelled to submerge his freedom or integrity in compromise for the sake of friendship, brotherhood, peace, or security. I must say this despite its apparent severity because it must be understood that faith is a very personal thing and that one cannot speak freely and honestly about faith and morals without hurting feelings. But neither friendship nor freedom is compatible with silence. If my views offend or wound anyone, it is done only as a friend wounds or offends. "Faithful are the wounds of a friend," the Scriptures say. (Prov. 27:6).

Oliver Wendell Holmes has said, "A man's mind, stretched by a new idea, can never go back to its original dimension." Serious and continuous study in the pursuit of truth leads to new plateaus and new relationships. Leo Tolstoy, in his *Reply to Edict of Excommunication*, said: "I do not believe my faith to be the one indubitable truth for all time, but I see no other that is plainer, clearer, or answers better to all the demands of my reason and my heart; should I find such a one, I shall at once accept it. . . . But I can no more return to that from which with such suffering I have escaped, than a flying bird can re-enter the egg shell from which it has emerged." And Samuel Taylor Coleridge has declared: "He who begins by loving Christianity better than truth, will proceed by loving his own sect or church better than Christianity, and end in loving himself (his own peace) better than all."

These men were advocates of honesty and believed that honesty demands a tentative faith. But a tentative faith does not imply spineless or weak convictions. I think it was Emerson who said once, "What I believe today I speak in words like cannon balls. If my belief changes before tomorrow, then tomorrow I will be speaking my new convictions like cannon balls." To follow a principle with constancy will not necessarily result in consistency of belief. The one thing I would like to have acknowledged in my case is honesty in faith. Accepted on that basis, I could be much helped in my efforts to live in harmony with honest faith.

I shall set forth, now, at some length, views which I realize are not acceptable in the Churches of Christ. I do not state them in order to shock, but because I believe they are in harmony with Scripture. I believe in the universality of truth, Christianity, the gospel, and the church, but I have found that in the Churches of Christ, *all* truth does not enjoy free course.

I am convinced, for example, that the Scriptures teach that the person who confesses sincerely Jesus as Savior, Lord, Son of God, and Christ, and serves him faithfully in that profession is a Christian despite any errors he may hold unintentionally. Further, I do not think anyone has the right to dictate how this conviction shall be expressed. But evangelistic techniques in the Churches of Christ exploit men's fears, promise a spiritual security which is secured only by man's obedience, and place every convert in a state isolated from all believers who are not members of the Churches of Christ.

I believe in Jesus Christ as the living Word of God, as the personal interpretive principle of the Bible, and as the Lord of the Bible. He is greater than the Bible and the Bible must fit Him, not He the Bible. I believe that the Bible is a trusworthy account of the Incarnation of the Living Word and of man's encounter with God. It is the normative witness for our faith and practice. But great as the Bible is, it is not big enough to exhaust the meaning of Christ for Christian faith. Once we learn of Him through the Bible, we will continue to seek Him "beyond the sacred page." The Bible was never intended as a detailed blueprint of faith and practice. When everything is forbidden that is not commanded, and everything commanded that is not forbidden, believers are no longer free sons but slaves of tyranny.

I believe the creativity of man is God's gift to be used in His service and worship. There is positively and absolutely no Scriptural warrant whatever for opposing instrumental music in the worship or in forbidding any other artistic talent's use for the glory of God. All music, painting, architecture, and other forms of art in good taste and capable of transmitting true devotion are acceptable means of man's adoration of His Creator. The Bible does not teach that human initiative and spontaneity motivated by adoration of God are to be penalized or outlawed as unscriptural.

I believe that church organization in the New Testament is functional, flexible, and pluralistic. There is no one form of church government dictated by the New Testament in word or in example. Therefore, differing patterns of church government do not justify religious divisions. Means are always subordinate to ends. The congregations of the church are intended by God to function as the body of Christ. To maintain each congregation in isolation from every other is to frustrate the church's mission, misrepresent its nature, and impoverish its fellowship.

I believe that unity is a major concern of the heart of Christ. But unity among believing Christians is not yet realized. It can be achieved only in a common loyalty to Jesus as Lord and Savior through mutual discussion, cooperation, give and take. Unity will never be achieved unilaterally by any fragment of Christ's body. The standard for Christian unity is the unity we see between the Father and the Son. This is the kind of unity our Lord desires. It is not doctrinal, organizational, or ritual unity, but a unity of character, purpose, action, love, fellowship, and will. The only real unity is one that is functional, dynamic, and sociopersonal.

I believe in the liberty of the individual conscience in Christ. Men do not have the right to dictate and determine the content and expression of a Christian's faith.

The Christian is the servant of his Lord and to his own Master he stands or falls. Freedom in Christ is the individual's right to act responsibly in the fellowship of the body. Responsibility is determined by the Lordship of Christ, the indwelling of the Holy Spirit, the insights of an enlightened and rational conscience, the fellowship of the body, the needs of the situation in the context where one is. The Holy Spirit works dynamically in sanctifying believers; His work is not limited to the effect of the words of the Bible on the human heart and mind. He works when, and where, and how He pleases, rather than according to predictable and fixed patterns.

I believe that the church must be involved with ministering to the whole man with a gospel unqualified by culture, nation, or race. The church cannot isolate itself from the problems of politics, economics, culture, health, freedom, human rights, and peace. I do not believe in the proselyting of other believers, in following a policy of isolationism, exclusivism, or neutralism. At the present time, we Christians should be supporting the war against poverty. But we should war also against prosperity when it is achieved at the cost of integrity.

I believe in distinguishing things that differ, in recognizing the priority of some values over others, and in living by a scale of values set forth in the Bible. Scripture speaks of some values in the superlative. "Now abideth faith, hope, and love, but the greatest of these is love." Some values are put in the comparative. Jesus is the surety of a better covenant, enacted on better promises, introducing a better hope. Some things are just good, others expedient, or lawful. Our Lord teaches "first things first." "Seek ye first the kingdom." He exalts the inward above the external, the substance above the shadow, the eternal above the temporal, the spiritual above the material, the principle above detailed minutiae, mercy above sacrificial obedience, His word above tradition, the ideal above the practical, and human need above ritual conformity even if a law must be broken.

I believe in the present activity of God in history and that history is meaningful as the stage of God's activity. I believe in the value and achievements of biblical scholarship, women's work in the church, the total involvement of the laity in Christian service, and in the dignity and authority of the Christian ministry. I believe in the aims of the ecumenical movement and that all Christians should partake in its work. I believe church work should be comprehensive, progressive, and relevant to contemporary life.

Holding all these things as important to spiritual growth, I found the Churches of Christ deficient. They seemed to me to offer poor environment for development in the Christian graces. They are growing numerically and their material expansion is astonishing. But quantitative growth is no guarantee of truth or approvedness. I can remember when smallness was used by them to some advantage when their size was pointed out. One would hear them say, "Only two out of two million who left Egypt reached the promised land!" "Only two out of twelve spies who spied out Canaan entered that land the second time." "Only eight were saved in the flood." They said, "Jesus says, 'Many are they that enter the broad way, but few enter the narrow way of salvation!' " We do not hear these illustrations used so much these days.

Let us note, now, some of the environmental conditions in the Churches of Christ which are not conducive to spiritual growth. The Churches of Christ identify themselves as a "Restoration Movement" which proposes to restore the New Testament Church in name, organization, doctrine, worship, doctrine, vocabulary, unity, conditions of membership, and creed. But the whole object of the "Restoration Movement" is improper. Restoration assumes the disappearance or cessation of the church in history. Now, we may think of the church ideally or actually. The ideal church never existed except as an idea in the mind of God. It has no real existence, members, organization, or place in time. The ideal church cannot be restored since it never existed. The actual church as described in the New Testament did not have a uniform organization, worship, practice, or faith, in all its congregations. The actual church was plagued by heresies, divisions, immoralities, ignorance, indifference, apostasy, and weakness. It has never ceased to be thus plagued. Since it neither disappeared nor ceased being, it is not an object of restoration. The Scriptures teach that the Lord's church cannot be destroyed. But, even if it could, would "restorationists" restore the actual church? Do they know what it is they are trying to restore? Actually, they should declare themselves no longer a "Restoration Movement," since they claim to have restored the church already.

In order to pursue their aim, they are compelled to interpret and present the Christian religion in terms of externals. But an external religion does not resolve religious problems because it misses the heart of man. The use of such external emphases reflects an intention to identify the church of Jesus Christ with external marks rather than by the presence of the Spirit of Christ and the regeneration of believers who exhibit the fruits of the Spirit. Man is not transformed or nourished by outward marks, but by a personal encounter and communion with God in Christ. Wherever this is possible is the place to meet and to worship, to learn and to serve Christ. But changing externals will not transform personality. "The dog (remaining a dog) turns back to his own vomit, and the sow (remaining a sow) is washed only to wallow in the mire" (2 Peter 2: 22). The cup and the platter are not cleansed by washing only the outside (Matt.

23 : 25-26). Changing externals still leaves man's heart untouched, unchanged, unhealed, and unredeemed.

A "Restorationism" which emphasizes externals as identifying marks of the true church degenerates into sectarianism. Alfred T. DeGroot, in his book, *The Restoration Principle*, states: "A cramped, or limited, or distorted estimate of the wholeness of Christian faith and life produces a fellowship with the same characteristics. Smug satisfaction with small success then inclines to insulate the little community from the major concerns and currents of life in the church as a whole. Failure to participate in the throbbing processes of the larger body brings a pallor of sickness and a withering of vitality to the degree of withdrawal" (p. 8).

"Restorationism" ceases to be a movement when it separates itself from the institutions and the society it seeks to restore. The vacuum created by the exclusivism of the Churches of Christ leaves nothing to be restored but themselves. A movement is a movement only so long as it retains universality, flexibility, spontaneity, and openness. But once it crystallizes or becomes stereotyped in an organization, in its dogma, and in its separateness, it ceases to be a movement and becomes narrow, sectarian, and arrogant.

The result is that it comes to embody errors similar to those it proposed to abolish. The "Restorationism" of the Churches of Christ has not solved a single one of its major aims within its own ranks! It is as badly divided and has as much disagreement as any other denomination. A religious group that thinks it has "arrived" is formalistic and legalistic; it can hardly avoid the concomitants of such attitudes. More frequently than not, its fruits are revealed as hypercriticism, arrogance, traditionalism, divisions, decline in spirituality, legalism, formalism, authoritarianism, uncharitableness, unethical treatment of those among its members who disagree with its orthodoxy, and witch-hunting. Jesus, speaking of the nature of such non-authentic lives, said: "By their fruits ye shall know them" (Matt. 7: 16).

The doctrines of the Churches of Christ are irrational. Their "Restorationism" is self-contradictory. They claim that they have achieved restoration of the true church while proposing to restore it. They measure themselves by themselves. Their attitude is, "If you doubt whether we are right, just ask us." They fail to distinguish means from ends. To them, everything is an end in itself. By absolutizing means, the ultimacy of true ends is obscured as well as the flexibility, temporality, and dispensability of means.

In the name of freedom, they deprive others of freedom. In the name of equality, they subordinate all to those who maintain "Restoration policy" and reserve for these latter the honors. They subordinate theological truth to atomistic conclusions drawn from biased exegesis of passages relating to salvation, baptism, communion, and the like. They ignore the biblical hierarchy of values, giving equal value to all points. But their authoritarian "blue-print" principle of the Bible is not carried out consistently. They gloss over the Biblical teaching regarding women's hair, women's silence, women's veil, and women's subjection. They have no teaching regarding singing when sad or alone, only when one is cheerful or worshipful (see James 5: 13). They ignore the Biblical examples and teaching regarding love feasts, ordination of church officials, deaconesses, the holy kiss, the orders of virgins and widows, wine in communion, church councils, the examples of the one cup in communion, solo singing, and mutual ministry. They are unwilling to follow Paul's example of religious fraternization with non-members for the sake of evangelism.

"Restorationism" as advocated by the Churches of Christ is unhealthy. It assumes that legalistic formalism will heal the sick in sin and the divisions among

believers. Many forms of neuroses and psychoses are
treated as sin. As a way of life, "Restorationism"
is irrelevant to man's needs. Too many members of the
Churches of Christ are dogmatic, implacable, and sectarian. The consequences of these errors are pride,
anger, suspicion, smugness, bigotry, and uncharitableness. Believers are encouraged to penalize one another
for deviationism. "Big brother" watches all the time.
They consider all but themselves non-Christian and
compel even the most devout and godly believer who
joins their group either to be rebaptized or to confess
publicly that he has been living in sin! They try constantly to proselyte believers from other denominations.
But if it was wrong for Roman Christians to rob pagan
temples, what about Churches of Christ robbing other
Christian Churches? (Rom. 2:22b). I gladly admit
that these policies are repugnant to some individuals
in the Churches of Christ, but they are accepted and
promoted by the generality.

There are, certainly, some good features in "Restorationism" as practiced by the Churches of Christ and I
do not want to overlook them. Many great souls in this
denomination hold and practice the highest ideals
despite the system in which they are members. Here
follow some valid and commendable features professed
by many in the Churches of Christ and which are
worthy of praise and encouragement:

With respect to authority, they aim to subordinate
all human authority, tradition, and the church to the
personal authority of Him to whom the Bible bears
trustworthy witness. They seek a valid and practical
interpretive principle and rightly uphold the superiority of the New Testament over the Old. They seek a
Biblical doctrine which is also psychologically valid
concerning conversion and initiation into church membership. They contend for a complete obedience to the
divine will.

With respect to Christ, they acknowledge Him as Son

of God, Lord, and Savior. They exalt Him as the only
Head of the church in heaven and on earth. He is presented as the perfect man, the Exemplar of the good
life. His atonement, resurrection, ascension, reign, and
return are all devoutly proclaimed.

With respect to the church, they stress the factuality
of its existence, the definability of its identity, and its
accessibility. They underscore the importance of
church membership. They emphasize simplicity in organization and sincerity in worship. They *profess* to
embrace all the redeemed as the body of Christ and are
committed to the universal mission of the church.
They exhibit courage, independence, and boldness in
proclaiming their message.

With respect to believers and unbelievers, they long
for the unity of the faith and the healing of divisions.
Loyalty to the church is stressed in every way and
is practiced well by the membership. They contend
for the priesthood of believers as a valid ministry. And
they restrain by reason and self-control the extremes
of emotionalism.

There are, as must be obvious from this essay, sug-
gestions for improvement which I would make, hopeful that the good I have praised will be increased and
the evils I have enumerated may be diminished. Here
are some of them:

The Churches of Christ should admit the reality of
their denominational status and humbly confess the
possibility that they may be wrong in belief and practice. They should stress the value of special training
for ministers, officers, and teachers, and reconsider the
public ordination of ministers, elders, deacons, and
deaconesses as the Bible teaches. They should practice comity with other believers in meaningful ways
and acknowledge them as brethren with real contributions to make toward unity.

They should cultivate existing unities and discuss
the *real* issues rather than continue to waste time on

peripheral matters. They should exalt the Lordship of Christ even above the Bible and the church, and learn to enjoy the freedom of the Spirit in Christian life. They should surrender and renounce the "blueprint" concept of the Bible. They should discover the unity of the Bible, its scale of values, its principles, and its subordination to the Lord Jesus Christ.

They should eliminate all sectarian barriers to fellowship, such as their opposition to instrumental music in worship, contention for one pattern of church government, communion only on Sunday, and salvation by baptism. The scholarship of the world does not support these views.

They should revitalize the worship by practicing the Presence of God. In many Churches of Christ, worship is not a moving experience. Communion is too much of a mere formality because it is considered little more than a memorial. A real sense that Christ is living and present at the table would bring warmth to their devotions.

They should make the gospel Christ-centered as it was meant to be, rather than baptism-or-church-centered. Neither baptism nor the church is primarily gospel. They should be willing to let consensus of rational opinion of all Christian scholars of whatever church and age be the decisive factor in matters of interpreting the Bible. And, finally, they should review and correct their conception of what needs restoration.

I do not know how soon these problems may be solved, but I found that for my own ministry it would not be possible to wait longer. I left the Churches of Christ because freedom and opportunity to speak became too restricted and because I believe these churches are in the unrelenting grip of false conceptions and purposes. I left because I believe they have drawn lines of fellowship contrary to the New Testament, because they have destroyed hope of achieving

through their system the unity Christ wanted, and because they repudiate the conclusions of the best scholarship in the world. I left because I believe they have
emptied worship of its spiritual depth and mystery
and because the personality of Christ is not for them
the reigning motif of their church life, worship, faith,
and work. I left, finally, because the effect of their
doctrines is to make one much more vulnerable to those
human weaknesses which lead to pride, hostile feelings
toward others, an uncharitable and unforgiving spirit,
social incompatibility, factions, implacability, ethical
weaknesses, and anxiety.

Let me assert firmly, however, that I love the people
in the Churches of Christ. I wish them only good. I
bear them witness that they have a fervent zeal, although I cannot believe that it is according to the truth
as it is in Christ. They have a form of godliness, but
they deny its power in human life by stressing the
form rather than the godliness. They are diligent,
aggressive, intelligent, self-sacrificing, and persistent
in their beliefs and works. I take no satisfaction
from pointing out their errors. My heart is heavy because of my separation from many dear friends. I must
say, too, that the criticisms I have written are not
true of all the members of the Churches of Christ.
There are many who agree with my views even if they
cannot imitate my action.

It is the system, really, which most concerns me.
There are thousands of good Christian men and women
in the Churches of Christ who could do much to im-
prove the situation by being true in word, attitude,
and deed to the mind and spirit of Christ. My prayer
is that we shall all grow more like our Savior, knowing
that as we make this progress our paths will merge
somewhere, sometime, somehow, in a deeper and more
loving fellowship in Christ. My fervent prayer is that
constructive changes will take place in the doctrines
and attitudes held by members of the Churches of

Christ that will reduce the unhappiness many experience as a consequence of them, and that the width of the chasm which separates them from other believers will be bridged over by love. understanding, and a meaningful exchange of ideas.

Meanwhile, dear reader, please believe that I have not spoken in anger or bitterness, and that I have not desired to make anyone angry. Just as you must do what your conscience in Christ leads you to do, so must I. I will close with an ascription of praise to Christ which is the will and sentiment of my own best self, and with a quotation describing His final victory, for which I work and hope:

"Worthy is the Lamb who was slain, to receive power and wealth and wisdom and might and honor and glory and blessing!" (Rev. 5: 12)

"The kingdom of this world has become the kingdom of our Lord and of his Christ, and he shall reign for ever and ever." (Rev. 11: 15).

MARGARET EDSON O'DOWD is the wife of John O'Dowd, one of the best-known Church of Christ preachers in the Southwest for more than a quarter of a century. Although Mrs. O'Dowd's conscience no longer permits her to attend Church of Christ services, her husband still ministers to a small congregation in Houston, Texas.

After a generation of faithful service as a preacher's wife, Mrs. O'Dowd published in 1958 an autobiography in which she set forth her reasons for turning away from some of the major doctrines of the Church of Christ. She titled the book *In the Great Hand of God I Stand*. The essay which appears here is a condensation of that first-person narrative.

The O'Dowds served churches at Chillicothe and Canyon, Texas during the time of his schooling. Later they labored with the Peak and Eastside Church of Christ in Dallas, and at the Wayside and Sherman congregation in Houston. They have a son, John, who practices law, but preaches occasionally; a daughter, Jeannine; and four grandchildren.

IN THE GREAT HAND OF GOD
I STAND

By Margaret Edson O'Dowd

If I should be lost, as many will think, for the thoughts of my heart as revealed in this essay, then my only reply is the title I have chosen for it. After years of struggling to find freedom in a legalistic religion, I have at last thrown myself upon the mercy of God and found the peace I sought. I write what follows only in the hope that my words may express the unuttered longings of many others who are still caught in the snares of authoritarian and exclusivistic religion. My testimony may have some special meaning for a few; I have been for nearly thirty years the wife of one of the most active preachers of the Southwest.

I married John O'Dowd in January, 1929, after he had already begun his college education at Abilene Christian College. At John's first church we were surprised by a wedding shower and got generously all we needed for housekeeping. My heart was filled with love for these wonderful people and their generous spirit. That was how we received our 'initiation' into our first local work. Together we were starting upon a career that would be both smooth and rugged, filled with sorrows and joys. The preacher twenty-one, his wife seventeen; ah, the bliss of youth!

After a few years of preaching and further schooling, we moved in 1934 to Dallas. Two years later we came to Houston where we have remained for almost thirty years at the time of this writing. As thousands of Church of Christ people know, John made himself a reputation as a debater during his early years. His dynamic pulpit personality and his fund of ready answers for every argument thrilled partisan audi-

ences everywhere. I was proud of him and often
wondered how anyone could fail to see how utterly
he had vanquished his opponents.

Only once was I bothered by an opponent's argument. A Baptist preacher was affirming the "once
saved, always saved" doctrine which we usually called
"The Impossibility of Apostasy" theory. John pressed
hard on the case of Ananias and Sapphira, asking
whether they could possibly be saved after dying with
a lie on their lips. I think the quiet reply to John's
argument may have been one of the first introductions
I had to a more gracious kind of religion:

"The case of Ananias and Sapphira was a special
case for a special purpose. I will not consider it a
comparison for us, for if I did I might be led to suppose that every time a church member lied he would
be struck dead. Mr. O'Dowd would have to draw the
same conclusion and if such were the case I'm sure
he will agree that the task of burying the dead would
soon become a major problem. Now Mr. O'Dowd
knows and admits that a Christian should not go to
sleep in the evening without asking forgiveness for
his sins during that day; every day we all sin in some
small way, though we might not even be aware of it.
If we should happen to die suddenly before we have
gone to the throne in prayer, we would be lost, according to Mr. O'Dowd. Then who could be saved?
Only those fortunate enough to be killed the moment
they arose from their knees? Even those who know
they are on their death bed commit little sins of dis-
courtesy, unkindness, or intolerance. But what saves
them from these little sins that are nearly always with
every man who dies? The grace of our Lord covers
that. Without His grace, who could be saved?"

As the years have passed, I have considered more
and more how much the grace of Jesus Christ means
and how futile all our efforts for salvation would be
without it. And looking back, I wonder if perhaps

the reason debaters like my husband stood out so far above their opponents was that they nearly always met men who were less talented in speaking, in quick thinking, in preparedness, and in pulpit magnetism. Perhaps this was where their real triumphs lay.

In all my years as a preacher's wife I have attended countless "gospel meetings," listening intently to sermons on first principles. Occasionally I heard a new illustration, sometimes the speaker's delivery was especially attractive, but the theme was always the same. I did not mind for a long time, but eventually something happened and a reversal began in my thinking. I found suddenly that some of my fervor was lost. One incident brought me face to face with this fact.

I was called one day to the home of a person very dear to me. She had been lax in church attendance, her husband had died suddenly, and she was reviewing their lives with regrets. "Oh, Margaret," she said through tears, "you have lived so wisely; you have gone to church so regularly and it has kept you close to God, and that is the most important thing in life, isn't it?" I wanted to agree that church attendance would bring her closer to God, but suddenly I felt unsure that all the numberless meetings with my brethren had brought me closer. I found myself evading the subject and turning instead to some comforting passages of scripture from which she might gain courage.

Later I pondered this change in myself. I could not fix a time when it had begun; I only knew that suddenly I could no longer speak words of assurance about how going regularly to Church of Christ services would automatically bring one nearer to God. I did not know what to do about the spiritual turmoil raging inside me. I had brought my children up to believe things I now doubted. My husband preached and taught these things via printed pages, pulpits, and radios. My son made plans to preach the same doctrine. My dear friends believed it and had the fullest confidence that I did.

Suppose I just tell them openly that it has come to seem empty to me, I thought; what would that do? I pictured the shocked and unbelieving looks from friends and brethren (many of them preachers and their families) whose friendships I had cherished for years and whose esteem I valued. Though I embraced, formally, a religion that now was empty to me, I was learning how hard it can be to renounce it. To deny the teachings of "our brethren" seemed virtual infidelity, so strongly does the tradition of our infallibility get into one's vitals. Yet to be silent and seem to condone our empty legalisms seemed an unbearable form of deceit.

After many hours of agony, tears, and prayers, I took the course of least resistance and kept silent about my doubts and my disbelief in many of the things we taught. I disliked the degree of pretence involved, but I argued that I must not hurt anyone or be a stumbling block to anyone in my family or in the church. I should have known, perhaps, that it could not work, but my heart struggled to evade wounding those I loved.

I kept attending church regularly and I taught a class, although I soon found myself hampered in my teaching. The lessons had to be "slanted" to add support to Church of Christ doctrine. I thought I might avoid this by using only the Gospels for study; I knew there were many valuable lessons in the life and ministry of Jesus. But the deeper I got into these, the more flaws I saw in our teachings. I was often asked direct questions to which I had to give half answers. To answer fully would be to contradict the hallowed beliefs of the church, yet it was impossible to parrot the old replies that satisfied my people. I found an excuse for giving up my class.

I went to fewer and fewer of our meetings, although I still tried to go to those held in my own congregation. They were the same to which I had so long given undivided attention, but now they had become to me as "sounding brass or a tinkling cymbal." They were words with no life, a form with no spirit.

All around me it seemed there arose perfect pictures of the Pharisees in almost everything my brethren did. What is wrong with me? I asked myself. Every time I read my New Testament and observed the inconsistencies, intolerances, extremes, and hypocrisies of the Pharisees, did I have to apply them to my brethren? I fretted over this critical looking at what I had formerly loved.

I had not wanted to become so, but I had not been able to control my thinking. Outwardly I could, in a measure, conform to the customs I had practiced; I could move along bodily in the same religious rut; but I could not command my thoughts to revert to the narrow realm that had bound them in previous days. Slowly I realized that I had changed in thought just as one changes in body, and that I could no more fit my thoughts into an outgrown shell than a child can wear the clothes he discarded in infancy.

I observed the people around me. Some had been members of the church for thirty, forty, and fifty years. I studied the way they listened to the sermons. Were they not weary beyond measure of hearing over and over the same limited teachings? Did they not yearn for a religion that had power to feed the spirit? It was evident that many of them did not; they were perfectly content.

Yet while I saw those who were content in their routine, I remembered others who had grown indifferent to "the church," as we universally refer to the Church of Christ. Among them were some very good people. When they were called upon or talked to about their back-slidden state, they gave no excuse for their actions. Usually they were silent as to why they had grown indifferent.

With my own mental change, I wondered if those people, and many more like them, had not hungered for a higher food than they had been fed in "the church." Wasn't it quite possible that when called on to explain their lukewarmness they were unaware themselves just what was wrong? As I looked back through my life, many individuals came to mind in whom I had seen all the symptoms of the spiritually hungry. Unable to nourish their spirits on the low-caloried spiritual diet they were being fed they had simply become cold and dropped by the wayside. Now I understood them better and wondered if their silence might not have been in part their feeling that it was useless to talk to people as certain and assured as my brethren.

For my brethren believe that they are "the church" spoken of in the Bible. They believe that anyone not a member of their group will be lost. They believe that all the churches around us are wrong and that their members are on the road to damnation. Even their prayers are not heard, because only those in the religious group called "Churches of Christ" have God's approval and God's ear. Regardless of how much good work may be done by Methodists, Baptists, Presbyterians, and the like, it is useless. Only the Church of Christ receives God's blessing and may rightfully call him Father. Penetrate the subtleties of expression and the public kindness of manner and this is the true picture of the religious world as it is seen by the faithful in the Church of Christ.

It is easy enough to subscribe to such a doctrine with our lips, but do we truly believe it in our hearts? What man can wholly accept this doctrine without some mental reservations? To believe it means that there is no hope for most of the godly men of the present or the past. Men like Wycliff, Huss, Luther, Knox—men who dedicated lives to Christian service and to giving us an accurate version of the Bible—these all died without hope because they did not belong to the Church of Christ. Their superb faith and courageous witness were all in vain because they were "in error," as we put it, on certain doctrinal issues.

My brethren feel some pity for such cases, but they shake their heads and say, "We can all see the truth alike, if we only will, and this is what God demands of us. They just didn't go far enough, or else they weren't quite sincere enough, that's all." To talk of "concepts of truth" or of different interpretations is to run into a stone wall with my brethren. They equate truth and men's conception of it, and they stoutly affirm that they do not interpret the Bible at all—they just let it "mean what it says."

Yet anyone knows how two different people may "view" an opera singer. One cringes with dislike at loud bellowing. The other is delighted by rich quality of the voice. Each is "right" in his reaction to the singer. One is not developed in musical appreciation and can only judge the singer with limited capacity, but his is nevertheless a "true" view. At some later date, better trained, he may have a quite different reaction, but it will also be a "true" one because it will correspond to his measure of knowledge at that moment.

So do we grow also in Biblical truth. We find new vistas of truth as we move up the plateaus of thought, but no one man or church can ever rightfully claim to have "the truth" as opposed to all others who are "in error." Listening to my preachers talk of how we had the truth and others were wrong, I found myself wondering about some obvious discrepancies. I saw other church members taught to be better citizens, I saw them feeding the hungry and clothing the poor, I saw them guiding their young people into spiritual truths, I saw them enlightening the minds of little children with stories about Jesus, and I saw many fruits of the Spirit through which they blessed the society I lived in.

How, I wondered, would Jesus regard their good works in His name? I spent hours wondering how they could do so much good and yet be so hopelessly lost. And then I remembered a scripture I must have read many times with blinders on: Luke 9: 49-50 " 'Master,' said John, 'we saw a man casting out devils in your name, but as he is not one of us we tried to stop him.' Jesus said to him, 'Do not stop him, for he who is not against you is on your side.' "

With those words ringing in my ears, so unlike the harsh judgments I was accustomed to hearing from my own leaders, I recalled how audiences had acted so often among our people when hearing sermons about why other churches were wrong. How many times I had seen members nudge one another with an elbow, or give a knowing wink or a slight smile of approval when points were made that showed how people of other churches were on the road to perdition. And how many times, after the services, had I sat with them while they talked of the "hot-headed Baptists" or "dyed-in-the-wool Methodists" who had been among our visitors, and how they had squirmed in discomfort during the sermon.

I do not believe these friends of mine were malicious, any more than I was, but none of us had really stopped to think about our attitude toward those we considered "lost." If we had, we could not have smiled at their discomfort or taken the slightest pleasure in their squirming.

It may be that we take pleasure in the discomfort, or supposed discomfort, of others because we are not ourselves happy. I think of a deacon in one of the congregations I attended. He would be called in our language a "faithful member of the church." He never misses a service on Sundays or Wednesdays or during the time of the gospel meetings. He has done this for years, but he does not hesitate to say in private talk: "Sure I have to go every Sunday! Man, do you think I'd be there if I didn't have to? If I had my way I'd be out fishing on Sunday morning, but I know enough to know I've got to get myself to that church building whether I want to or not." He will suffer through his religion the rest of his life, but without much happiness from it. And it will soothe his misery when the preacher attacks someone for failing to do what he has so dutifully done. It isn't hard to see how such a religion fails to enlarge or beautify the spirit.

We have taught the duty of going to church, but we have given little thought to making our worship really reverent and lovely. We have insisted upon regularity in prayer, but those one hears in our services are far too often cold and stereotyped. We have magnified the office of the pulpit, but the lessons that come from there are too often shallow and trite. We have exalted correctness and knowledge, but we have not been successful in bringing to people the peace that passes all understanding.

Not everyone who feels as I do will want to speak so frankly as I have done, or act so decisively. Thousands will continue to attend Church of Christ services while their hearts hunger acutely for something better. They deserve to be given something better. I say to all of them that my love and sympathy is with each of them. But I can no longer settle for a faith less than the one I now hold. I am not satisfied to have just life, but I want it as Christ promised it— abundantly. The religion I have known most of my life is fat with argument, but lean on spiritual depth and richness. I cannot pretend to be learned in theology, but like the blind man of John 9, I know that I now see what once was dark to me and I thank the same Lord for His precious gift.

WILLIAM K. FLOYD has served as minister for fifteen congregations of the Church of Christ, sometimes working full-time for them in the summers. He is presently a member of and teacher at the Broad Street Church of Christ, Cookeville, Tennessee, and is actively engaged in preaching for Churches of Christ in the area.

As a student at Harding College, Mr. Floyd was president of the student body, an outstanding intercollegiate debater, and a member of Who's Who in American Universities and Colleges. He majored in Bible and Speech, receiving his B.A. degree in 1958. He took his M.A. degree in Speech from the University of Oklahoma and has done graduate work toward his doctorate at Pennsylvania State, Wichita State, and the University of Tennessee.

Mr. Floyd has taught at the University of Oklahoma, at Southwestern State College in Oklahoma, at Pennsylvania State, and is now on the faculty of Tennessee Technological University as Director of Forensics. He has been president of both the Tennessee Speech Association and the Tennessee Intercollegiate Forensic Association. He has sponsored many academic and church youth organizations. He is 29, married, and has two children.

WHY I COULD NOT BE
A CAREER PREACHER

By William K. Floyd

Before I went to the Church of Christ college I chose, I had planned to be a minister. This was partly due to the inspiration of my father, who is himself a career minister in the Church of Christ. He had long ago won my admiration for his courage to think and speak straightforwardly, for his love of people even when it cost him, and for his interest in a cause above a career. But the inspiration waned during my years in that college and I am now a teacher in a secular university. My interest in the ministry remains high and I believe it can be a worthy calling. Still, I chose another means of service, as have hundreds who once felt as I did. The reason undoubtedly lies in part within my personality and theirs, but it also lies in great measure within the very nature of the Church of Christ and its schools. I want to explore this problem.

Church of Christ journals have been decrying the preacher shortage for several years. While college enrollments have gone up, the number of preaching students has gone down. Both the Church of Christ and the general population are increasing faster than are the ranks of preachers. It is estimated that there are fewer than half as many preachers as there are congregations in the Churches of Christ. The problem worsens and demands our concern, but concern is not enough. Nor is exhortation. There must be some analysis of the situation in the Church of Christ which causes the problem.

The articles so far published have made only superficial explorations of the problem. One man of repute among us writes that what we need is more "men's training classes!" An editor of one of our most influential papers lays out his solution: encourage our young men to lead in prayer, to read publicly, and to make announcements. Another writer suggests that materialism is drawing young men away, even though he must know with the rest of us that salaries for preachers are better than they have ever been. Still another says that in spite of ample support it is hard to find ministers who have adequately prepared themselves. The unprepared are being used, he laments; the qualified are turning to other forms of service.

A Church of Christ college president lays the blame elsewhere: "The picture of the preacher as presented in modern literature and in movies, on television, and on radio has certainly been less than noble. . . . This image of God's man has been so debased as to cause many young people not to desire the work of the minister." He does not mention, though he might, that many bright young ministerial hopefuls are appalled to learn that in the larger academic world they are viewed as men committed to dogma rather than truth. Painful as it is, we must confess that the images portrayed are not altogether untrue.

The Gospel Advocate, a Church of Christ publication, has finally hinted at one of the basic causes of our preacher shortage. It notes that there is too much politicking in the church, too many closed minds, and too much apathy to challenge either of these evils. Perhaps the problem of the closed mind is best illustrated, albeit unconsciously, by the editor of the *Firm Foundation,* another such paper. He made this amazing admission:

"We have often said that among the greatest dangers we face is that of having to send our brightest young men off to sectarian schools for their doctorate work. Most of the work in the doctorate area is under the domination of very liberal forces. We cannot expect to keep it from affecting our own teaching in our schools. I am personally more interested in at least one of our schools becoming able to train teachers to the level of a doctor's degree, so that it may supply sound teachers for at least the other schools supported by brethren, than I am in any other phase of their development. . . . The church can always profit from a better trained minister. Until recently they have had to go to sectarian schools for any such training. In these schools they must constantly be on guard against teaching which would undermine their faith. We have lost any number of good men because they could not stand up under the strain."

Why do our "brightest" leave? The answer is inherent in this editor's view of education as propaganda! The bright young men, sooner or later, begin to wonder what there is to a faith that needs such cloistered protection.

My own college responsibilities gave me unique opportunity to know the preacher boys and those who had meant to be, and were able, but who had rejected the ministry. It always seemed to me, even before I made my own decision, that those who decided not to be fulltime preachers were the most capable students. Those who chose to stick were, all too often, the pastoral lackeys who were short on imagination. They could speak glibly to little congregations which were dead in their pews. They warmed over sermons from sermon outline books which they purchased in the college bookstore. Their creativity consisted in thinking up new word gimmicks for outlines. They impressed their parishioners by regurgitating revered and stock patterns, and they enjoyed the inevitable praise. They played the sycophant without qualms. They accepted without question. Was it a clear vision of this kind of life that made the others forsake the ministry?

Since there is a crucial shortage of preachers, my analysis may be helpful. It can do service even for those who disagree with, or deplore, my point of view, for it will acquaint them with the way many young people think today. If some do not agree that the Church of Christ is as I describe it, they may at least become aware that many view it this way and so have not given themselves to the ministry.

We cannot understand our problems in the church without seeing what is happening in our world. We are in the midst of social and cultural revolutions more drastic and rapid than any generation has experienced. Some of the major problems which have resulted are these: technological and scientific innovations so wide-ranging that we are unable to keep up, new sources of power that demand controls we have not yet devised, new social and ethical values we have not yet tested adequately, the nearing end of white supremacy and the consequent necessity for new modes of thought, disturbing new patterns of work and living habits, loss of the church and the family as sources of authority, and the loss of a sense of identity and belonging as a result of our amazing physical mobility.

The world of 2000 A. D. (I shall be 63 years old) will not be merely 1966 with more gadgets. Basic concepts of society will be radically different. There will be new modes of thought. That our religious concepts will be greatly affected should go without saying if we recall the modes of thought and action in our own group fifty or one hundred years ago.

Young people today read the future by their knowledge of history. They are aware of the larger patterns of change and they put their world in new perspective. They want little part of any movement that is not cognizant of change and progress. Any reverence for the past which seems to them an obvious attempt to maintain the status quo will fill them with disgust. And when they see that their church interprets the ancient message via a nineteenth century mode of thought, they will conclude that it is out of touch with reality.

Those my age and younger have not despaired of idealism, only of institutions that have surrendered to traditionalism and the status quo. Unfortunately, this has often included the church, so we are finding and creating new forms for the expression of our idealism: civil rights groups, benevolent enterprises, the Peace Corps. In these activities we are not obliged to sit silently while our Church of Christ teachers tell us that the world is only six thousand years old, that there are no textual or canonical problems in the Bible which should worry us, or that biology textbooks are naughty because they present frank and objective truth about human anatomy and procreation.

The last comment above is no fiction. The editor of a most influential Church of Christ paper indicted biology texts in his state because of their "graphic descriptions of the male reproductive system, the female reproductive system, stages of human birth" and the like. He said that all this constituted "Godless, materialistic, atheistic preaching." It is astonishing how far removed from young men and women this editor is. In or out of the church, young people will not take seriously a high school biology text that has for its section on sex a photograph of a bird, a bee, and a stork. Nor will they kindle to any spirit represented in so patronizing a way. When they see church leaders react this way, they lose respect for them, and because they equate (with the abrupt conclusions of the young) the church with its leaders, they lose respect for the church too.

A Gallup poll in 1965 showed that since 1957 three times as many adults as formerly are saying that religion is losing its influence upon American life. Younger adults (21-29) are even more inclined to take a pessimistic view of the influence of religion upon

American society. And among persons now attending colleges, belief in the power of religion is waning even more. These last claim that religion fails to meet the challenge of science and the intellect; that it fails to solve contemporary moral, social, and economic problems; and that church involvement has not proved itself necessary to the fulfillment of life.

But it is *institutional* Christianity that has brought the greatest dismay. The church's introversion, her preoccupation with outmoded forms, her use of embalmed theological jargon, her hair-splitting over dogmas, and her refusal to re-examine interpretations in the light of twentieth century knowledge—these are the failures bright young men and women quickly point to. Significantly, religion which expresses itself in terms of social action and improved interpersonal relations is *increasing* its influence.

It is popular to blame higher education for loss of faith. The truth seems rather that certain religious approaches betray the young men and women who accept them. As one minister put it recently in a national magazine: "The problem of fundamentalism is that it cannot withstand critical Biblical scholarship and scientific facts. . . . And the moment small-town boys go to college, they take a course in biology and their faith is gone. Our great sin is never having offered them a real alternative."

The enrollment in colleges and universities goes ever higher. The time is near when the man in the pew may have an education superior to that of the pulpit speaker. In most Churches of Christ a sizeable number of auditors will have received better educations than their preacher. They tolerate warmed-over sermons and generalizations offensive to their minds only because they still believe that loyalty to this particular denomination will eventually save their souls. When they grumble about the meagre fare they get, the preacher generally stiffens and denounces them as liberals and radicals who are not "sound" in their faith. This tension has already created many serious splits in the Churches of Christ and will create more unless an atmosphere of respect for learning and of insistence upon freedom can be achieved.

This antipathy toward learning and questioning is widespread in the Church of Christ. In an Oklahoma college town the director of the Bible Chair, where college students took courses for credit under the sponsorship of the local Church of Christ, told a friend of mine that he (the director) was familiar with modernists and their ways. He said that he had read a question-and-answer book written by a modernist. "But," he added, "I only read the questions because I knew his answers wouldn't be worth reading." Not many would be so blatantly open, but the arrogance of such a remark is not unusual among some of our leaders.

I had an experience with some of my relatives once which illustrates the same point. Although the adults in this group (a family reunion) liked to avoid controversial religious issues, we always found the children greatly interested in new ideas. Talking to some of the teen-age boys present, I tried to acquaint them with views about a certain issue which are not normally expressed by our church group. One of the teen-age girls overheard our talks and became interested. She thought of something she wished to contribute, but needed to ask her mother where the Scriptural passage was that she felt would support her point. Her mother said, "Don't be disturbed over their discussion; just don't listen."

This attitude is still far too common among us and children treated in this way sooner or later realize what is being done to them. Their reactions are often violent when they come. And come they must, to many, because these children will be living far beyond the year 2000 A. D. The revolution of thought now taking place will affect them beyond our foreseeing. To present only one view and to protect them from all else will leave them without the tools or temper to analyze their complex world.

The situation is similar with respect to the clichés spoken so glibly by too many ministers. Today's students are taught to condemn the meaningless stereotypes. What, then, is their inevitable reaction when they hear their preacher solemnly intone such incrusted platitudes of the party as, "We speak where the Bible speaks and keep silent where it is silent"? It takes little mental exercise for them to see that what the preacher asserts is violated repeatedly by himself and his auditors. And a bit more reflection will bring them to wonder why the principle is valid even when observed. For does not God still speak? he will ask himself. The first century church was one that looked forward. Today the church that claims to partake in the spirit of the early church looks backward. Has God's revelation in Scriptures called us to a closed system, or liberated us and set us on a new road of discovery? Must we see all religious truth limited to the Bible, or see the Bible rather as a means of pointing us to religion as it is everywhere manifest?

Young men and women of intelligence and sensitivity are not much concerned anymore with the claims of rival sects to be the "true church." They grapple, instead, with such basic issues as the nature of God, the spirit of Christ, the relevancy of the church's message in a world of ever-shifting values. The kind of legalistic preaching which turns the Bible in upon itself and thrills to an introverted involvement with it will never again capture the finest young minds.

Nor do they want to live in a state of submission and fear. When they raise really significant questions and are met by charges of heresy or "getting out of line," they quickly lose hope that they can find freedom to grow in the church. With no vested interests to defend, they can afford to put more stress on integrity than on safety; the result is that many of them simply walk out.

Alexander Campbell recognized the pressures which authoritarian religion puts upon men. "It is a rarity seldom to be witnessed," he said, "to see a person boldly opposing either the doctrinal errors or the unscriptural measures of a people with whom he has identified himself and to whom he looks for support. If such a person appears in any party, he soon falls under the frowns of those who either think themselves wiser than the reprover, or would wish so to appear. Hence it usually happens that such a character must lay his hand upon his mouth or embrace the privilege of walking out of doors."

Eager to be popular, many Church of Christ ministers must hide their own values and insights, at least until they are convinced of enough support to keep them in service. Some of them find it convenient to learn which side of a controversy has the most influential members, then arm themselves with proof texts and become fearless spokesmen for the "church's" viewpoint. To act so is to play the hypocrite and to rebel against God by refusing to be the person He would have His minister be—a man of integrity who exemplifies moral courage.

One cannot but wonder what the Churches of Christ would think of Paul were he to speak to us today. He once (at least) preached a sermon on the existence and nature of God without quoting a single verse of Scripture; instead, he cited pagan poets in making his points. Could we tolerate such "liberal" tendencies, we who virtually worship the firing of Biblical prooftexts at the audience? Would we not charge Paul, also, with ineptness in handling race problems? After all, his associations with Gentiles gave the Jews grounds for stirring up mob action against him. We would likely charge him with "poor timing" because he insisted on pushing ahead with his universal religion and antagonizing many Jews. And we would be aghast at his audacity in challenging and exposing a "big preacher" in the "brotherhood" for following the dictates of expediency in this matter. Doesn't he know, we would wonder, that the "social gospel" has nothing to do with the Christian religion?

In other words, the vibrant, live message of Paul has become a dull, but respectable sermonizing. Ministers in the Churches of Christ find it generally wise to avoid involvements with the great crucial issues of their world. Nationalism, integration, population control, the sexual revolution, war, euthanasia— these and a host of other pressing problems must be ignored lest the congregation brand them as "unsound." Yet these are the very problems which today's college student debates vigorously. If his church hides its head from them, he will simply conclude that the church is an embalmed society for the preservation of peace and comfort.

One of these problem areas, that of racial relationships, is especially vital for Christianity. We live in a world where three out of four people are non-white. No amount of money, prayers, or missionaries will counteract the undermining influence of our segregated churches. In the face of our moral cowardice, God may be passing us by to raise up others more willing to fulfill his redemptive purposes. Many young men and women seem to sense this today and they do not intend to be found wanting. As Dante might have put it: "The hottest places in hell are reserved for those who, in a time of moral crisis, maintain their neutrality."

The Church of Christ has placed itself on the sidelines of the greatest moral struggle of our times. Without exception, every one of our southern Christian colleges have waited until it was safe before they integrated. And when they finally integrated (mildly), they blew trumpets and waved flags and sent articles to newspapers announcing their courage and humanitarianism! All this, to their everlasting shame, after they had worked for years to stave off integration as long as possible.

One of our top college presidents told me in private conference that Negroes really want to attend school "with their own people," and that he had personally contributed to their educational support elsewhere. But, he admonished me, "many Negroes have venereal disease," and we must protect our present students. God did not intend integration, he said, and it was not expedient, anyway, at present because the school might lose monetary support and not be able to teach "Christian principles" to as many students. Yet when it finally was "safe" to integrate, in fact imperative lest they be exposed in the newspapers, this president publicized the school's action as an act of Christian witness! One knows little about today's intelligent youngsters if he thinks they are blind to such hypocrisy or willing to partake of it.

My father ministered to an Alabama congregation during the Birmingham riots. He preached on segregation, his text being: "Do unto others as you would have them do unto you." He was called a "son of a bitch" and a "devil" from the audience while he was delivering the sermon. When the elders defended his right to preach what he believed, the elders were dismissed by the men of the congregation and my father was fired. Why have more Alabama Church of Christ ministers not been fired? Where is the church of our group that is in danger of being burned because of its stand for decency?

In another of our "Christian" colleges, located where all state colleges have been integrated for years and in a city in which other private church-related schools have been integrated for years, segregation has until very recently been an iron-clad policy. At this Church of Christ school, Negroes were excluded from tournament events that involved other schools for on-campus participation. And when faculty members were hired it was made a specific condition of employment that they must refrain from making any public statements (even in the capacity of private citizen) favoring integration. This will shock readers who believe in responsible freedom in integrity for faculty members, but it is a fact easily verifiable from men who formerly taught in this college and are now in respected positions in other colleges and universities.

When I was serving as president of the student body at Harding College, some students asked me to help them circulate a petition demanding an end to the de facto policy of racial segregation at the school. I suggested that we were not in a position to make demands and asked for time to draw up a *statement of attitude* that would indicate clearly the feelings of students and faculty. With the advice and assistance of some faculty members, the statement was readied. Before any signatures were obtained, the administration was told of the contents of the statement and what was about to occur. The administration immediately requested that the action not take place. I met that evening with the student council and told them of the administration order. They voted to go ahead with the circulation of the statement. The administration announced in chapel the following day that it did not favor the statement's circulation. When an overwhelming majority of people at the college signed the statement, we sent it to each member of the Board of Harding College, along with the following letter:

"November 10, 1957. Attention members of the Board of Harding College: The following is a statement that was circulated on the Harding College campus: To the administration and Board of Trustees of Harding College:

"A number of members of the Harding community are deeply concerned about the problem of racial discrimination. Believing that it is wrong for Christians to make among people distinctions which God has not made, they sincerely desire that Harding College make clear to the world that she firmly believes in the principles of the fatherhood of God and the brotherhood of man. To that end, the undersigned individuals wish to state that they are ready to accept as members of the Harding community all academically and morally qualified applicants, without regard to arbitrary distinctions such as color or social level; that they will treat such individuals with the consideration and dignity appropriate to human beings created in the image of God; and that they will at all times face quietly, calmly, patiently, and sympathetically any social pressures intensified by this action.

"Furthermore, the undersigned individuals wish it clearly understood that this statement of attitude is by no means intended as an attempt to precipitate action by the Administration or Board of Trustees of Harding College, but that it is instead intended entirely as an expression of the internal readiness of the Harding community to end discrimination, such expression being tendered as one factor for the consideration of the Administration and the Board of Trustees when a re-evaluation of the admission policies of Harding College is undertaken."

"The copies bearing the signatures of those supporting this concept have been sent to the Chairman of the Board and to the Administration of the College requesting consideration of this problem at the next Board meeting.

"Forty-nine faculty members signed, forty-two staff members and eight executive directors. There is a total of nine hundred and forty-six signatures affixed to the statement. There are nine hundred eighty-six regularly enrolled students in the college.

"We appreciate your continued individual thought

and expression given to this problem, which is of great concern to us.

"Sincerely, Bill Floyd, President, Student Body."

In later sessions with the administration I learned a great deal about the power structure of the Church of Christ. The president told students in chapel that the action was improper and that the signatures were not an accurate expression of student feeling. I never understood how he determined this, when such a vast majority signed. His explanation was that "they didn't understand what they were signing." Any reader who can believe this does not seem to me to fathom the mind of today's college student. In the same address, our president explained to us that God made some blue birds and some black birds and that they were not intended to mix, that Negroes in America have more cars than the people in Russia, and that we would lose students and financial support if we were to integrate. I was told in private by one administrator that I had betrayed my trust as student body president, that no employer would ever hire me, that when one works for an institution he should accept all its thinking and keep silent about contrary beliefs, and that if I wanted to crusade for integration I should go where everyone believes in it. Another administrative official told me that the student government should be an agency to indoctrinate the students with the ideas of the administration.

During this time the state of Arkansas was much in the national news because of its racial problems. The *Arkansas Gazette,* never hesitant to print uncomplimentary stories about Harding College, would have been more than willing to print the story of the student statement and its reception by the administration. *Time* magazine, I feel sure, would have printed the story of a small southern college whose faculty, staff, and students had voted overwhelmingly to end segregation. But it seemed to me that sending the story to these media would not be the proper response, so it was not done.

So ended the 1957 attempt at Harding to end discrimination. When it was safer, several years later after it had become "the thing to do" around the nation, Harding at last made a mild, token integration and promptly released stories to news media acclaiming its action.

Our feeling about the civil rights struggle is akin to our ideological alliance with the political right wing. This alliance should surprise no one who knows us well. The right wing movement is characterized by intolerance under the name of conviction, by suppression of inquiry for the sake of propaganda, by counting expediency above principle, by the principle that the end justifies the means, and by a basic anti-intellectualism. I have seen far too much of all these traits in the church I grew up in.

One of our colleges is nationally known as a propaganda mill for far-right political groups. It has been called by name by several national publications, including *Look, Atlantic Monthly,* and *Time.* It has been described in complete chapters in three books dealing with the far-right movement in America. It has been discussed by name in articles in *The New York Times News Service,* the *Kansas City Star,* and the *Nashville Tennessean.* Yet, amazingly, one of the school's best-known teachers says that when people say this of his school they are bearing "false witness." He says: "The motives of various individuals who do this may differ—they range all of the way from Communists, socialists, and various other degrees of collectivists to the ignorant and the opportunists. . . . " This from the *Gospel Advocate.* I must list myself with those individuals who label his school a far-right propaganda mill. I do not think their witness false, and the only appellation above that comes close to describing me accurately is "ignorant." But that very kind of name-calling is typical of the radical far right.

The right-wing spirit is not found merely in our colleges. It is heard on radio from some of our preachers. It can be found scattered throughout gospel papers. In a *Firm Foundation* issue of 1964, one of our best-known preachers said: "The founder of the Christian religion said: 'the POOR ye have always with you' but these modern pink prophets actually think that the church should launch a campaign to prove that Jesus was a liar. They would turn the sacred hours of the pulpit and holy precincts of the Lord's Table into a discussion of the political and economic problems that face our troubled world. . . . Men need to be saved, not from bodily aches and pains; not from poverty and social injustices, but from SIN."

Not many intelligent potential young ministers want to be part of a church group that not only tolerates but in general approves that kind of approach to social evils. The great political polls show that young people are moving ideologically in the opposite direction. The talent drain away from Church of Christ pulpits is awesome. We are left with many handsome, glib, extroverted young men, but with too few thoughtful ones.

One of my most distressing realizations has been this one: that I am expected as a preacher to be an "answer factory," rather than a man expected to *struggle* with problems of life and the relevancy of Biblical principles to them. In my Sunday school classes, too many students think there aren't really any serious problems. There just *seem* to be, but answers are available from any good Church of Christ preacher or teacher worth his salt. There is a psychological mania to provide all the answers. Any hesitancy, any deliberation, any confession of alternate possibilities proves that the teacher is not really sound, not really well-prepared with his arsenal of quick answers.

Since I cannot be a man with a bag of answers, I cannot be a career minister for the Church of Christ. To salvage integrity I must turn to other forms of professional activity and be independent of those who would squeeze me into a party mold and rob me of God-given freedom. As a college teacher I can encourage students to think for themselves, something I am not often allowed to do in the party. I can urge them to enter into life and religious experience directly, not vicariously. I can encourage them to be free—a condition fraught with dangers, but glorious beyond all measure.

I confess, too, that I am dismayed by "preacher worship" and the dangers it poses. When I go away from home to meetings and songfests where I am not known and meet strangers, I introduce myself simply as "Bill Floyd." They give me their names in a bland, uninterested way and prepare to move on (I am not an impressive-looking person). But when a member who attends the church where I preach is with me, he quickly announces with pride: "This is the minister where I go to church." Then the quick, schizophrenic change invariably takes place. The stranger brightens up, smiles, often regrasps my hand (this time warmly) and shows interest in me.

Am I not worthy to be shown interest and respect as a human being? Can I not be given respect simply as a person, rather than because of some artificial appellation and status assigned to me? It is no credit to me to have an obsequious sycophant fawning at my feet. I am somebody only because *God* made me. Every other person in the whole world is worthy of every bit as much respect as I am. I glory only in being respected for what makes me respectable—that I am a creature of God.

Preacher worship can be a kind of self worship. If

you cannot gain personal status, you give it to your preacher and then identify with him. By insisting that he is intelligent, you can believe that you are intelligent to perceive his intelligence. His rightness makes you right. By and by, this blind worship makes it impossible for one to see clearly that what he has standing before him in the pulpit is, after all, only a man whose words must be evaluated thoughtfully before they are accepted.

Too many preachers foster this worship and dote on it. They foster it by talking of preachers as a special breed, by writing the kinds of articles they write, and by the way they praise other preachers at all the big lectureships.

"Even preachers," one preacher said, "sometimes are competitive and find it hard to be free of envy when one of their colleagues is successful." We think: "How big of him to admit this; what humility!" But the humility is false; pride looms behind the thin veil of pretence. "Even preachers," he says, as if preachers are truly a special breed expected to be above the temptations common to ordinary men. Such a comment is not humility; it is merely skilful boasting.

Still, it is hard to blame preachers. They are only responding to the environment created by their members. They want to be prominent and they know how to do it. I once knew a young man who was determined to be president of a Church of Christ college someday. He knew what to do. I have been following his career with much interest. He has the required smooth personality, good looks, and the proper amount of intelligence. He owns the right kind of car, has the right kind of wife, follows the party line. Occasionally he will express an objection to some unimportant party view, to prove that he is a free-thinker and courageous, but he knows exactly how far he dares to walk on this dangerous ground. He supports no controversial programs. He reads the church papers to know what to think about issues and to see what is in vogue. He cultivates the right people. He goes to graduate school, for one must have the educator image. He gets a job as dean of students at a Christian college. Knowing that it is also vital to have the "big preacher" image if one is to become president in our colleges, he gets a job as minister at one of the biggest churches in the brotherhood. He needs the writer image, also, so he blitzes the gospel papers with bland articles (he can write more thoughtfully, but he *must* get the items published). He holds as many gospel meetings as possible. He will be president someday of a Church of Christ college.

One Church of Christ minister, disfellowshipped long since as a heretic, said candidly that he hoped to see this power structure destroyed. "Disciples are awakening everywhere, and those of us who preach are losing steadily our power to mold audiences into puppets who rubber-stamp all our views. This is long overdue and will be a blessed and wonderful thing when it comes in fullness. Among other things, it will mean that the preacher has a corrective, some intelligent force able to counter his interpretation with others, so that he may be able to check the validity of his own. It is no wonder that so many of us who preach are arrogant and sure of our infallible interpretations when, within our party, there is seldom ever a strong voice to question us."

Congregations that insist on thoughtful and provocative lessons will get them from a minister worthy of his calling. Such a minister will devote himself to *wide* reading, careful and arduous study, and contemplative exercises. The sad thing is that there are few congregations who desire deep, honest, free thought from their ministers. The result is that one sees impoverished personal libraries too often. The standard fare on Sundays is still too much stagnant thought and stale sermonizing. Gimmicks are popular, whether

in the form of clever little outlines, alliterative sermon
titles, or ingenious "object lessons." This is not surprising; when men are penalized for thinking they will
cultivate mediocrity.

I think one of the most penetrating comments I
have ever seen about this kind of mental laziness was
made by Charles Fort in *Wild Talents*. He said: "I
am in considerable sympathy with conservatives. I am
often lazy myself. . . . When I'm somewhat played
out, I'm likely to be most conservative. . . . My last
utterance will be a platitude, if I've been dying long
enough. If not, I shall probably laugh. . . . One can't
learn much and also be comfortable. One can't learn
much and let anybody else be comfortable." The judgment these remarks makes upon our pulpits need not
be elaborated upon.

With such views as the foregoing, it must be clear
to anyone versed in party politics and party thought
that I anticipate no calls to large churches or Church
of Christ college jobs. I look with some regrets upon
the dead-end street, but I console myself with the
thought that the cost of success would be too high. I
prefer to see Christianity as a stance, rather than as a
system. I think no Christian need guard the faith; I
think it needs to be exposed, not protected. I believe
the truest disciple must live with the courage of faith:
calling prophetically for change before the climate is
right or safe, throwing himself on the barbed-wire so
that other troops may reach over him to victory, knowing that he may not himself survive to see the glory
of triumph. This is the courage of love, this defines
for me the genuine "man of God." I hope that I may
find some part of it in my life, despite my failure to see
how it can be realized in the present climate of our
pulpits.

CECIL L. FRANKLIN, who became Rector of the Church of Christ the King (Episcopal) in Arvada, Colorado in 1960, was born in 1927. His father was a Disciples of Christ minister who later became a minister of the Church of Christ. Mr. Franklin attended Abilene Christian College as a ministerial student in 1943-45 and received the A.B. degree from Phillips University in 1947. He attended Harvard Divinity School and received the degrees of S.T.B. (1950), S.T.M. (1951), and Ph.D. (1961). He was ordained a priest in the Episcopal Church in 1957. He has been active in writing religious materials, in social services, and on a wide variety of church and civic committees. Currently he is a Lecturer in Bible and Religion at Monmouth College (Illinois).

WIDER HORIZONS

By Cecil L. Franklin

It is with a large measure of reluctance that I have
been persuaded that my contributing to a collection of
critical essays about the Church of Christ might serve
a useful purpose. There are several reasons for my reluctance. It was in the Church of Christ that I first was
taught the Christian faith, was baptized, was nourished
in Christian teaching and behavior. It is mere decency
to hesitate to join in a criticism, no matter how well-
intentioned, of a church from which one has received
so much. Furthermore, I have friends who are faithful and loyal members of the Church of Christ. I
should not like in any way to offend or alienate them.
I can only ask the reader to believe that I have no
consciousness of any present hostility against either the
Church of Christ or any of its members.

*   *   *   *

A biographical note will provide a useful and necessary background for what I have to say. My father
was a minister of the Church of Christ, having entered
that church from the ministry of the Christian Church
(Disciples of Christ) when I was a small child. During
my senior year in high school, I became convinced
that I, too, ought to devote myself to the ministry.

I entered Abilene Christian College in 1943, at the
age of sixteen. I left in 1945, having, for all practical
purposes, lost my "fundamentalist"[1] belief, and with
it all that I cared to call Christian faith. At that time,

---

[1] I am not sure whether this term is honored as much within the Church
of Christ now as it was then. I know that in some circles the term "conservative evangelical" is now preferred. Even at that time it did not mean
precisely what it had originally meant, in terms of the set of books, The
Fundamentals, published in 1910. In this essay, I use the term chiefly to
denote the point of view which holds firmly to Biblical inerrancy, and rejects
the historico-literary approach to the Bible which has the unfortunate name
of "higher criticism."

I did also acquire some degree of hostility and bitterness towards the Church of Christ and some of its members.

Here, I think I must interject a reflection that comes from later years. It is my opinion that at that point in my adolescence I would probably have rejected any religious view with which I had been brought up. This appears to be, for many people, a part of the psychology of that stage of development. It is possible that if my associates during that period had been more understanding of that psychology, there would have been less of hostility and bitterness. But I believe that neither the faith itself nor anyone connected with the church was in any appreciable degree responsible for my rejection of fundamentalist Christian belief. The fact of my rejection of the Church of Christ at that point in my development is not so significant, in my opinion, as the fact that, at a later point, return to the Church of Christ was not something that I was able to consider as a live option.

My situation during that period was not comfortable. On the one hand, I felt almost a glee in emancipation. But I did not know quite who I was or where I belonged. Most of my friends were members of the Church of Christ, many of them studying for its ministry, and I did not have the feeling of personal security to enable me to speak freely of my doubts and growing disbeliefs. Furthermore, to do so would usually have been interpreted in terms of personal hostility. It was all somewhat tentative, but I was coming to the opinion that I could no longer be a member, let alone a minister, of the Church of Christ. Yet I knew that study of religion was the one thing that interested me most, so I continued to pursue it, not knowing where it might lead me.

My next two years of college, in Phillips University, were not very happy. Though the conservatism there was not so extreme as at ACC, it was sufficient to make me feel not-at-home, and to cause me to be far less than candid in the expression of ideas.

Only when I went to Harvard Divinity School in 1947 did I feel quite free to express myself, and to pursue my studies in the way I wanted. I reveled in the "liberalism" and "modernism" which then (more, I think, than now) characterized the school. I felt myself drawn to Unitarianism, a religion in which my beliefs—or lack of them—were easily tolerated. For a few years I felt largely comfortable in the Unitarian context, though I never actually joined the Unitarian Church.

Slowly, however, there began to grow in me a conviction that Unitarianism was inadequate. I yearned to believe the Christian faith. Intellectually, and perhaps also emotionally, I could not accept the fundamentalism which I had been taught in my childhood; yet it was very difficult for me to separate the Christian faith from fundamentalism. When I was finally able to do this, I was also able once again to examine the Christian faith. As a result of this re-examination, I became a member, and subsequently a priest, of the Episcopal Church.

*   *   *   *

I believe that I can make my contribution to this collection of essays most effectively not by pointing at things in the Church of Christ which I believe to be wrong, and saying why I think so, but rather by suggesting something in the way of broader vistas and wider horizons which I believe would contribute significantly and fruitfully to thinking within the Church of Christ.

1.   The first of these has to do with *reverence for truth*. This is something in behalf of which virtually all men would make protestations. We all believe that truth is to be preferred over error. And yet we some-

times become peculiarly defensive about the truth, as
though it were intrinsically stronger than error.

I am not here about to propose some kind of liberalism that teaches that we should, within the Church,
permit every opinion which someone holds to be truth.
Once I might have done that, but not now. The Church
is a community of faith, not a debating society.

I do, however, modestly suggest that our attitudes
towards people who sincerely disagree with us on what
the truth is, sometimes partake of a personal hostility
that is both irrelevant and un-Christian.

Although we believe that truth is real and absolute,
we recognize that the minds of men are finite and
fallible. Of course, we recognize this about the minds
of other men more readily than we recognize it about
our own. But even when we are able in some degree
to recognize it about our own minds, we have the conviction that we must pursue and proclaim truth as
best we can with such finite minds as God gave us.
What we must also recognize is that every other man
must also do the same. We know, from observing
others, that it is possible for other men to arrive at a
position (though erroneous to us) which is the conclusion of their thinking and the criterion for all truth
thereafter. We must learn that this is possible also for
us.

What, then? Must we give up our convictions? Must
there be a diffident and qualified tentativeness about
all that we believe and say? Not at all. As Christians,
we must have a firm faith, and must proclaim it firmly.
But at the same time, we must in humility recognize
our own fallibility, and re-examine our understanding
of that faith from time to time. We must also recognize
the full sincerity of people who disagree with us. We
must, in brief, take seriously the motto that ends,
"and in all things, Charity."

2. The second point is closely related to the first.
Most people recognize, upon reflection, that it is pos-

sible for two persons who are equal in intelligence and sincerity to arrive at diametrically opposite conclusions about something. This reality causes a problem for many who would like to think that if a person is reasonably intelligent, and genuinely sincere, he can infallibly arrive at the truth, or at least at any really important truth. But it is only a person who has isolated his mind that is able to believe this with confidence. For we readily find people whose intelligence and sincerity we cannot easily doubt, who believe things that are very far from the truth as we understand it. Surely the type of mentality that assumes that all disagreement with truth as one understands it is due to deliberate, wilful, and sinful insincerity is the epitome of sectarianism.

This is a threatening idea, for it suggests the possibility—however remote we may deem it—that we ourselves are in error, and no matter how hard we try, cannot arrive at the truth. This idea destroys the security which we would like to get from our firm conviction. But perhaps that security ought to be destroyed, because it is a security that attaches to intellectual propositions. Our true security ought to be in God Himself, rather than in intellectual propositions about Him. But here, we find ourselves further entangled in the difficulty that we can think of God only through intellectual propositions: that He *is,* and that He is supremely *good,* and *holy,* and *just.* This entanglement is one of the conditions of our creaturely finitude. We have no right to expect the security that God Himself has. We can seek security only in Him, with childlike trust.

But again, the question arises, if our convictions are such as to be subject to conditions and qualifications, whether we can firmly hold and proclaim them. If they are the result of the best and most sincere thought we can give them, we cannot abstain from holding and proclaiming them. But we must do so in the knowledge that God Himself is inconceivably greater than any convictions about Him that we can hold. This knowledge will help us to govern our relations with our finite fellow-creatures.

3. The third point I want to make concerns the fact that there are many millions of people who profess and call themselves Christians. Many of them are persons who, with great piety and devotion, offer themselves to God through Christ in worship, both in the congregation of fellow-believers and in the secrecy of their closets. They read their Bibles regularly with all the intelligence and devotion that they can muster. They partake in the supper of the Lord with regularity and frequency. In their daily lives, they try to follow Christ, and, as members of His Body, to give themselves as instruments of His will. For their hope of everlasting life in the presence of God, they trust, not in their own works, but in the merits of Christ, who died for them.

But the people who believe in Christ and try to follow and obey Him are divided. This ought to be a source of deep sorrow to every Christian. Christ prayed that His disciples should be one, but they are separated from one another. The apostle Paul proclaimed that there is one body, but that body is tragically broken.

Some people are able to calm their minds about this in an easy way: "We are right. Therefore, Christian unity can be achieved if the others will join themselves to us." This is an attitude which, until recently, has characterized the Roman Catholic Church, though there is some evidence that there may be a beginning of change in this. It is an easy way that can be adopted only by what is essentially a sectarian mentality which refuses to take seriously and attempt to understand a different belief.

Certainly, we cannot say that all the things that divide people who call themselves Christians are unimportant. There are deep and important convictions that divide Christians, and if we take Christianity seriously, these divisions cannot be done away with at once. But also if we take Christianity seriously, we cannot rest comfortably in our sectarian security, untroubled by the divisions which separate us. On the contrary, we must take one another seriously, and take one another's convictions seriously, fervently praying that the Spirit of God will further enlighten us all, and draw us closer together, and in His time reunite us.

4. Not only is Christianity far vaster than the particular brotherhood of Christians to which you, or I, belong; it is also vaster historically than our generation, or than the history of America, or than the history of England. Ever since that Day of Pentecost after Christ's ascension, the day on which the Spirit of God fell on the disciples as a divine enthusiasm, there has been a great company of men and women calling themselves Christians and devoutly trying to follow Him. Of course, some Christians have made bad mistakes. Some men who pretended to follow Christ were scoundrels, and some of them got into positions of prominence and leadership in the Church. There have been tares among the wheat. And even some of Christ's faithful sheep have sometimes been misled. Yet we have His promise that His Spirit will continue to guide His Church, even though the members of that Church appear not always to have heeded and followed His guidance.

But sectarianism obscures the fullness of that history. In some circles, one gets the impression that there is a long, dark tunnel between the times of the apostles and of Martin Luther; in others, that the tunnel extends still further, to the times of Alexander Campbell. In yet others, one might get the impression that the track ran straight from Jerusalem to Rome, and stopped there; or to Constantinople, and perhaps to Moscow. But the fact is that the history of Christ's

Church is far vaster than any of these sectarian views
would suggest. Even Canterbury is not the end of the
line!

We, then, are the heirs of almost two thousand years
of Christian history, in many countries, among peoples
of many tongues and races. We are the heirs of their
insights into the truth of God in Christ, of their piety
and devotion to God through Christ, and also, alas, of
their mistakes and errors. To cut ourselves off from
any of this heritage is to impoverish ourselves.

5.　Not the least of the achievements of these centuries of Christianity is the development and sys-
tematic formulation of Christian belief. Some of the
results of that process are sometimes taken for granted
by Christians, without their realizing that they came
about in the course of Christian history. Most notable
of these is the New Testament itself. The books of the
New Testament were all written in the very early
period of Christianity. But they were not all immediately accepted as Scripture. Nor are they the only early
Christian writings that were sometimes accepted as
Scripture. Indeed, it is not until the fourth century of
the Christian era that we find a list of books identical
with the list that finally came to be accepted among
Christians as the books of the New Testament. It is
thus due to the sifting process of several generations
of Christians that we have the New Testament in its
present form.

Many theological doctrines which some Christians
take for granted are likewise the end-product of a
process of devoted Christian thought in the light of the
Scriptures: the Trinity, the Incarnation of God in
Christ, the atonement, etc. Many of the same problems have been present to every generation of Christians. Many of the same questions have been asked by
members of every generation of Christians.

Certainly, there is no other area of study in which
one would presume to start from scratch without learn-

ing of the history of that study. For example, one would hardly try to find truth in physics or pyschology without learning what preceding physicists and psychologists have learned and believed. Similarly, it behooves one who wishes to learn the truth of God in Christ to study what earlier Christians have learned and believed. We do not stand alone. We are members of a great procession, marching through the centuries.

6. The Bible has always been, and must always be, central in the thinking of Christians. It tells us all that we know about that great central event of human history: God's sending His Son to earth to become man and to die and rise for mankind's sake. But we ought never to assume that we know every thing of importance that can be learned about the Bible, nor to close our eyes to new methods of approach to it. An unwillingness to consider new ideas about the Bible may be related to a desire to defend the truth against falsehoods. But we ought to examine carefully whether we are really defending the truth itself, or rather defending ourselves against the hard and uncertain work of seeking the truth with the energy which it deserves.

During the past few generations, new developments in historical and literary research have thrown new light on the probable historical origins and backgrounds of the Bible. We must be willing to examine these developments fairly, and ask, not whether they support what we have been accustomed to believe, but rather whether or not they are probably true. It is hard to suppose that we can be genuine disciples of Him who is the Truth at the same time that we defensively protect ourselves from what are claimed to be new discoveries of fact. That is not to say, of course, that we ought uncritically to accept every new theory that is proposed. An idea is not by any means more likely to be true simply because it is new. Quite to the contrary, we ought to move slowly. But we ought to move; we cannot ignore the newer researches.

Virtually all who call themselves Christians attribute authority to the Bible and call it the inspired word of God. But these words are subject to a number of interpretations. It is necessary for us conscientiously to re-examine periodically just what they ought to mean. I believe that several centuries ago, when it began to be suggested that the earth moves around the sun, one Christian theologian repudiated that notion, quoting some such passage as Psalm 93: 1, "the world also is stablished, that it cannot be moved." None of us today would use that as a reason for rejecting this commonly held astronomical belief. Nor do we suppose that this idea destroys the authority and inspiration of the Bible. But we concede that it gives us a clue for defining a little more accurately what we mean by authority and inspiration.

Important researches are continuing in the area of study that is called "Biblical theology." Many scholars are contributing to this study, on the basis of presuppositions which do attribute authority and inspiration to the Bible, not in terms of the idea of infallibility, but rather in terms of seeing the Bible as consisting of the basic data for understanding the work of God among His people, and especially of that central work, the incarnation in Christ. If we cut ourselves off from this new learning, again we impoverish ourselves.

7.   My last point concerns the relation between the Church and the world. Sometimes we become so involved in our own narrow concerns that we act as though the world existed for the sake of the Church, whereas in reality the Church exists for the sake of the world. God became man in Christ for the sake of world, because He loved the world so much. When we cease to think of the Church as existing for the world, we lose our entire perspective.

What can and ought the Church to do for the world? What can and ought the individual Christian, as a member of Christ's body, to do for the world? This can be answered in many ways. One might point to the works of mercy enumerated in the parable of judgment: feeding the hungry, giving drink to the thirsty, welcoming the stranger, clothing the naked, visiting the sick, going to the prisoner. This is at the center of what once made the "social gospel" so popular in certain circles. That movement sometimes took on utopian overtones. But the excesses which may be connected with that do not diminish our social responsibility in the social context in which we find ourselves.

The Christian, loving the world because God loves it, must concern himself with the problems of the world, both on a large scale—problems of war and peace, of poverty and famine, of overpopulation, of national and racial hostilities—and on the most local scale—the Negroes or Mexicans in our town who are not getting a fair shake; the people who are unskilled and untrained in habits of thrift and enterprise, and cannot get a job; the people whose married life is so fouled up that there appears no way out of the mess; the people who are burdened with the disease of alcoholism and are unable even to recognize their problem, let alone remedy it; and the people in the next block who are lonely, aimless, and lost. It was to such as these that Christ Himself ministered as He had opportunity; it is to such as these that the body of Christ must minister today, as its members are able.

* * * *

I cannot close without a further personal word. Some of what I have written could be interpreted as coming from one who considers himself intellectually or morally superior to his readers. I suppose this is the perpetual danger for a preacher. Like most people, I preach better than I practice. Probably like most preachers, I rarely preach without the gnawing consciousness that I could be a better Christian if I would yield my life more fully to God's grace. What I have written, I have written in love and sincerity, and I can only hope that it will be read in the same way.

CHARLES E. WARREN was born in Rogers, Arkansas, and grew up in Paducah, Kentucky. Since his family were all of Church of Christ background, he entered David Lipscomb College in 1947. In the winter of 1949, he left to serve the Valparaiso, Indiana Church of Christ. While there, he completed his B.A. degree at Valparaiso University in 1952 and in the fall of that year entered McCormick Theological Seminary in Chicago.

After a year at McCormick, Mr. Warren gave up efforts to maintain a relationship with Churches of Christ and served for two years as assistant minister in Faith Presbyterian Church in Chicago. Upon graduation from Seminary in 1955, he became minister of the First Christian Church at Deer Lodge, Montana. In 1957, he accepted a call to the Englewood Christian Church, Portland, Oregon.

Mr. Warren is now serving as associate minister of the Gordon Street Christian Church in Kinston, North Carolina, having gone there in 1961. This church is fully cooperative in the Disciples of Christ brotherhood and associates itself with the National and World Council of Churches.

NO CREED BUT CHRIST?

By Charles E. Warren

It is quite a challenge to retrace one's spiritual and mental travels, especially if one feels that he has come a long distance from where he once was. The intention of this essay is to state some of the ways in which I still feel some kinship of life and thought with my early background, but primarily to relate the ways in which I now feel removed from it.

It may be well to state that I did not originally wish to leave the Church of Christ. Outward and inward pressures compelled me. There is a saying in the Restoration movement: "We have no creed but Christ." This certainly seems to be a wonderful emphasis on unity of faith and love, while at the same time leaving plenty of room for variety and difference of thought. But in my experience in the Church of Christ, the slogan did not work out that way.

After a short tour of duty in the Air Force in World War II, I realized that I had confronted a larger world than I had known before. As I began college I found myself wrestling with some new-found ideas in psychology and philosophy. A questioning mood possessed me. I recall a day in the Church of Christ college I attended when I heard with some shock a conversation between a teacher and a student. In their talk they were agreeing that things of the Bible and of our faith should simply be accepted and taken at face value without any questions or theories about underlying reasons. I interrupted them with the remark, "I believe a person *should* ask questions, and *should* seek underlying reasons." The teacher cut me down with a blunt *ex cathedra* utterance: The secret things belong to the Lord our God; but the things that are revealed belong to us. . . ." (Deut. 29:29). He seemed to think it rebellious and sinful to have a curious mind, to ask questions, and to seek more adequate understandings. But I kept asking myself if it were not part of every free man's dignity to seek truth wherever it led without fear and intimidation.

The writings of men like Darwin and Freud unsettled me. One Church of Christ philosophy teacher did a great deal to help me struggle meaningfully and constructively with the theory of evolution, but none helped me struggle meaningfully with Freud. In fact, the whole world of clinical and therapeutic psychology seemed taboo.

A brother of mine, serving at that time as a minister in the Church of Christ, became embroiled in a conflict over some broader attitudes and ideas which he had come to hold. I loved him, but I was not able to accept all aspects of his thinking at the time. So I sought to discuss some of the ideas he was wrestling with, hoping that teachers and others in the Church of Christ could help me put them in proper perspective. I wanted to remain in that particular fellowship.

I found no one with the willingness (or perhaps with the religious perspective) to help me with this personal crisis. Outwardly some were very kind and showed good will toward me. But nearly all seemed to have some fear of me and of the situation I was in. This contrasted sharply with the attitude of Jesus, who showed no fear of the troubled nor any reluctance to go near those in crisis. I would today consider myself disloyal to Christ if fear kept me from drawing near and helping with all the grace and wisdom in me any man caught up in trouble or crisis.

I left the Church of Christ college before I graduated and moved to northern Indiana to preach for a small Church of Christ congregation and to finish my college work. In a Missouri Synod Lutheran liberal arts college a whole new religious perspective began to grow in me. Teachers who took differing views from my own, which were still loyal to the Church of Christ interpretations, opened up for me the reality of the grace and love of God. Much of the Bible that had been meaningless to me before came alive. Yet here were teachers who, according to my belief, were outside the pale.   ,

The mental conflict was intense. I had to know what to do about teachers who had revealed to me so much more about the Christ than had those of my own party. So it began to come to me that a true, personal laying hold of the grace of God in Christ is more important than correct outward observances. I came to know that it is much better to have personal grace and goodwill toward others and be wrong about facts and externals, than to be perfectly right about facts and externals without any personal grace and love. "The code killeth, but the Spirit makes alive."

My growing insistence within the Church of Christ was not that externals were to be changed, but that a new attitude and spirit must be breathed into their way of thought, life, and worship. I still very much wanted to stay within the Church of Christ tradition of simplicity of worship, adult immersion, weekly observance of the Lord's Supper, and use of the Bible as the basis for preaching and Christian living. But it seemed increasingly clear to me that members of the Church of Christ were making themselves out to be the only Christians. I felt that a return to the saying, "We are not trying to be the only Christians, but Christians only," was urgently in order. After all, I had already found Christians outside the Churches of Christ who had taught me more of Him than those inside. And I had been taught from youth up that Christ was the only proper creed, not some unwritten tradition of a religious party.

After finishing college I moved to Chicago to attend a Presbyterian seminary (reflecting, meanwhile, that all the founding fathers of our Restoration movement had Presbyterian educations!). I preached for Churches of Christ for about another year before leaving their ranks. My brother had written an essay called "The Heresy of Legalism," which had offended many leaders and members in the Church of Christ. I was soon to realize what this meant. I preached for a few Sundays in a Church of Christ north of Chicago; the membership was gracious enough to call my preaching helpful and Biblical. But another preacher, eager to purge the church of any who might be tainted, came along and explained to these good people who my brother was. That slammed the door in my face.

I was hurt by this growing exclusivism on the part of the Church of Christ. I had no creed but Christ; I was using no book but the Bible. For a movement that claimed to have no written creeds, it seemed to me that the Church of Christ had an amazingly potent unwritten creed and anyone who dared deviate from it was in dire trouble. For all practical purposes my association with Churches of Christ was ended.

The last two years of seminary I worked part-time with a Presbyterian church in Chicago. One may wonder why I did not stay with that group. The simple reason is that I could not bring myself to give up immersion and weekly observance of the Lord's Supper. These things, however, I saw in a different light than did most members of the Church of Christ. It seemed to me that the Churches of Christ had made adult immersion merely an arbitrary command of Christ's, to be conformed to or else. Little or no emphasis was given to baptism as a personal response to Him, an acceptance of God's free grace and love, and a total commitment to live according to the Spirit and teachings of Christ in all that one did. Church of Christ baptism seemed to take seriously neither the free and abounding grace and love of God, nor the radical nature of becoming totally responsive to the Spirit and will of Christ. Baptism itself seemed to constitute the obedience, rather than serving as the symbol of a commitment to be Christ-like in all things.

To illustrate how baptism seemed to be put in false perspective, I recall studying carefully the first five verses of John 10. How often I had heard these verses used to prove that if anyone tried to get into the Kingdom of God without believer's immersion he was both a thief and a robber. But it became clear after more careful study that Jesus was speaking of his own credentials as Christ and Savior. He was also speaking of the personal recognition that will cause people to become his followers. This discovery shocked me, slight as it may seem, and opened a vista before me of how strongly external acts and laws were put before a personal confrontation with Christ in the church I had served. Believer's immersion became much more significant to me, but in a totally different light from that in which most Church of Christ members see it.

In somewhat the same way the Lord's Supper seemed to be observed as an arbitrary command of Christ without being seen as symbolical of one's continual participation in Christ and the Christian fellowship, as a way of keeping in touch with God's Spirit in Christ, and as a way of drawing strength from other committed Christian souls. From Acts 20:7 it seemed clear that the Christians gathered for the express purpose of participating in the Lord's Supper. I felt that the Supper, then, should be the center and high light of Lord's Day worship. But in the Church of Christ the sermon got the lion's share of time and emphasis, while the Lord's Supper was handled routinely and briefly. I felt that this gave scant attention to our need for continual participation in Christ through the Spirit, and to our need for continual participation in the company of those committed to Him.

Again, the tendency of Churches of Christ to identify the Holy Spirit with the written words of the Bible revealed a deistic bias. Eighteenth and nine-

teenth century deism thought of God as creator of the
world, but as one who had set it going and then left it
to be governed solely by natural, scientific, and moral
laws. Like a railroad engineer he had set the controls
on the engine, then jumped off to let the train run
along the tracks by itself. But the Bible seemed to me
to teach that God was always active and working in
His world through the Spirit, that Christ had promised
the Spirit to His followers, and that we should not
think of God as limited by any so-called natural, scientific, or moral laws. Certainly the science and philosophy of the twentieth century have called into question the dated eighteenth and nineteenth century concepts of "law." It seemed to me, therefore, that the
Church of Christ attitude toward the Holy Spirit
seemed to be of the nineteenth century rather than
of the first century.

While deeply appreciating much about the Presbyterian church, I decided to become a Disciple of Christ
(Christian Church). As stated earlier, this was due
to my convictions about baptism and the Lord's Supper. A good friend of mine in seminary asked me once
who the Churches of Christ were. I answered, face-
tiously, "Non-fiddlin' Campbellites." He laughed and
wanted to know something about the Campbells. Later,
when I decided to become a Disciple, he wanted to
know who they were. I answered, "Fiddlin' Campbellites." This oversimplification at least serves to
bring up the question of proper music in worship, a
matter of great urgency in the split between Christian
Churches and Churches of Christ.

The first Christian church I served was in Montana
and it was this church which ordained me as a minister. On the afternoon of the ordination service a thun-
derstorm knocked out the electricity so that the organ
would not play. When the service was over a good
friend of mine, a minister who was also of Church of
Christ background previously, joked: "The Lord was

giving you that last warning about the organ, Charley."
I laughed, but I knew that to members of the Churches
of Christ this was serious business.

A cappella singing can be moving and beautiful. It
is also true that an organist or pianist who knows
what he is doing can bring some excellent singing out
of a congregation. To me the question of instrumental
accompaniment to singing is of minor importance.
Through the beauty of a building, or of words, or of
various material objects, all churches seek to add
beauty and dignity to their worship.

My most serious quarrel with the Church of Christ
emphasis is that it often separates faith and life, putting religion in its proper pigeonhole and secularizing
the rest of life. This is well illustrated in the matter
of music. In my home we often sang hymns around
the piano with my mother playing. This was a mem-
orable worship period for me. I recall reading an argument by some Church of Christ ministers on the matter
of whether it is sinful to play religious hymns on instruments outside the formal church worship. One of
them seemed to cinch the argument to his satisfaction
by explaining that singing hymns to instruments *outside* the church worship was practice, and therefore
not intended for worship. In this way, he said, it was
not sinful.

But Jesus said that where two or three are gathered
together in His name there He would be with them.
If three or four of us around the family piano forgot
that we were merely practicing, if we fell into the
spirit of what we were singing, and if we reverently
used Christ's name, did that mean we had suddenly
begun to sin? Is the only true church that which
meets for formal worship in the church building?
Where persons live in reverence and in the Spirit of
Christ in the home, is this not also a church?

If one attends a concert or a symphony and the
beauty of the music leads him to deep reverence before

God's work in His creation, is this not worship? Is it at the same time sin? Is the religious only that which takes place within the confines of the formal worship service? Is the temple of God really a *building*? Or is it the totality of one's life, inseparable from all one does? Churches of Christ often permit instrumental music in a wedding ceremony. Are not these vows of fidelity and these prayers for God's blessing in one of life's most important relationships an act of worship? Does the music turn this worshipful attitude into sin? Surely the genuinely religious is more than a fragment of one's life and includes far more than he does in the formal worship service.

Then there is the matter of church government. I remember a situation in the Church of Christ once when it was suggested that the members of the group should vote on certain issues and not just follow the will of the elders. Some prominent ministers in the group protested with indignation that the church is a kingdom, not a democracy. They appeared to me to be arguing the "divine right" of elders. I am ordained, and the elders of the church I now serve are ordained, but none of us would get far arguing "divine right" to our membership. I have long felt that elders must justify their leadership directly to the congregation; in the Churches of Christ I knew they seemed to be a self-perpetuating body of leaders who would not let their minister share the fruits of his studies, but who refused to study seriously and deeply themselves. It may be that such an eldership is the most urgent problem for the Churches of Christ today.

In another area of government, Churches of Christ claim autonomy for each congregation. In the Christian churches I now serve we have state societies and a national convention, plus other agencies through which we cooperate to do much work. It does not seem to me that one finds any uniform or fully developed method in the New Testament for church organization.

There are references made to the church in a certain city. Does this mean that there was just one congregation in that city, or did a number of different home congregations make up the church in that city with one group of elders? I really do not know. Certainly there were many apostles and evangelists traveling from church to church, exerting influence on many different persons and serving as agents for missionary and benevolent work. The early churches did not live alone without being influenced by other churches, and they joined together in many cooperative enterprises.

Pure local autonomy is probably something that never really exists. No person or group lives totally apart from others. In the Churches of Christ it seemed to me that college presidents, teachers, and editors were centers of influence and authority. To cross or to ignore some of these leaders was to put one's standing in grave peril. I must say that I have seen no leader in the Christian churches wield such immense personal power as I have seen editors, college presidents, and teachers wield in the Churches of Christ. As a minister in the Christian churches I feel quite free, though at the same time responsible to the church I serve and to our brotherhood at large. I really do not know what a perfectly Biblical organization would be. Whatever it is, I am positive that only the Christ can claim "divine rights" to rule.

And there is the Church of Christ's attitude toward the Bible itself. For me, this book is simply an accurate record of God's revelation of Himself to man, culminating in His final and complete revelation through Christ and the first apostles and Christians. The Bible is not a revelation of mathematical, scientific, or purely rational truth. It was written out of the background of the world views of the times of the writers and it is colored by the situation and temperament of each one of them. It was written in the language of the time and in terms of the thought patterns of the time; otherwise its message would have been gibberish and no revelation at all. To try to prove the Bible to be a collection of mathematical or scientific truths is a hopeless endeavor. Yet the Churches of Christ feel compelled to do this, no matter how literally and woodenly they must read some parts of the Old Testament in order to do so.

I felt that Church of Christ folk unnecessarily fear scholarly study of the Bible. They are afraid that acknowledgement of the contributions of historical, linguistic, and archaeological students will somehow weaken the power of its message. They are often frightened by study of the Bible which treats it as, among other things, a collection of various kinds of literature. My own feeling is that the Bible contains self-authenticating truth, carries immense authority within itself, and will lead us to God. But I do not fear to examine it carefully and to accept a great many of the findings of dedicated men who have pondered its nature for their entire lifetimes. I fear that the Church of Christ tends to worship the book, rather than the Savior; to become bibliolaters, rather than adorers of Christ. This makes their study of the Bible rather inflexible and leads them into some curious situations.

I want to mention briefly the ecumenical movement and the attitude of Churches of Christ toward it. Like any group claiming to be the only true church, the Church of Christ feels that any significant involvement with other churches is a dangerous compromise. They do not allow their ministers to join ministerial alliances for this reason. But I cannot see this quest for Christian unity in our time as an exercise in compromise. Each church is expected to bring into the quest the strength of its own convictions. Real unity will exist, but it will be unity in diversity—a very real kind of unity despite those who believe that only in conformity can there be such harmony. I deplore the unwillingness of the Church of Christ to join in this enterprise. In the face of threats from communism, from nationalistic religions, and from mushrooming materialism and secularism, it is imperative that churches seek unity in Christ so that their witness may be strong. Denominational separateness is an expense we can no longer afford.

The ecumenical movement is not really an effort to build a super church. I remember that in Churches of Christ I often heard that it was wrong to belong to a church that one did not *have* to belong to in order to be saved. In other words, there was no justification for any church if it were not the *only true church*. There is little room for freedom and diversity of opinion in such a position, of course. But this always seemed to me like saying that if my home were not the only home where true grace, love, and responsibility reigned, then I should not be a part of it. Homes do differ widely and we treasure the differences; so churches may keep their freedom and individuality without becoming sectarian and divisive. There are many ways in which differing denominations can work together in labors of love without conflicts over theology.

I have been startled in recent years about another matter: the deep involvement many in the Church of Christ have with certain social and political concerns. The identification of the Christian faith with radically conservative views in politics seems to me a distortion of the best in the Church of Christ tradition. As I always understood this tradition, the church was to maintain some detachment from such matters. This did not mean that one's faith did not have meaning and implications in such areas, but there was no effort to describe a "Christian position" in social matters and in politics.

It would certainly be tragic if persons became members of certain churches because of positions these churches take on social and political matters, rather than because of the churches' ability to lead them to firm faith in God and discipleship to Jesus Christ. There should be room in all churches for responsible conservatives and responsible liberals, both of whom see in God and in His Christ a deep and powerful basis for unity. With such a viewpoint they can be free to hold differing judgments as to how good is best realized in this life, while at the same time respecting one another.

I must say before closing that I have deep respect for the zeal and concern of many members of the Church of Christ. Paul Tillich has defined faith as "ultimate concern." Certainly Church of Christ folk have such strong concern. Disciples of Christ could use more of it. As this essay has indicated, I suspect that the *object* of Church of Christ concern is all too often a God of legalism rather than a God of love and eternal hope; but if their great zeal could be fused with the spirit and greater universality of some other kinds of Christians, it would be a happy and useful marriage.

This short essay is simply the way one man sees his past involvement in the Churches of Christ from the viewpoint of his present commitment to the Christian Churches (Disciples of Christ). I claim no infallibility for my convictions, obviously, nor do I maintain that they are representative of views held by my fellow Disciple ministers. My convictions have been born out of the crucible of my own study, some tearing life experiences, separation from many I loved, and a deep desire to know as intimately as I could the life and teachings of Jesus. Happy in my work, I am thankful for God's blessings and hopeful that He will enable me to communicate the story of His grace, love, and salvation to others.

RALPH MILTON STOLZ, a graduate of Abilene Christian College, is unique among writers represented in this anthology in that he has found himself unwilling to unite with any religious organization following his separation from the Church of Christ as a formal body. He affirms dependence upon the guidance of the Holy Spirit and moves freely among all believers.

After his graduation in 1955 from Abilene Christian, where he majored in Bible, Mr. Stolz studied at Southwestern Theological Seminary for two years (1958-60). His ministerial work in the Church of Christ includes service as an assistant minister of the Harris and Irving Church of Christ in San Angelo, Texas (1955-58) and service as an educational director for the Southside Church of Christ in Fort Worth (1958-60).

Mr. Stolz is presently a developer of commercial properties in Dallas. Married, and father of three children, he was born March 12, 1932, in Dallas.

OUT OF THE WILDERNESS

By Ralph Milton Stolz

"I did know thee in the wilderness, in the land of great drought." *Hosea* 13:5.

On Saturday morning, October 19, 1963, I was introduced to a vast new dimension in worship of God: worship in and by the Holy Spirit.

There were about 150 people who had gathered in a banquet room of the Executive Inn in Dallas, Texas, all of them active members of various churches in the city. They met once each month just to worship God, seeking a "liberty in the Spirit," and a restoration of the Holy Spirit's position as the One who should properly direct all meetings of the saints. I had to admit that my own church leaders had refused the Spirit's leadership and substituted programs and techniques of human wisdom. There was simply no other explanation for our sterile and ineffective witness.

At the Church of Christ we had just completed a study of the fruits of the Spirit as recorded in Galatians 5. My obvious lack of such qualities in spite of many years of trying to possess them, coupled with a non-acquaintance and lack of understanding of the Holy Spirit, had begun to seriously bother me. And although some of the proceedings of that Saturday meeting caused me to react with both scorn and fear, I had to confess that their acquaintance with Jesus seemed genuine and real.

I remember that what impressed me most was the boldness with which they praised God. They had such heart-felt joy and were so free-flowing in their thanksgiving to Jesus that I was pricked in my heart. I knew that I did not possess such joy or thanksgiving. And my lips never uttered such praise.

I am unashamed to thank God for the faithful witness of these misunderstood and often persecuted Christians. He used their testimony to deliver me from the wilderness of unbelief. Sanctification by means of self-effort is a horrible pit, so dark and deep that it requires an act of Divine power to lift a soul out of it. Equally binding is the miry clay of constant failure in the time of temptation. God used their love to point me to His Love which brought me out and "set my feet upon the Rock and established my goings; and he put a new song in my mouth, even praise unto our God." (Psalm 40:2,3).

I am not set to attempt doctrinally to persuade anyone to agree with me. The Father has freed me from the bondage of forcing all men to accept my opinions. But I am delighted to share my conviction that God calls men to fellowship His holiness, and that He works out this holiness in the yielded spirit of a man by His Spirit.

All my Christian life I have earnestly longed for a walk of practical holiness, but it always seemed to escape me. I thank God that he implanted such a longing, for I believe it to be a certain sign that I was born-again. But the miserable man of Romans, chapter seven, was a photograph of my life. Like a lot of men, I had begun to suspect that this was the normal Christian life, and that there was no use to expect any better.

Today I know differently. In a series of experiences that can be classed as nothing but supernatural, God led me into Romans 8, and to increasing victory over temptation. I am not so foolish as to think or claim that I have attained perfection, but beginning with my introduction to God's Holy Spirit on that Saturday morning, I have embarked upon the most exciting adventure of dominion, peace, and joy that I have ever known!

It is an adventure of communion with God; of progressively becoming more knowledgeable of Jesus; and of experiencing the power of His resurrected life. My future is wholly in the hands of God, to whom I look for sustenance and guidance.

When I began asking questions about vital faith and communion with God through the Holy Spirit, I found I was not the only one uninformed about the Holy Spirit. No one seemed really to know Him, although a few could quote a Biblical passage or two that mentioned Him. My search led me to attend various churches and to talk with their preachers. When my attendance at these churches was made known, I was contacted by my own local preacher and warned against such associations.

When I came to believe that God had illuminated my spiritual understanding, and that this heavenly fellowship is the basis for our earthly fellowship, my church began giving serious consideration to expelling me. I had no intention of leaving them for I wanted to share what seemed to me a marvelous understanding. I was not led of God to affiliate with or join another religious group, but I did gladly accept their invitations to speak and testify of God's faithfulness to His promises.

These speaking activities caused the elders of my church some embarrassment. People began calling them and asking questions about my speaking. At length they felt constrained to write the *Firm Foundation*, a Church of Christ publication, and ask them to print the charge that I had "given fellowship to various denominations," and that it was necessary to mark me "as a factious teacher of doctrines that cause divisions." I felt I was testifying to God's fulfilling His promise to give me "rivers of living water," but it was construed as "serious doctrinal heresy."

The thought of excommunication was almost unreal. But the pain turned out to be real enough and it became necessary for God to strengthen me to "go with-

out the camp, bearing the reproach." I can appreciate
the action of my brothers and understand why they
feel that I have left not only my senses, but what is
far worse, the very Body of Christ. But believe me,
although I have lost security and approval of what
presented itself to me as the "established" church, I
have never felt more secure!

When Jesus promised to manifest Himself to all
who believe and follow Him, He meant actually and
personally. The security of this spiritual communion
with Him is peace beyond understanding. Let me
repeat that I did not choose to leave the church of
my boyhood; I was forced to leave because I could
no longer exclude from my fellowship those with whom
God has fellowship. God grants an exhilarating freedom to all who thrust themselves upon Him in complete reliance. Included is an awareness of one's
uniqueness to God. The thought of loss of position,
honor and approval by my religious party was of little
consequence when compared to thoughts of approval
by God.

I now worship God "in the Spirit, rejoice in Christ
Jesus, and have no confidence in the flesh." Indeed
God is cleaning out all trust in externals. But since
many have been deceived into trusting in what they
have done (or left undone), let me be exceedingly
foolish for a moment and present my "case" for confidence. I was born into a home where Christ is professed as Saviour; trained in Sunday School from
nursery age according to the traditions of the Church
of Christ; baptized in water when twelve; and taught
by men of great Biblical scholarship at Abilene Christian College. Thus I have been fashioned according
to the perfect manner of orthodox doctrine. My family
has worked for our "Restoration Movement" with
devotion.

My manner of life from my youth up is well known
among members of the Churches of Christ in Dallas,

how that I have been zealous for God. In fervor I outdistanced many of my contemporaries, being in the front guard of the defenders of the faith. In perfect conscience and righteous zeal I have persecuted all those who differed from our accepted teachings, denying them fellowship and openly branding them as messengers of Satan sent to deceive the poor and unlearned. I truly believed within my heart that the Church of Christ was the only scripturally correct group, and I tried for five years in full-time work with two large congregations to extend her borders.

The above list of "spiritual assets" has always commended me and I have been accorded certain honors and recognition. But I have now written off all such assets and count them as so much trash. What is more, I will to lose everything that would separate me from constant communion with Jesus.

My early Christian experience does not differ from many others. I was brought up in an ordinary Christian home with an ordinary concern for the Christ. There are many exceptions, but most preachers give major emphasis to the church doctrines of organization, mission, and ritual, and leave untouched the Biblical teaching concerning the indwelling Spirit who is experienced in reality. Thus the vibrant Spirit of power is not in abundant evidence in the lives of most of us.

In the spring of 1951, when I was eighteen, I came under the conviction of the Spirit regarding sin. I did not know it was the Holy Spirit who was causing me such misgivings, but His message reached my heart. He overwhelmed me with His insistence upon my need of a Saviour. In fear and trembling I ran down the aisle one Sunday evening at the Hampton Place Church of Christ and told the preacher my story, how that I had entered church membership almost by osmosis, because my parents were members. I was no more than a "grandson" of God and He doesn't

have any grandsons! But, since I was a regular at-
tender, and had gone through a certain ritual when
I was twelve, and had led singing in the services, the
preacher suggested that I was unduly concerned. He
dismissed the service, saying he would talk with me
in his office later.

I sought at this time no "walk in the Spirit," for
I knew of no such walk. But I desperately wanted
release, and in spite of the fear that all my church
friends would scoff, or laugh, or suspect the worst, I
went to Him.

God honored my baby-trust. There were about five
young people who remained that night. They heard
me confess my faith in Jesus as Saviour. The preacher
decided to immerse me in water, but the Spirit immersed me in the body of Jesus and I was born again.
God gave me a new spirit. I went home that evening
with a great sense of relief and peace, and two months
later entered Abilene Christian College to prepare myself to be a worker for God.

The next four years were blessed years. Many warm
friendships resulted. Yet as I look back, I see that
the carnal man dominated my walk. I was born of
the Spirit, but not led by the Spirit. Jesus had brought
me out of the Egypt of bondage to sin, but I was still
walking around in the wilderness of unbelief. And this
same frustrating experience prevailed through five
years of attempting to serve God full-time with two
congregations, first in San Angelo, Texas, and later
in Fort Worth. May the Christian people of those
churches forgive me for keeping them so busy in various programs and dulling their ears with so much
carnal noise that they never had time to keep still before God and listen to Him speak. I sincerely felt that
if I kept them busy they would somehow be made holy.

It was not until after three years of this that I first
became convicted that my work was only "wood, hay,
and stubble." The people needed spiritual bread and

I was giving them a stone of mere "success techniques." However, the Spirit was not to have His way
with me yet. I decided that what I needed was more
scholarship. So I asked the Lord to let me move to
Fort Worth where I could attend a seminary. Surely,
I thought, if I could get all of the "horses and chariots"
of the Southern Baptist folk and combine it with "the
truth" of my church, then I could win the religious
battle and lead our people to complete victory! Perhaps the greatest lesson the Spirit has taught me this
year is that "it is not by might, nor by power, but
by my Spirit, saith the Lord."

The fact is that no elaborate program, no church
traditions, not even a true doctrine can make up for
the absence of the living presence of the Lord Himself. And the marvel is that we can travel so far—
singing hymns, being orthodox, hating false cults, and
keeping up spiritual appearances—without realizing
that Christ is not in our midst! It took two more
years for me to admit to myself that I was being unfair to Christ to say that I believed Him when my
life was lived according to *my* desires. Even my desire
to be a sucessful church worker was keeping me from
Him. I have learned that He is to be Lord of even
my smallest thought, so that "it is God which worketh
in you both to will and to do of His good pleasure."

At the Seminary I met a young man recently brought
out of the darkness of sin and so in love with Jesus
that he wanted to tell everyone about Him. I was
impressed with his enthusiasm and thought to convert
him. May God forgive me for all the times I have
quenched His activity in some soul by my legalistic
insistence upon some doctrine I felt necessary for
salvation.

Each time we discussed religion I was able to tie
him up in a theological straitjacket. Yet, though I
knew more about the doctrines of Jesus, he seemed
to know Jesus better than I. At the time I despaired

of converting him to what I thought the right way, but five years later he was to be instrumental in my own absolute surrender to Jesus as Lord. He had a simple faith in Jesus, in His reality, that I often envied. My faith lacked that ever-present reality; I even doubted upon one occasion the ability of Christianity to solve any man's problems. The husks of church doctrines do not satisfy one who is hungering for vital communion with God.

Since I could not, in complete honesty, persuade this friend to give up what he had for what I had, and since self-surrender was still too difficult for me, I decided I must get out of full-time church work. I reasoned that I could "make tents" and still try out my plans for leading the church to victory. This way, perhaps I could escape the nagging conviction that I needed to give up my life completely. It was an out-and-out case of running from God; a foolish attempt to hide in some far country away from His insistent demand to be Lord of all my living. I praise Him now for His unwillingness to let me go, but at that time it was pure misery.

As I left the horrible pit, I entered the miry clay. I was in one line of business after another, never satisfied, and going deeper into godlessness with each passing year. Released from the watchful eyes of the church members, I began to experiment with the passions of the flesh. But the born-again believer can never be happy in sin. I began to hate myself. My body showed the inevitable signs of a dissolute life. My former friends left me and I couldn't trust the new ones. I can say from experience that there is no fun in sin. It eats like cancer and is rottenness to the bones.

I had literally fulfilled the story of the Prodigal Son. But God heard my heart-cry and brought me out. To my surprise, however, He didn't point me back to my church organization. The fact is, He didn't point me to any church organization. He lifted the veil and set my eyes on the only answer He has for all our questions: Jesus.

Christ had said, "If any man will come after me, let him deny himself and take up his cross." The cross may be different for each man, but it is always the will of God for his life. My cross included the loss of former religious ties. I didn't seek it. I don't want it. But, with Him, I am content to have it so.

On that Saturday in October, a man named Sam Phillips was the speaker. He related his experience of surrender and subsequent baptism in the Holy Spirit. Because his church superiors didn't understand, he said, he was forced out of his ministry and in eight days he was to leave his house. In spite of my fears and the strangeness of the meeting, I found my spirit going out to him. But I was not prepared for what happened next. As Sam finished speaking, a man suddenly stood and began rapidly speaking in some language that I did not know. He spoke for only a few moments. But when he finished another man began speaking, this time in English. It was a message of hope and encouragement to Sam, but it was in the first person and ended with a "Thus saith the Lord," identifying its source. It was so appropriate and beautiful, and yet so against my beliefs, that I just stood there and marveled.

The thought that God was actually present and active through a man's voice; that He was concerned and intended to help this preacher; and that He was letting His intentions be audibly known was more than I could take into my understanding. Yet in a realm somewhere above my logic there flashed an awareness that it was indeed real. A recognition of the Divine presence, discerned in my spirit, filled me with a sense of awe and fearful wonder. It made such an indelible impact that, after several weeks had elapsed and I was dissecting and analyzing the event, I could not dismiss it.

I left the meeting engrossed with the thought of God's nearness and willingness to make Himself known. Instinctively I turned to my Bible. I went home, got on my knees, and asked God to enlighten my mind on these things. For the next three weeks I spent every available moment reading the Bible, devotionally, reverently, and prayerfully. This was in contrast to my usual hunting for proof-texts. Teachers and commentaries were not called upon. God and I were alone in His Word. To my amazement, passages which had before been puzzling began to unfold a meaning. 1 Corinthians 13, for example. I had traditionally understood this passage to teach the cessation of the gifts of the Spirit. Now a mist lifted and I saw clearly that they will cease, but only at that time when we see Him "face to face."

And Isaiah 66:1-3 almost jumped out of the page as I saw the futility of trying to "do something" for God. I saw that God is looking for men of humble and contrite hearts, not men who can boast of religious position. I was not learning just Bible doctrines. God was revealing spirit-freeing truths.

With my automobile as my prayer-closet, my Bible as my library, and the Holy Spirit as teacher and guide, God led me out of the wilderness of unbelief. He caused me to see that the root cause of all my problems was my refusal to take Jesus exactly at His word. I was going to have to lay down my self-directed life, voluntarily, and take up His Life, through the Spirit, if I were to be perfected and have peace.

It was amazing how much it hurt, how desperately my self-life fought the death it had to die. When my flesh would begin to weaken, I would pray, "Lord, don't pay any attention to my complaining. Just give me His Life." He continued His work amidst many tears. I have never been so thoroughly humbled, so reduced to ashes. He had to take my pride in my accomplishments and throw the light of eternal values upon them for me to give them up as filthy rags. He revealed to me the glory of Jesus, and I saw myself as unclean. My last fears were quieted when I really accepted the blessed truth in *Luke* 11, that my Father would never give me a stone when I asked for bread.

I considered telling of the assurances God has given me that He was guiding me, and also of the first time that I spoke in "other tongues." These would be terribly hard to accept for all who have known only the cold code of legalistic religion. But just as wonderful to me have been answered prayers, power in witnessing, dominion over the desires of the flesh, and the experiencing of some real fruit of the Spirit. These experiences assure me that God continues His work in me, not stopping with His gift of my first taste of the "powers of the age to come." And, anyway, none of these things commend me to Him and I no longer seek to commend myself to men.

The one dominant identifying characteristic of the early church was not its name, or its organization, or even its ritual of worship. It was its supernatural witness. God has individuals everywhere today who do His will, filled with Himself, by whose prayers in the Spirit He is bringing in His kingdom.

God can still use the "Church of Christ," but it must humble itself and repent of its intellectual pride. It must do this or God in mercy will have to break it, as He broke me.

DAVID DARNELL has roots that go deep in a Church of Christ past. Brought up in a Church of Christ home, he attended Abilene Christian College (1950-51) and Florida Christian College (1953), returning to the former for graduate study. He preached for Churches of Christ during his college days and until 1958.

Additional academic work followed at the University of Toronto and at Brite College of the Bible in Texas Christian University. Mr. Darnell is currently studying towards a Ph.D. in Biblical Studies at Duke University. Now minister of the First Christian Church in Fayetteville, North Carolina, he was earlier minister for the First Christian Church in Archer City, Texas, from 1958 through 1961.

MUSINGS OF A PILGRIMAGE

By David R. Darnell

All of my grandparents were members of Churches of Christ and lived out their lives in active Christian service among that brotherhood. The Will Ranciers, my maternal grandparents, were leaders of the Church of Christ in Killeen, Texas. The David N. Darnells, my paternal grandparents, were life-long leaders of Churches of Christ in Texas, including Thorp Springs, Abilene, and Sweetwater. Before her death, my grandmother, Mrs. D. N. Darnell, was distinguished as having held the longest continuous subscription to the *Firm Foundation* of any living person.

Both of my parents, the Dewey R. Darnells, were reared in the Churches of Christ; both attended Abilene Christian College; and both served for many years as active influential workers among Churches of Christ, especially at the Fifth and Marble Church of Christ in Albuquerque, New Mexico.

It is therefore no surprise that I was born into the spiritual atmosphere and nourishment of the Churches of Christ; that in 1940, at the age of nine years, I was immersed for the remission of sins in the baptistery of the Fifth and Marble church; and that throughout my youth I rarely, if ever, missed a church service on Sunday mornings or nights, or on Wednesday evenings.

Upon my graduation from Albuquerque high school in 1949, I enrolled in Abilene Christian College, at Abilene, Texas. During my first year there I decided to give my life to the preaching of the gospel of Christ. Deeply influenced by the teachings of Homer Hailey, I followed him to Tampa, Florida, in 1951, and enrolled for my last two years in Florida Christian College. In 1953 I graduated with a bachelor of arts degree, *magna cum laude,* and moved back to Texas, where I became minister of the Eighth Street Church of Christ in Cisco. For six years I preached for Churches of Christ and shared in revival meetings and fellowship with many of the leading ministers and missionaries among Churches of Christ today.

I mention these facts to show that my roots are deeply planted in the Churches of Christ. In their midst I was taught to pray and to read the Bible. There my faith was nurtured. There I was baptized into Christ. There I received my call into the proclamation of the gospel. *For all of this I am deeply grateful.* I am thankful for that little band of Christians in Albuquerque who shared with me their faith and Christian nurture; thankful, too, I am for the fellowship and love of the broader fellowship I came to know as I went to college and as I began my ministry. There are so many dear friends, too numerous to mention, whose memory now brings joy to my heart. I am thankful for the deep respect and concern for the Biblical message which I learned to share in their midst, and for the vivid sense of my standing before God which I came to know in their fellowship. I give thanks to God for this rich heritage which is mine because of the Churches of Christ.

But while there is so much for which I am thankful, there is also much among the Churches of Christ with which I cannot agree, and which I personally can no longer uphold. Since this is an essay and not a book, I must limit my statement to two broad attitudes among Churches of Christ which I have found impossible to maintain.

The first is this: *a "closed" attitude towards religious learning.*

As I grew up in Albuquerque, I was taught by my parents and my church always to be open to truth, wherever it might lead me. We had nothing to fear from any truth, they said; only half-truth and error needed to withdraw itself from open investigation and criticism. I remember well how a minister from the Christian Church came once to speak to my father about the possibility of his preaching among the Churches of Christ. He asked what he would have to preach. My father replied that he could preach the truth as he saw it. He would have to endorse no peculiar position or belief, but simply study the Bible for himself and proclaim the truth that he learned.

I rejoiced in this openness toward truth and supposed that it reflected a general attitude among Churches of Christ. It seemed to me to be the distinguishing mark between the Lord's church and the churches of men that were bound down by human, creedal limitations. Early in life I read much from Richardson's *Memoirs of Alexander Campbell*, and thrilled at his willingness to publicly and openly present his views and let them be subjected to the most able criticism that could be brought against them. Campbell, sitting in his study surrounded by the writings of leading thinkers of his day and of ages past, listening fairly and calmly to all who wished to speak, respecting others in spite of their differences from him, and yet boldly teaching the truth as he found it—this was my idea of the Christian minister's attitude toward truth. And this, I believed, was the attitude that marked the Churches of Christ: an open willingness to hear and to be heard, a refusal to reject others unheard or to burn books, and eager readiness to proclaim the Biblical message in the arena of human thought, and an impulse to lead mankind in its struggle to understand the deep problems of human existence in the light of God's revelation.

But as I reached out beyond my home congregation and sat in classes at Abilene and Florida Christian Colleges, I soon came to realize that the Churches of Christ did not hold such an attitude towards religious learning at all. In the preaching and teaching which surrounded me, I found myself exposed to one viewpoint and one only—a viewpoint hammered into my thinking from every angle. The leading thinkers from the Churches of Christ were not joining the great battle with unbelief, they were not leading mankind in wrestling with the crucial problems that cry out for religious answers in the twentieth century: economic and social injustices, war, national and racial unrest, population explosion, division in Christendom, the need for and scarcity of depth psychology and pastoral counseling, Biblical criticism and comment. They were writing no significant books. They had withdrawn themselves from the mainstream of human thought to build up and defend their peculiar, narrow party beliefs—to fight nineteenth century battles in our twentieth century world.

When we studied what we called "Denominational Doctrines," we did not study them sympathetically, to seek to understand and appreciate what earnest and sincere Christians believed and were trying to say—not at all. We studied them to know how to answer them, and how to convert them to our conception of the truth. We could easily dismiss a giant like John Calvin and his *Institutes,* or Augustine and his works, by a passing reference to their being the sources of most denominational heresy! And this while we ourselves refused to grapple with the great problems which they had sought to solve!

In all of this we were being taught to defend and maintain the peculiar tenets of our party in Christendom, but we were not being taught to be open, to go on an intellectual pilgrimage ourselves, to seek to wrestle with the great issues of Christian faith and human destiny on our own. Our constant assumption was that we already "had the truth," and we either refused to listen to the voices of others or else we studied their views only to point out their weaknesses and reply to them. It was never a matter of really seeking to understand them; we never allowed for the possibility of actually changing our own viewpoint because of what we learned; and our approach to religious knowledge was therefore sterile and irrelevant to the crying needs of our world.

This same attitude was expressed constantly in almost every class I attended. (There were exceptions, and for them I am very thankful now, although at the time I suspected those very teachers of being "modernists"). We were always told which books, and which men were "sound"; and we quickly learned which scholars, and which positions were "poison," to be handled only with extreme caution and suspicion. We learned to study and appreciate scholars who supported our own assumptions and conclusions; we looked upon all others as pathetically lost and hopeless, even though we had never read a line from their own writings.

I remember well the first day of a class in Biblical Criticism, in which the instructor began his lectures by asking, "If you were the Devil, attempting to destroy the Christian faith, how would you begin?" Someone replied, "By attacking the confidence of people in the reliability of the text of the Bible." The instructor said that this was correct, and with that comment we began our investigation of textual criticism—as the Devil's fiendish attempts to uproot Christian faith and destroy belief in the Bible! And we were the ones who said that all "sectarians" looked at things through colored glasses!

Examples could be multiplied, but this will suffice to illustrate what I am saying. Churches of Christ have taken upon themselves a closed attitude towards religious learning. In so doing, they have isolated themselves from the rest of the Christian world and they are no longer making an effective contribution to the thorny problem of division among Christians. By adopting this closed attitude, they have unconsciously taken to themselves an unwritten creed and they have become victims of the need to promulgate their own peculiar way of thinking, instead of speaking in Christ's name to the real problems of this century. Religious learning has ceased to be the challenging adventure of dedicated disciples who would speak His word to their world; it has been sidetracked onto the endless defense and promotion of a narrow, irrelevant kind of Christianity. It is for this reason that I think the Churches of Christ no longer constitute a "Restoration of New Testament Christianity," as they so forcefully proclaim. Instead, they have substituted a legalistic and artificially patterned religion for the rich, dynamic truths of the New Testament.

And this "closed" attitude towards religious education has violated the very basis of real learning. When one begins by assuming that he has all the truth and then proceeds to defend that assumption without ever really questioning it, or honestly listening to other views of "the truth," he may get his prejudices bolstered but he is not going to get an education. Real education questions and examines all assumptions, listens sympathetically to all proposed solutions, and seeks out new truths for itself. Real religious education is "open." It reaches out into the mainstream of human thought, both present and past. It does not assume its conclusions before it gets to them. It exposes its assumptions and opinions to the full light of public, critical examination. There, in the open arena, in honest give and take, genuine faith is born and takes root.

During my college days I studied New Testament Greek; after graduation I did further work in the language. As I began to read the Greek New Testament in earnest, I began to wonder about the words *psallo* and *psalmos*. The more I inquired into their usage, the more I became convinced that these words describe singing accompanied with an instrument, and that they do not at all imply *a capella* singing. Because of this, I decided that I could no longer preach that people who sing with musical accompaniment in Christian worship are acting in violation of the New Testament, and I so informed the elders of the Lake Worth Church of Christ in Forth Worth, where I was preaching. I did not want to make an issue of this in any way, and our agreement was that I would make no mention of it in my teaching and preaching. The only change that I made was that I stopped saying that the use of the instrument would condemn people.

Over a year later, I was asked to teach Bible in Fort Worth Christian College, and accepted. But the week before school began, I received a phone call from the president of the school, asking me what I believed about instrumental music. I told him how I felt, and stated that I certainly did not want to make this an issue in any way, or even bring the matter up in my teaching. But this did not satisfy him. He asked me for a direct answer, yes or no, as to whether a man who used the instrument in Christian worship would "go to hell." When I answered, "No," I was told in reply that my services could not be used at Fort Worth Christian College. I had failed in my "creedal examination." It was not a question of my loyalty to Jesus Christ, or of my ability and desire to teach the Bible. I had refused to utter the proper shibboleth; I could no longer be trusted to teach our young people the Bible.

When I informed the elders at the Lake Worth Church of Christ that I could no longer keep silent on this matter, they told me that I could not again speak in the pulpit of the church. The following Sunday, a visiting minister "tried out," and at the close of the service I was allowed five minutes to say goodbye to the congregation I had loved and worked with for some three years.

Needless to say, this was a heart-breaking experience for me and my family. But what seemed at that
time a very terrible experience seems to us today one
of the most blessed events of our lives. That separation
broke the hold of a narrow, unwritten creed on our
minds. I became, in a very real sense, a "free man
in Christ" on that day. I began to turn from a narrow,
sectarian view of religious truth and to drink afresh
from the living water. I ceased to call any man, or
group of men, "Master." I entered into a joyous fellowship with *all* who honor Jesus Christ, and I began
the arduous but joyous process of working through
to my own theology in the open arena of world-wide
scholarship and criticism, looking to the original docu-
ments of our faith with a freshness that continues to
thrill and challenge me to this very day.

So it was this basic attitude towards religious learning that led me to reach out beyond the exclusive fellowship of the Churches of Christ. The question was
whether learning should be conducted in a closed,
creedal atmosphere, or in open, questioning discussion.
I chose the latter. I would choose it again today.

The second attitude which separated me from those
with whom I had so long worked was this: *a lack of
love and a suspicious fear of other Christians.*

For some three months following my dismissal from
the pulpit of the Lake Worth Church, I continued to
attend Churches of Christ regularly. But it was never
the same again. I was no longer "Brother," but "Mr.
Darnell." I never again was asked to lead in prayer,
nor recognized in any public way. I was only told
that I ought to repent and "come back."

I was doing construction work at the time, and one
rainy day, when we could not work, I went by the
seminary building of Texas Christian University and
spoke to the dean of the seminary, Elmer Henson. In
the course of our talk he told me that I could attend
classes there and that they would expect me to "ham-

mer out my own theology"—that what I believe and preached would be a matter between me and God, but that the teachers and library of the University were mine to use. At the time, I didn't believe him. Surely they held some peculiar view that I would have to espouse! But as I began taking courses, and as I continued with my B.D. program, I came to realize that the dean had meant every word. Here were devout Christian men who were interested in helping me grow as Christian scholar and minister, but who did not consider it their responsibility to predetermine the conclusions at which I would arrive.

One day I went to Archer City, Texas, and preached for a Christian Church. I did so with much fear and trembling. How it shocked my ears to hear the singing with piano accompaniment! What a shock to hear the whole church sing "Happy Birthday" to those who had had a birthday that week! How different it was to what I had known! But those warm-hearted ranch people listened eagerly to what I had to say, despite the fact that much of it was new and strange to them. I went back to that little church for almost four years. I found there acceptance as an individual even though we differed about many of our understandings.

This was the beginning of a wonderful experience for me. I began to reach out to know and share with Christian people and ministers from varying religious backgrounds. I found in them the same fruits of the Spirit of God that I had found among Christians in the Churches of Christ. I came to know that the Holy Spirit of God is much larger and more all-encompassing than the narrow bounds I had found erected among Churches of Christ. And I began to see that what is really wrong among the Churches of Christ is a sickness of heart, a fear of others who differ with them on doctrinal issues, and a lack of love for such persons. It is a kind of spiritual paranoia that looks with suspicious distrust on those who are different, that demands credentials before it will give its love, and that destroys all possibility for real growth in Christian thought.

One evening I went to the home of a very well-known evangelist for the Churches of Christ and met there four other prominent ministers for a lengthy discussion. We talked of the meaning of Acts 21:17-26, and I said I thought that this, and other passages, show clearly how first century Christians felt free to continue observing the religious customs of the Law of Moses. One of the ministers, a speaker for the "Herald of Truth" (a national television program), said: "But if that is true, how can we condemn the Catholics?"

Indeed, how can we condemn the Catholics? Is that an essential to our faith, that we condemn others? Why should we not look for grounds for fellowship, understanding, and agreement instead? Why not build bridges instead of walls?

As I look back now, this attitude seems to me to be decisive in my religious pilgrimage. Churches of Christ do not teach or practice genuine love for their religious neighbors. They do not really come to know their religious neighbors, nor to share sympathetically in their religious longings and convictions. They have so separated themselves that they are left "high and dry," unable to enter into real dialogue and constructive criticism with other churches. They miss the strengthening which such mutuality would give, and which all of us so desperately need. After all, if we are right about necessity of weekly communion, and of immersion, why should we run away and hide? We cannot convince others of the correctness of our plea by refusing to know them—really *know* them. If we do indeed have, as we say, the one workable plan for Christian unity, it seems odd that we should pull away from all others who claim to be Christians and spend our time quarreling and dividing among ourselves.

It is my constantly growing conviction that we disciples of Christ have nothing to fear from encounter with others, whether in an academic way, or in religious fellowships. Rather, we have much to gain. Only when we truly know others can they begin to hear what we are saying. We gain nothing by isolating ourselves and refusing to listen to anyone else. There is so much for us to gain that we cannot afford any longer the tragic luxury of self-centeredness and separation from our fellowmen, whose loyalty and devotion to Jesus Christ are every bit as strong as our own.

As the years have passed, my family and I have grown to know the validity of God's providential guidance of our lives. We have been enriched spiritually. Our faith has deepened year by year as we have learned to love, and appreciate, and share with Christians of Roman Catholic, Greek Orthodox, and Protestant backgrounds. Our love and respect for Jesus Christ is much stronger today than it was ten years ago. Our belief in the validity and relevance of His teaching has grown yearly. It is our deep longing and prayer that our brothers in the Churches of Christ will be blessed and used by God's Spirit, and that new days of fellowship and understanding in the light of Jesus Christ lie before all of us. In a world desperately needing the Light of Life, may we, the "light-bearers," not let our candles be hidden under any of our creedal bushel-baskets!

> O God, forgive all of us our pride, our self-centeredness, our divisiveness, our ignorance, and our lack of understanding. Cleanse our hearts from suspicion, mistrust, and party-spirit. Fill us with deep, out-reaching love for all Thy children, our brothers, and a deep faith that will leave us unafraid. Open to us anew Thy truth, that the Spirit and power of Jesus Christ may be in us, and that we may speak Thy Word to the crying needs of our lost world. Give unity to all who love and honor Jesus Christ as Lord, that in oneness of mind and purpose we may proclaim the gospel to the nations. In His name, Amen.

MARTHA ARMSTRONG was educated at two Church of Christ schools, Gunter Bible College and Thorp Springs Christian College, and has been deeply interested in the Restoration Movement most of her life. For many years a member of the Pearl Street Church of Christ in her hometown, Denton, Texas, Mrs. Armstrong is now a member of the First Christian Church.

Since coming to Denton with her husband, Boyd, in 1916, Mrs. Armstrong has opened the doors of her home to many gospel preachers, both from the Church of Christ and from the Christian Church. A recent high spot in her life occurred in late 1965 when she visited the National City Christian Church while President Johnson was in attendance. Seated just in front of him, she was impressed when he went out of his way to shake hands with a soldier who had placed membership with the church that morning.

The Armstrongs have reared two sons, Kenneth and Oramel, besides a grandson who lost his own mother at an early age. Owners and operators of the Armstrong Nursery for years, the couple are known in Denton for having one of the most beautifully kept lawns in the city. Mrs. Armstrong was 70 on October 17, 1965.

THE HEART HAS ITS REASONS

By Martha Armstrong

It seemed like an impossible task to talk with a minister of the Church of Christ about *leaving* the Church of Christ! After all, I was the third generation of my family to be brought up in the Church of Christ, and how could I leave the church of my parents and grandparents?

This was the question that burned in my heart one pleasant summer evening in 1927 when Brother W. F. Ledlow was again a visitor in my home. For thirty years Brother Ledlow had been a prominent evangelist among the churches, and he had served as president of the old Thorp Springs Christian College. He had taught at the University of Texas and was at that time on the faculty at North Texas State Teachers College. Even though he was a man of great learning, his faithfulness to God and to the church could not be questioned. He was often in our home, and I had grown to admire him greatly. If a member of the Church of Christ could have a "priest," then Brother Ledlow was my "priest." He was tender and loving, like the One he served, and I could talk with him about anything—yes, even about leaving the church of my fathers.

I spoke softly, as if to speak of someone's death. "Brother Ledlow, I simply cannot stand it any longer. I must, for conscience' sake, leave the Church of Christ. I suppose I'll go to the Christian Church in search of the peace I long for."

If I was surprised that I could ever say such words, rooted and grounded in Church of Christ thinking as I was, I was even more surprised at what Brother Ledlow said to me in reply. These were his shocking words:

"I understand, my sister, I understand. If it were not for the many people I have baptized, who look to me for guidance and encouragement, I would take the same step you are taking. I would have left the Church of Christ long ago were it not for these people; but if I should leave, I fear they might become discouraged and lose their faith in Christ. By staying, however, I have lost part of my own family. It is a sad thing. I understand why you have decided to do as you are doing."

Hardly anyone could have been more firmly rooted in what we called "the New Testament church" than was I. Immersed by Horace Busby when I was only twelve, I went on to attend the old Gunter Bible College under N. L. Clark, and Thorp Springs Christian College under A. W. Young. I heard most of the prominent evangelists of those days, including G. C. Brewer, Thomas Milholland, Jim and Gus Dunn, G. H. P. Showalter, R. L. Whiteside, Cled Wallace, Foy Wallace, Jr., and Foy Wallace, Sr. The preachers who were "running a meeting" at our congregation often stayed with my husband and me, or at least took a meal or so at our table. I recall with fond memories the extended visits of G. C. Brewer during at least two meetings in Denton.

At both Gunter and Thorp Springs I was thoroughly grounded in sound doctrine. Brother N. L. Clark was a dedicated man of God, and I learned to love and respect him deeply. It was at Gunter that I first met Brother Ledlow. He came there as a grown man with a family, but with only a second grade education. I admired him for his willingness to sit with children in order to get a common education. I admired him even more as he went on from there, under terrific difficulties and with almost no encouragement from the brethren, all the way to a Ph.D. from the University of Texas. In those days a Ph.D was a rarity, and for a Church of Christ minister it was unthinkable.

Gunter Bible College was the last word in sound doctrine. Everything was done "according to the Book," and it was here that I witnessed my first brotherhood fuss. The question was whether it was scriptural on the Lord's day to ring the school bell for the gathering of the saints who met in the school building. This question was thoroughly aired, with lots of scripture quoted by both sides, and it was finally decided that it was unscriptural to have sounds of an *instrument* bellowing forth from the belfry to summon the saints to the assembly. One might conclude that we were a bit narrow-minded at Gunter! But I learned my lessons well, and I loved the old school.

I was 32 years old, married, and had a growing family when I decided to leave the Church of Christ. Why did I finally leave? It was because of years of embarrassment and harassment—and a freedom so limited it often became downright enslavement.

I say *embarrassment* because some of the finest people in our community were scolded for being "sectarians" whenever they were kind enough to attend our meetings. *We* never attended *their* services, for they were "in error," and so, when they visited us, we berated them soundly, naming their particular church and showing how their doctrines were wrong and ours right.

I say *harassment* because I was continually subjected to the notion that *we* were right and *all others* were wrong. I grew up believing that we were "the true church" while all others were "the denominations." We were careful to speak only of our ministers as "gospel preachers"; all the others were "sectarian preachers." Even if a preacher of the Christian Church visited with us, he was treated as any other "outsider," no matter how pious and dedicated his life. Whenever "a sectarian" came to our services, the word was passed along to the evangelist, and the visitor was sure to get skinned. This deeply grieved

and embarrassed me, but I endured it for almost half
a lifetime, and might have continued enduring it had
it not been for Foy Wallace, Jr.

Brother Wallace came to Denton in 1926 as the minister of the Church of Christ in that city. He was
young, handsome, intelligent, and arrogant. He came
at a time when I was maturing as a Christian, studying and thinking for myself, and becoming increasingly uncomfortable with the view that we were the
only Christians. Sunday after Sunday I listened to Foy
Wallace as he strode back and forth across the ros-
trum, profusely quoting the Scriptures (which he must
have known entirely by memory since he hardly ever
used his Bible) and "skinning the sects" as only he
could do. The more I heard him, the more resentful
I became.

He became to me the sum and substance of all
resentment toward our negative religion. All the
preachers were not like Foy Wallace, Jr., but his attitude and behavior were nonetheless consistent with
what the Church of Christ stood for, as well as with
the image it had with the general public. The "outsiders" thoroughly understood the Church of Christ
viewpoint: that we thought of ourselves as the only
true church and the only Christians, and that all besides ourselves would go to hell. I cannot see that this
image has changed any since 1932, unless perhaps our
preachers are now saying the same things a little more
subtly.

With Foy Wallace in the pulpit, I simply could not
stand it any longer. I had to leave. If I could have
been exposed more to men like G. C. Brewer, Horace
Busby, and Jim Dunn, it might have been a different
story. But even with these men the viewpoint was
the same. They simply were more subtle and more
gentle. Yet despite the narrow views they were genuinely Christian men.

I left in order to be a free woman in Christ. I felt

that I was in bondage in the Church of Christ. I can explain what I mean by telling more about W. F. Ledlow, who tried to be a free man in Christ. When he was holding a meeting in the little town of Valley View, near Denton, he called on the local Presbyterian pastor to lead a prayer. It was like a shattering clap of thunder out of a clear sky! We members were all shocked and amazed, and we could hardly listen to the prayer because of what had happened. And yet the brethren seemed to appreciate it, however surprised they were. I was then a young girl and worked as the town's only telephone operator. For days after that the phones buzzed all over town, and "the sectarians" delighted in telling about "that Campbellite preacher that called on Brother Baker to pray."

Brother Ledlow had to pay for such transgressions, of course. Not only was he criticized for fraternizing with the sects, but also for getting an education. Even though he sacrificed both pride and comforts to return to elementary school after becoming an adult, and stayed with his studies through the years until he finally earned the Ph.D in his fifties, his brethren (especially preachers and editors) offered nothing but ridicule. He was "written up" in the pages of the *Firm Foundation* as some kind of heretic. He was highly respected at the University of Texas (a professor there wrote a lofty eulogy of him for the *Firm Foundation* when he died) and at North Texas State Teachers College (the dean delivered a high tribute at his funeral), but his own brethren were constantly harassing him for being different. His constant theme as a preacher was the wonderful love of God, and the beauty of His grace to us through Christ. He spoke of Christ with great reverence, as if His presence were a living reality. His preaching and conversation were much different from most of his fellow ministers. And *he* could understand why I just had to leave, even though he chose to stay.

Since beginning work on this personal message I have recovered the December 6, 1932 issue of *Firm Foundation* from the bottom of an old trunk. The paper is filled with tributes to W. F. Ledlow (I recall resenting such tributes from a paper which had been so critical of him). I wish to quote from one of these testimonials to Brother Ledlow, written, by W. W. Freeman:

> Brother W. F. Ledlow for twenty-five years found his progress in religious thought hindered by preachers of less learning who easily capitalized their traditional loyalty at the expense of his reputation among conservative brethren. The student of religious history knows the travail of all religious reformers, and Ledlow was well able to interpret generously the envious opposition and criticism sometimes met, heard or felt. He never became bitter, for he knew from his own growing experience the good intentions of critics.

This is what I mean by being enslaved. A church that is so cramped in its ideas that a respectable minister in a community cannot be recognized in its services without causing a commotion is an unfree church. Except for the time Brother Ledlow called on that Presbyterian to lead a prayer, I have never witnessed any visiting minister called on to do anything in the service of a Church of Christ unless he, too, were a Church of Christ minister. Even to this good day the Church of Christ will not treat a Christian Church minister as a brother in Christ. If he dares to go among them, he will be treated as any man of the world would be.

And when Brother Ledlow attempted in a brotherly way to reach across the barriers that divide men, not only in recognizing ministers in other churches but in his general attitude, he was, as Brother Freeman said, "hindered by traditional loyalty."

Well, that is why I left. I did not want to spend my life with a church that impressed everyone with the idea that they think they have all the truth while others have none, that they are the only Christians while all others are sectarians. I left because I wanted to be free and to think for myself. I had been stifled long enough. I left for conscience' sake. I left for the same reasons that some give for leaving the Roman Catholic Church. To me there are striking resemblances between the Roman*ism* and the Church of Christ*ism* that engrossed me for half a lifetime. Both suppose that they alone have the truth; both suppose they are *the true church* while others are heretics; both are right about everything, infallible interpreters of the Word; both teach their people to stay away from other churches; both are authoritarian and dogmatic; both suppose their priests or ministers are the only true servants of God; both claim that the way to unity is to join them and to do as they do in every particular.

So that is why I left, for the same reasons people sometimes leave the Roman Catholic Church. I can belong to Christ, and love Him and serve Him and be free in Him without belonging either to the Roman Catholic Church or to the Church of Christ. I must admit that there now seems to be one important difference between these two churches: the Catholics seem to be changing, while I can see no real cracks in the wall of Church of Christ exclusivism. The Roman priest here in Denton is president of the ministerial alliance. Years ago I could not have imagined such a thing. Even now I cannot imagine the Church of Christ ministers in this city having anything to do with any ministerial alliance. Even yet, I suppose, they would dare not join such a group lest they be "written up" in somebody's paper as Brother Ledlow was years ago.

That the Church of Christ attitude is still what it was a generation ago was made evident to me recently as I lay on a hospital bed extremely ill. A lifelong friend and an ardent Church of Christ sister sent me a kindly greeting with an attending note that read: "Read your Bible." That is always good advice, and of course I do read the Bible. But knowing the good sister's religion as I do, I knew quite well what she meant. She was calling my attention to the fact that I am in the wrong church, where there is instrumental music, and that I had better read my Bible and get right before it was too late. Her advice was well-intentioned; that is the way the thinking of her people goes. If people would just read their Bible, they reason, they would all believe like the Church of Christ. The conclusion must be that if we disagree it means we are either ignorant or we do not want the truth. I myself shudder to think that I might once have been so cruel.

For some thirty years I have belonged to the Disciples of Christ, so I am still a part of the Restoration Movement, which I love. Do I agree with everything in the Christian Church? I should say I do not! Then why do I not leave them as I did the Church of Christ? Because I am now free to think for myself. They do not try to push anything down my throat, and I can worship with people who believe Christians can be different and still love each other and work together.

While I still resent the narrowness in the Church of Christ, I certainly love these brethren and have no bitterness toward them. I have always been thankful that I attended Church of Christ schools and had contacts with so many dear Christians. For the sake of the young women now growing up in the Church of Christ, as I did long ago, I would urge the leaders to have more feeling for those with whom they differ, and to work more realistically for the oneness of all Christians. The Church of Christ's plea for unity will never be listened to seriously until its leaders learn to share in conversation with others. It is rather childish for any of us to suppose that we have so much of the truth, and others have so little, that the answer to division is for everyone else to become like us.

I would urge those with whom I once worshipped to extend to others the graces they assume for themselves. We must not suppose that a person is either ignorant or dishonest if he does not see things the way we do. There are such things as *honest* mistakes, even when men are searching eagerly for truth. And must we not keep in mind that *we*, too, might be wrong about some things? We want others to be gracious enough to understand that our errors are unintentional. Let us judge only to the extent that we wish to be judged. The truth is that most of us are what we are because of the circumstances of birth. Most of us would have been a Mormon or a Moslem if we had happened to be born that way. Few of us are what we are because of a long, painful search for truth. It is not gracious of us, after accidentally being born into the "right church," to be severe on those who have done exactly what we have done—remained where the circumstances of birth placed them. Let us learn to be kind and gentle.

Our Lord assures us that "If the Son shall make you free, you shall be free indeed," and this has been my blessing. My cup overflows. While I am not a woman of letters, I might quote Pascal in a further effort to summarize my testimony: "The heart has its reasons that reason knows not of." I have tried to set forth a reasonable account of what I did and why I did it. If I have failed in this, then let us simply say that it is a matter of the heart. It was for Him that I did as I have done. Most of those in the Church of Christ will disagree with me. They will choose to remain where they are. This is as it should be, and may the Lord bless them as they serve Him. For them, too, I say: "The heart has its reasons. . . ."

WILLIAM P. REEDY was reared in the Church of Christ and became a minister at 21. After several years of traveling in various states as an evangelist, he moved in 1915 to Long Beach, California, where he served the Church of Christ for eight years as a located minister. In 1923 he moved to Los Angeles, helped establish the Southwest Church of Christ, and worked with this congregation for thirteen years. While there he earned a B.A. and an M.A. from the University of Southern California.

Attempting to share the new insights resulting from these studies, Mr. Reedy found himself described more and more often as a liberal. He taught Bible at George Pepperdine in its first year of existence as a college, but soon found himself at odds with the administration. Although urged by some to seek a less restricted religious environment, he hesitated to break old and dear ties. He chose to involve himself in studies again, spending three years at Yale Divinity School, from which he earned the B.D. degree.

Returning, Mr. Reedy found himself unable to change attitudes and decided at last to switch his religious affiliations. He was granted ministerial status by the Congregationalists and worked first with one of their churches near San Diego. Given a later assignment with the Temple Street church in Los Angeles, he spent some ten years in service before resigning because of declining health. He now teaches a class in a congregation of the United Church of Christ. He is chaplain of his service club and active on committees.

WHY WE CHANGED

By William P. Reedy

Editor's note: This explanation by William P. and Jessie T. Reedy appeared in the *West Coast Christian* in 1945. Mr. Reedy has added recent comments in a postscript at the end of this essay.

My "changed attitude toward the church" has not come about suddenly without due consideration of all that is involved in such a change. It is not the result of any one thing which has happened at——— church or any other church. It is not due to any real or fancied slight or wrong done to me. Moreover, I was not motivated by an ambition for place or prestige or distinction, nor moved by "preacher pride," nor by concern over loss of "professional" status.

No, it is far deeper than that. I will confess that I have struggled for years within myself, trying to reconcile certain practices and attitudes of the Church of Christ, as I know it, with the Spirit and teaching of our Lord and His apostles. When it came finally to the point that I had to say and teach what I sincerely believed in order to be true to myself and to my God, I found that I could not do this without being criticized, ostracized, and regarded as "off color," unsound," "not loyal," and the like.

The church has devised a formal pattern, to which one must conform even to stereotyped phraseology, if one is to retain favor with "those who seemed to be somewhat" (Galatians 2:6). A deep conviction which told me that I must be true to what I believed was right and what God wanted me to do, moved me to rebel against such intolerance. I could not be true to myself and to God, and remain within the fellowship of the Church of Christ.

Yes, I have changed. I am glad I have changed.

But to many, this is an unpardonable sin. There are those who speak with pride of their "unchanged and unchanging position." I do not think it is smart to be smug. But there are some who consider change-lessness a mark of "loyalty," of religious superiority. Those who are entirely filled with the spirit of con-servation have no spirit of exploration or advance.

I offer no apology for having changed my mind on many subjects. I am not ashamed to admit that my mind is not yet made up on many other matters. I do not feel that my present judgment represents the last word. No one has heard the last word—it has not been spoken. I hope to outgrow tomorrow what I think and preach today.

Ultimate truth is, of course, fixed, but my conception of truth is not fixed nor should it be. If it were, all possibility of growth would be ended. Within the Bible itself there are great growths—great develop-ments in the basic concepts of truth. The attitude of the Church of Christ at this point constitutes her gravest error. She has crystallized her concepts of God, Christ, the Bible, the "Plan of Salvation," and all the rest, into a closed pattern, and by so doing she has identified these concepts with the total truth on such subjects.

This is wrong. It is not right to identify truth with our concepts of truth. This attitude on the part of the Church of Christ makes her intolerant and causes the good that is in her to defeat the best which she might have. This attitude closes the door against all prog-ress, and forbids the voicing of any newly discovered truths or the expression of honest convictions. This is exactly what the Pharisees did in our Saviour's day. This was the cause of His break with them.

All churches (fellowships) are human in many re-spects, including the Church of Christ. And in so far as they are human, they are imperfect and sinful. It is therefore obvious that all have truth—and all have error. I have, frankly, not found it very satisfying or fruitful to compare and try to determine which church is nearest to the "divine pattern," seeing that one is "nearer" in some things, while others are "nearer" in other things. One will never find a body, a church, a fellowship, which is right in every thing and at every point, and I do not think that one can ever belong to any church and believe or accept everything it teaches and practices.

I did not do this when I was in the Church of Christ fellowship, and of course there are certain tenets held in Congregationalism (my present commitment) to which I personally do not subscribe. But in the Congregational Church there exists an attitude which tolerates, even *appreciates*, points of view which are different. So, if I want to believe in immersion and preach it, I may, without being disfellowshipped. Could I follow that principle in the Church of Christ as we know it? In the Congregational Church one does not have to subscribe to any creed or dogma or to any certain belief other than that of belief in Jesus Christ as Lord.

All the while that I was identified with the Church of Christ I was preaching unity and practicing division. The unity of Spirit, or unity in diversity, which is in my judgment, the unity taught in the Bible, is all but unknown among those who are with the Churches of Christ. I feel very strongly that the Congregational Church comes "nearer" to demonstrating what the real unity of the Spirit is, as this is taught in the New Testament, than any other fellowship I know.

Now let me hasten to say that I do not consider that I have left the Church of Christ, nor departed from the faith. As a matter of fact, all I have done is to shift my fellowship from one group to another. I have not believed for a long time that the Church of Christ, as we knew it, could boast properly that it was the only true Church of Christ. As a matter of fact, it is not. No group can make such a boast; no group can claim to be the one and only Body of Christ.

Yet it does not follow that Christ has no Body. He does have indeed. The Body of Christ is bigger and better than any one group or all of them together. I would not even say that all of the churches, as such, constitute the Body of Christ. I do not know who all of God's people are—in this world, in the USA, or in any local fellowship. I imagine the names on any one "church book" are not the same as those God has enrolled in heaven for that church. But we are not the judges of that.

I admire the words of a dear brother in Christ, written a few years ago. They are appropriate and I here make use of them. He said: "Some one may say that the church consists of the 'faithful,' or 'loyal.' But who are they? We must remember that no one is absolutely 'faithful' or 'loyal.' We can be so relatively, not absolutely. Some are very faithful in some respects, and very unfaithful in others." All are unfaithful somewhere. When we try to answer the question: Who is 'faithful' or 'loyal,' we are faced with the fact that every one will raise or lower the standard according to his measure of understanding as to what is important as a basis of fellowship and as a formula of salvation. In the Church of Christ alone, as we know it, we can get twenty-two or more different answers. In calling a divided church to unity, it would depend on who was doing the calling as to what the *basis* of unity would be!

What modern, model church reaches up to the brotherly love, benevolence, unity, missionary zeal, personal purity of life, discipline, radiance and joy of the true, divine church of God? Why isn't it just as fatal to lack apostolicity in one respect as to lack it in another? Why is it more important to restore the "form of doctrine"—outward, objective forms—than to restore the true "spirit" of the early church?

I believe that I find some of God's people every-where, in all of the different fellowships, and that the Spirit of Christ which prevails in them will invariably find expression. This Family of God, this Church of Christ, is the all-glorious Body which concerns itself with great issues and does not parley over matters of trivial import.

As to the name, just this comment: if one thinks of the church in terms of that heavenly, spiritual Body which is composed of all redeemed, past and present, in heaven and in earth, and not in terms of some small group or sect or denomination, he will have no difficul-ties. It is the former thing that is the Church of Christ, and to this truth all Christians will give assent.

I must say, quite frankly, that while it is most likely that the first church did not use instruments of music in their worship, I am not convinced on that account that it is wrong. I shall never again make an issue of it. I feel now that it should never have been made an issue. The slogan has been, "Where the Bible speaks, we speak; where the Bible is silent, we are silent." Actually, the Church of Christ has often spoken where the Bible is silent, and has often been silent where the Bible speaks.

One good brother whom I esteem very highly wrote and "wondered if I could say with Paul, 'I have kept the faith.' " All I may say is that I still love the Church and the Bible and my reverence for God is deeper and more meaningful and my peace of soul is far more satisfying now than it ever was. I would have you remember, however, that Paul left the Jewish Church and was himself accused of "persuading men to worship God contrary to the law." (Acts 18:13) Just as he broke with the traditions he had known so that he might lay hold on the new truths that had come to him, so have I. I cannot regret it.

I might have continued in the Church of Christ fellowship. I turned down many invitations from brethren and churches in various places. Why did I not accept, continuing to preach and teach within the limits of the "brotherhood"? One good and influential brother told me frankly: "You will be accepted if you will go back and preach the sermons you preached twenty-five years ago and hold protracted meetings as you did twenty-five years ago." That, of course, I could not do. This ought to be obvious to anyone. The gospel of Christ means infinitely more to me now than it did twenty-five years ago. How can one "go back" when the whole genius of the gospel says "go forward"?

I want to be tolerant toward sincere Christians whose convictions differ from my own. This does not mean that such tolerance dissolves convictions. On the contrary, Christians must have positive convictions about the truth. We all need to grow in our comprehension of truth. But this is not possible without tolerance, without the spirit of respect for a clear, personal faith on the part of another.

I share the feeling and spirit of an honored contemporary who writes, "I have come into the Congregational-Christian Churches seeking for a more flexible and adequate instrument with which to work for the Kingdom of Jesus Christ on earth. I have come hoping for that combination of honesty and freedom, breadth and tolerance, and spiritual earnestness and passion, which is by no means always wrapped up in the same bundle. Thus far I have been disappointed in my search. I am grateful beyond words for a communion which is as wide in its welcome and outreach as the Spirit of the Living God. May I say in conclusion that no one should be compelled to depart from his inherited church home base in order to find freedom, tolerance, and spiritual vitality."

POSTSCRIPT

During the years that have intervened since I wrote the foregoing in 1945, much has happened to me, and

I believe all to the good. The change I made at that time was not a sudden impulse nor an afterthought. It was the result of several years of inner conflict and prayerful meditation . It was a struggle against an attitude of narrow provincialism and arbitrary theological dogma, a struggle against an attitude that assumed it was right while all others were wrong. In my earlier years I was led to conform to and accept a narrow pattern of thinking which would allow little or no change.

I was glad then and I am glad now that I changed. I have never regretted it. True, I had many friends among the Churches of Christ whom I loved and still love. But many of them did not understand. I was forced to be true to myself and to my God. My conscience forbade me to allow myself to be a slave any longer to narrow, arbitrary and inflexible patterns. I challenged this attitude; I dared to be a non-conformist. This, predictably, was my undoing with the Churches of Christ. I was sorry, but I was under compulsion to be a free man in Christ Jesus my Lord. I could no longer consciously be pressed into a mold of human traditions. The liberty I yearned for and sought out gave me a sense of dignity as a man; I no longer felt as if I were a puppet manipulated by pulling of strings.

The change that I made has done much for and to me. I have experienced a sense of freedom of thought and action, both in and out of the pulpit, that I did not and could not have before. I was relieved of a load that I had tried to carry for years, but with misgivings. The human spirit must not be bound. Freedom under God is the most precious possession one can have.

Let me hasten to add that one must not take freedom to mean license. Freedom under God has a built-in quality called responsibility. It will not allow one to follow every whim and fancy or "cunningly devised fable." It will not permit one to use a passage of Scripture out of context simply to bolster a preconceived idea. It allows one to search and find the truth that is vital to the needs of one's own soul. Freedom with responsibility leads one into a genuine encounter with the Eternal.

With this freedom I have found the Bible more interesting and challenging than ever. My appreciation for it grows from day to day as I search for deeper insights into the meaning of life. I plead that many in bondage to dry legalism can find a new lease on life if they only will. We should look at the Bible as a library, rather than a codebook. When one interprets some fragment and gives special emphasis to it, a schism is started.

An overly-literal interpretation leads us far afield, too, although the most ardent fundamentalists find this hard to accept. Men of old had experiences with the living God and they tried to tell us in song and story, myth and fable, symbol and law, parable and metaphor, what the meaning of life was. Their revelations were guidelines for generations to come. From them we learn about the age-long search for the living God. In my present church framework I have enjoyed a wonderful freedom to study the Bible fearlessly and to see how Jesus emerged into history as the true light of our world. I shall be forever grateful.

Soon after I made my change, I received ministerial status in the Congregational Church. I was given a cordial welcome and was assigned to a church. I entered the pulpit without the slightest misgivings. I was able to preach what I believed to be the truth of the Gospel. If any disagreed, I was not ostracized. All of us were happy in the exchange of ideas. There seemed to be none of that fear and insecurity I had so often seen before. With grand cooperation from the congregation, I was able to give renewed hope and to put the group in position to be a greater force for righteousness in the community. No one can imagine the thrill of this experience unless he has struggled through long years, as I did, in frustration because of authoritarian attitudes.

Most importantly, I came to know God in a personal way after I realized clearly that I was an individualization of the Eternal Spirit. This consciousness sustained me in many dark hours of blighting circumstance. Some may think that all this would have come anyway in the passage of years, but I am deeply convinced that in my own case the blessings came because I escaped the restrictive world in which I had so long lived. I am a free son of God today, responsible only to Him who will be the final judge of us all. What comfort, what peace of mind, what joy of life came to me as a result of my decision, no one can know for sure except those who have been brave enough to step forth and "stand fast in the liberty wherewith Christ has made him free."

ROBERT MEYERS has been a minister in the Church of Christ for twenty-five years. He attended Freed-Hardeman College (1941-43) and graduated *summa cum laude* from Abilene Christian College (1948). He was awarded an M.A. from the University of Oklahoma (1951) and a Ph.D. from Washington University (1957). During World War II he took special courses at Oxford University and at Salisbury, England.

Now serving as a professor of English at Friends University in Wichita, Kansas, Mr. Meyers has taught at the University of Oklahoma, at Washington University, at Harding College, and at Stetson University in Florida. He has twice received $500 awards for excellence in teaching.

Mr. Meyers is entering his sixth year of service as a minister for the Riverside Church of Christ in Wichita. He is a book reviewer for the Dallas *Times-Herald* and writes frequently for religious and educational journals.

BETWEEN TWO WORLDS

By Robert Meyers

I remember clearly when it all began. There were those long Sunday afternoons in Uncle Clell Martin's living room on that farm in Oklahoma. I was a boy of five or six during those summer months and I could not understand what it was that my father and my uncle talked about so seriously and for so long. Their voices would rise stridently at times to startle me out of some childish reverie. Later, in the languorous evening, they would talk quietly, exhausted by their efforts to communicate. What I did not know then was that Uncle Clell was converting my father to a new set of religious values.

My father had been a Methodist first. His parents had worshipped with less inhibition than most do now. They "got the Spirit," as they explained it, and they were never greatly interested in arguing the logic of it. They put their hands upon their hearts and said, "Jesus lives here. I know He does. Nothing you can say will make me change my mind about that." I was taught later to ridicule that way of talking as "better felt than told" religion, a foolish thing when compared with my own legalistic, argumentative head-religion.

As my father grew up he turned away from the religion of his parents. Perhaps some parts of it embarrassed him. Perhaps a friend influenced him. He tried the Baptists for a while. He embraced the Dunkard faith. He believed for a time that he had gotten religion in the cornfield and owed no one any further explanation than that. By the time he married my mother in Oklahoma, he was adrift religiously. She was a member of the Christian Church.

Uncle Clell, who belonged to the non-instrument Church of Christ, won my father to that church. From the time I was six I went to its services every time the doors opened. I can still vividly recall my parents' beaming pride as I sang lustily the first church song I ever learned, "Bringing in the Sheaves."

Always a person of strong enthusiasms and deep attachments, I became the most loyal Church of Christ youngster imaginable. I liked to read, so I read all the literature that church provided. I learned the arguments by heart and recited them glibly. It was not long before I could vanquish any of my childhood playmates with barrages of prooftexts. What a heady joy it was to dominate them so completely! I was secure and, as I now see, religiously arrogant. I could not imagine the ignorance of people who knew the Church of Christ was right there in their own towns but who persisted in being Presbyterians or Nazarenes. I was discouraged from visiting them, so I knew nothing about them firsthand. This did not matter, of course, since my own preachers assured me that they were foolish folk who did not seem to care how far they missed God's teachings. Once or twice I sneaked off to sit on some back pew and watch them curiously, but no one had helped me know how to understand them, so I only laughed. May God forgive me.

I was baptized at eleven under the preaching of the famed Negro evangelist of the Churches of Christ, R. N. Hogan. I began immediately to memorize huge batches of prooftext verses so that I might crush the "sectarian" religionists as R. N. Hogan crushed them. The fact that he required police protection around his tent in Okmulgee, Oklahoma did not make me wonder about his methods. I merely thought it exciting and believed that the true man of God must expect hatred from other and false religionists.

The initial fervor diminished after I had learned several hundred verses but at fifteen it returned with extraordinarily powerful impulse. Will M. Thompson, a famed old debater, became minister of my local church. Under his guidance I began preparing bulging notebooks loaded with points to make in debates with "sectarians." Ultimately I had a stack of these over a foot high, laden with typewritten clinchers. For example, after each one of the thirty-six arguments made by Baptists who believed in the impossibility of apostasy, I would have an extensive reply which made the argument appear puerile. I would not have confessed it then, or perhaps recognized it fully, but my answers were replete with quibbles, dodges, evasions and satirical sallies. I used many exclamation marks and happily jotted down all the clever ways Will M. Thompson taught me about winning debates and emerging as party champion. There seemed to me to be no more glorious life imaginable than that of defender of the faith against all the diseased Protestant sects that differed from my church.

In my junior year in high school I began to preach. It was a wonderful experience. By the time I graduated from high school, I knew what my life was to be. I rejected the senior year of football so that my father would buy me a desk, a typewriter, and some books. When Abilene Christian College offered me a four year scholarship to play football (mainly because they hoped a friend of mine, an all-state player, would be thus encouraged to come), I turned it down and went instead to Freed-Hardeman College, a Church of Christ Bible school in Tennessee. I had heard that ACC preachers spoke too often on "love" and were therefore, perhaps not so "sound" as those at FHC. Above all else, I wanted to be sound.

Packing all my debate notebooks and my small library, I went away to Tennessee. I engaged in those mock debates which were often featured at our Monday night preacher's club. I enjoyed excellent "appointments" in area churches. H. A. Dixon, a minister in Jackson, Tennessee and later to become president of Freed-Hardeman, once predicted from his pulpit that I would be one of the great defenders of the faith (i.e., Church of Christ interpretations). This heady praise only confirmed my conviction that I was on the glory road, destined under God to point the way to all who had an ear to hear.

Then came Pearl Harbor and, shortly, three years of military service. The experience was cataclysmic. Not because I was in mortal danger in foxholes. On the contrary, I was lucky enough to be a newspaper and radio correspondent and seldom in any real peril. But because I moved outside my isolated Church of Christ world for the first time in my life. I met Seventh Day Adventists whose devotion to Christ put mine to shame. I met Presbyterian lads in whose hands I placed my life with full confidence. I watched thirty different religious groups worship together in army chapels, carried above their differences of tradition by a consuming faith in Jesus Christ.

Suddenly my beautifully structured world began to crumble. I lay in a pup tent or on a cot many nights and cried quietly into my pillow because the house I had built was falling apart. I had intended it for a lifetime and it had seemed to excite the admiration of all my friends, but it was being shaken to pieces. The friends around me in the army were bound to be lost; I knew this because dozens of preachers had told me so. Yet how had it happened that they had such beautiful faith in Christ? How was it that their characters had taken on more of the Christ image than mine, the defender of the faith? I could beat any of them into subjection in a few minutes with my formidable array of prooftexts and my debate-sharpened mind, but I began to feel hollow after the victories. I had some fellow Church of Christ friends to chum with for a time. A few were splendid fellows, generous and loving; others were pinched and narrow, unhappy and loveless. I saw clearly that my religion did not inevitably turn out superior people. And I saw that religions I had been taught to scorn as hopelessly false often turned out men more Christlike than any I had met before.

Always an avid reader, my reading now underwent a marked change. Whatever I had read of religious material before, I read from a fixed position. Whatever differed from that position, I rejected easily without being troubled. Now, with my certainties tottering, I opened up to what I read and discovered a completely new world.

One day in North Wales, lying on a straw mattress, I read a book I had bought in a bookstall in Llandudno. It was called *In Quest of a Kingdom*. I would doubtless have bought another volume of Hardeman's Tabernacle Sermons, since I had already memorized five volumes of them, but none were available. No Church of Christ material was to be had. I think this study of parables by Leslie Weatherhead was seminal for all my later development. In it I caught a glimpse of a kingdom of right relationships which surpassed in loveliness anything I had ever heard about in my boyhood church meetings. The book is no profound theological study, but it was the door through which I walked into a new country. I shall always remember gratefully the debt I owe to the London preacher.

From that time, I read everything of the kind I could get my hands on. And I observed people. I watched from jeeps, trains, and marching columns as peasants worked the turnip fields in Belgium under gray skies; I watched old women grabble in GI slop cans for fragments of food; I watched desperate boys and girls try to live life quickly before a bomb or a bullet ended it. And I knew that none of them had ever heard of my Church of Christ, southern style, USA. They might as well have been on Mars.

How would I be able to return to the pulpit and condemn them all with a wave of the hand? How could I accept, even silently, my church's dictum that there was no hope for those who had not reached our plateau of understanding? I knew at last that I could not. I came home to finish my work at Abilene Christian College, but this time as an English major, not as a Bible major. I saw all things in a new light. I preached, but it was apparent to those who heard me that I was no longer a candidate for honors as defender of orthodoxy.

The years of graduate study followed. My doctoral work involved me heavily in textual criticism. I could not help but see how it transferred to Bible criticism. Families of manuscripts, kinds of textual errors, collations to show divergencies in parallel accounts— such academic exercises I applied to Biblical problems. My emphasis on Renaissance literature led me deeply into study of the sixteenth century as the great age of English translation of the Bible. I shared all these things with the Central Church of Christ in St. Louis, a wonderful group who were not afraid to listen and to encourage. We studied the development of the canon, the apocryphal books, the variant accounts in the gospels, the transmission of the English Bible, what inspiration is, and kindred topics. I felt that in such an atmosphere any Christian might live and grow.

But the time came when I felt I must return to Harding College, where I had taught two years before beginning my final studies in St. Louis. Dear friends at Central doubted that I could find sufficient freedom there after the invigorating years away, but I believed I had to return. A twenty-year dream of teaching in a Christian (i.e., Church of Christ) college was not yet dead. I had known dear friends and fine students at Harding. Perhaps, I told myself, I can continue to grow there and share with others in frank talks the attitudes I had come to cherish.

I was wrong. Over a period of three more years I

learned slowly but surely that I was no longer party champion enough to be happy at Harding. When the president of the school, under urging by some members of the Bible faculty, decided against renewing my contract, he acted wisely. As for me, perhaps nothing has happened to me that was better than this severance. I might soon have reached a point where cherished friendships and hallowed ties would have urged me to compromise convictions and fall into line.

I came to Friends University in Wichita where the forty-two different denominations represented accepted me as fellow Christian and teacher. Having had previous experience with students and ministers of my church, the president and dean of Friends asked me only one serious question: "What is your attitude toward other believers?" I understood at once. They wished to know whether I could work with them and accept them, or feel constantly prompted to convert them to my understandings. I explained that my attitude was one of acceptance, that I did not hold to the infallibility of any pattern of interpretation, and that I could happily maintain my personal convictions while talking without rancor to those who held others. On such a basis the Quaker-sponsored liberal arts college employed me. The Riverside Church of Christ in Wichita engaged my services at the same time and permitted me to talk freely and openly about all kinds of Christian concerns. The two labors have teamed well and have been immensely fruitful and satisfying to me. At the time of writing this essay, I count myself one of the fortunate few who are genuinely happy not in one job, but in two.

To this point I have deliberately made my essay autobiographical because in other places I have tried to set forth structured criticisms of the religious system in which I grew up, and in which I remain. But I must now honor one of the purposes of this book by speaking explicitly of the failures of that religious system which so long held me in thrall.

I know now that I suffered tragic losses as an adolescent. I was taught narrowness by those who fashioned me. Deliberately isolated from other religionists, I came to think of them as insincere people who simply did not care enough about being right. By speaking always only to those who approved what I said, I lost the priceless opportunity of receiving correction from older and wiser heads whose religious orientation was radically different from mine.

I was taught to be so completely sure that my interpretation of the Bible was the only correct one that I could not even understand that the Bible is one thing and individual interpretation of it quite another. It was excruciating to learn that my interpretation might be as fallible as the next man's and when, one day, I finally knew this, my rigidly authoritarian religion crumbled into dust.

The plasticity of children is a beautiful and a terrifying thing. I idolized those authoritative and impressive-looking men who told me that my religion was the only correct one, and that no other could be of use to any man. I accepted happily my amazing good fortune at having been born into a family which embraced this true religion. Sometimes I was puzzled to observe how much of our time was spent in fighting among ourselves over proper interpretations. I knew that we had "the truth" and that any deviation from that was heresy, but occasionally I was not sure when we had a violent internal quarrel just which of the two parties was the "right" one.

It now seems terrible to me that I have no distinct memory of having been impressed, ever, with the extraordinary transformation which the Spirit of Christ may work in a person. I was impressed by fluency, by authoritativeness, by strength of conviction about interpretations, by party solidarity—by many such things—but I had to be grown before I found the full, glorious flowering in the human spirit of the Spirit of Christ. The result was that my religion was a head religion. It performed precise exercises, added and subtracted with marvelous skill, and knew how to dissect and analyze. But its only rapture was the joy of conquest and of correctness. It knew no other warmth.

Little was said about love in the sermons of my boyhood, except that the vital thing was that if one loved God he would *keep His commandments*. I can hear that now, ringing down through the years of my growing up. The first and greatest commandment was inevitably reduced to this, and only to this, and I knew scarcely any other possibilities for it. Those ministers who occasionally tried to explore the limitless suggestiveness of the word "love" were called "soft" and said to be in danger of losing their doctrinal purity if they were not careful. Little was said of the Spirit and its indwelling power, except that we were warned that it operated only through the written word and must never be considered as mysterious in the least.

We split terribly once, when I was a lad, over whether it was right to have a kitchen in the church building, or whether it was right to use literature in our classes—I have forgotten which. But half of us went one way, and half the other, and the town hid its face behind its hand and smiled at our quarreling. It took fifteen years before the bitterness of that tragedy wore off, and by then hardly anyone knew anymore what had started it all.

Yet I repeat that my tragic loss was not in learning this, that devout men may divide sharply over interpretations. My loss was that I met no singularly gracious human being whose whole life literally sang of Christ. I knew firm men, fighting men—but no man whose spirit had been so changed by Christ that he could, under almost any circumstance, display serenity of spirit and true greatness of character. And because of this I was into my twenties before I knew that the essential thing in religion is the difference it makes in the character of a man. When I began to meet such beautifully humble persons, to my great shock they often came from groups I had been taught to view as heretics because their interpretations of the Bible were unlike mine.

This little history is not unique. Thousands have shared it. It is, in fact, of importance only because it *is* common. It suggests that many of us have an initiation moment when we see all our training in a new light and for the first time evaluate it by a different set of standards. My new standard became this question: Is the winsome personality of Christ visible in this man? If it were not, despite lifelong church attendance and constant talk of dogma, I concluded that something basic was wrong with his kind of religion. He was part of a body from which the spirit had departed. He had a form of godliness and talked persuasively of what was scriptural and what was not, but he had no power within him to change his personality. Truly believing His word that by men's fruits they are to be known, I found my closed system of religious values radically altered.

My church's approach to religious unity failed me. I once saw a newspaper cartoon which summed it up classically. A parson is shown sitting on a stump in the moonlight, looking out across a meadow. Beneath the picture is his reflection: "Christian unity seems simple enough—all it would take is for everybody to agree with us." Most of us are not quite so honest as this parson is made to be. Instead of saying "agree with us," we prefer to say, "All it would take is for everybody to agree with the Bible." That is, we equate our views with the Bible itself, and thus we become unassailable. No professing Christian wants to argue against the teachings of the Bible, and if a sect is convinced that its views, and the Bible, are identical, its position becomes invulnerable.

When my people talk of unity, most of them really mean conformity. Conformity decrees that everyone shall be exactly alike, thinking and talking alike about all the party interpretations. The total experience of humanity proves that this is not possible, but we go on talking as if it were. Only conformity can be enforced. An environment can be created in which it is easier to keep quiet than to express a dissenting view. Once it is clear that men who think for themselves will be persecuted as violaters of tradition, all the more cautious men in the group will be careful to keep their true views hidden. This is the unity of conformity. It is the only unity some religious groups know. But it is sterile, and ultimately self-defeating.

The other kind of unity, unity in diversity, unity of spirit and purpose, is the only sort that works. Everywhere in the world are Christian people who see the true image of Christ in other believers. Spirit is linked with spirit in a holy bond of fellowship. When such Christians find that they differ about interpretations, they are not so much dismayed as intrigued. They seek to learn from one another, respecting convictions on both sides. They talk *with* one another, rather than *to* one another. I know well what the difference is, for I was trained to use my opponent's comments as welcome interludes in which I might be fashioning my next attack upon his position.

It is ground for hope that so many of us manage to unlearn this approach to religious differences. Exposure to Christian neighbors from other church groups often upsets the applecart. We find it hard to believe that such persons are wilfully stubborn, as our ministers tell us, and we are uneasy about what attitudes to hold toward them. It puzzles us that God should have granted to a few of us the proper interpretations, while denying them to millions of other in-

telligent and honest men. It is this deep-rooted honesty
and the uncertainty that arises from it that cause
many thousands of my people to stand ready to be
more charitable when they find ministers who will
permit them to be.

I have been appalled by the degree of party spirit
within my church. Like John in Mark 9, we seek too
often to build a fence around a clique and leave on the
outside all the people who do not possess our special
knowledge. Like John, we have yet to learn that the
Kingdom of God has God's dimensions, and that those
who truly do the works of Christ, and bear the fruit
of the Spirit, belong to Him.

John was looking for labels. He wanted to be sure
that the man doing good belonged to the right party
and wore the right name. Jesus said, in effect, "Look,
instead, for actions, attitudes, and dispositions. When
you find the things which delight me—mercy, justice,
faith—welcome them. Do not meet them sourly." How
desperately my people need to learn this lesson. We
often find it hard to be glad about work done by those
who do not share our interpretations. We talk of
missionary enterprises without happily acknowledging
the ground-breaking done earlier by Adventists, or
Friends, or Methodists. After other religious groups
had gone in and gentled the local population, civilized
them, and introduced them to Christ, then we went
in with what we were pleased to call the "real truth"
and sought to convert them to our own particular set
of dogmas. This is painful to confess, but it is the
best way to purge ourselves of the shame.

Christ once met a Roman, a pagan according to
Jewish standards. He said of the man, "I have not
found so great faith, no, not in Israel." I have sometimes tried to imagine the reception this remark would
get among some of my people today. If Christ were
to make this statement about some religious group,
it is quite likely that one of us would reply, "If the

man has so much faith, why is he not a member of the right church?" Some of us have come that far in bigotry.

One of our greatest needs is to realize to what degree most of us are prisoners of our heredity and environment. We like to think that we make our own choices, but the truth is that only a small part of our commitment in any area is the result of deliberate choice. I know Southern gentlemen of strong religious drives who simply cannot throw off all the racial prejudice bred into them. Other men find it impossible to be completely unbiased about politics. Try as they will, they over-value evidence on the one side and under-value it on the other. Religion is not different. People as wise as ourselves, and quite as sincere, are honestly unable to accept all of our views. If we are to rule all such people out of the Kingdom because they cannot share our interpretations, we elevate ourselves into judges and announce ourselves as keepers of the gates of Christianity.

We have failed through being inconsistent in our assessments of others and of ourselves. We emphasize the weakest positions of those who differ with us, minimizing their strengths until it is clear that no sensible person could possibly believe that way. At the same time, we overlook our own deficiencies and exaggerate our strengths until we appear far more superior than we are. Our refusal to measure our best against the best of others, and to confess our weaknesses as no less obvious than theirs, puts the lie to any claim of objectivity which we make.

A year or so ago I read in the pages of one of our widely circulated church newspapers a story about some nuns at a Roman convent who disgraced themselves by getting in a fight. They pulled at one another's garments and had to be subdued. The implication of the report in our paper was that here was proof of the perfidy of the Roman Catholic Church.

What else could one expect to come from a group in such hopeless error? Yet a more sympathetic view might explain such conduct quite differently. I recalled the sudden, unreasonable fights that broke out among my soldier colleagues in war time when they had been cooped up together too long. I pitied the nuns, who undoubtedly were shamed and embarrassed because of their lapse.

And then I remembered the Church of Christ minister in Texas who floored one of his elders with one looping punch, but whose lapse was never reported in the editorial page of this newspaper. And the Church of Christ minister whose three-time robbery of a supermarket and subsequent prison term was never once thought of as proof that Church of Christism is a perfidious religion which could only be expected to turn out robbers.

It is not wrong to throw the mantle of charitable silence over the failings of our own. But to say nothing of *their* defections while we trumpet loudly the defections of those who differ with us, this is abominable. To print gleefully the tales of a Baptist minister who runs off with a choir girl, but to keep conspiratorially mum about that minister of ours whose cottage meeting activities resulted finally in life imprisonment for double rape—this is to cheat against all rules of gentlemanly or Christian conduct. We must not use human failures among our religious neighbors as proof of their doctrinal errors, when human failures among our own people are hushed up and forgotten.

But all these things will pass. A great change is in the air. Those who have vested interests, who would have to reverse a lifetime of word and action if they moved across to another world, are fighting desperately to isolate my people from these ideas. They must preserve the system, because it is under the system that they have grown powerful and prominent, and it is under the system that they can enjoy the heady excitement of guarding orthodoxy and punishing those who offend. But "our little systems have their day," as Tennyson affirmed, and God is greater than they. Our system has had its day and we are, even now, poised between two worlds.

Our system is our apprehension of God's eternal truth; it is forever partial and incomplete. We are fragments; only our Lord is whole. But once we have humbly confessed this, we may do much good. With a membership of more than two millions, the Churches of Christ can exert influence for good in a world which urgently needs all the moral leadership it can get. But no large group will ever listen seriously to an organization which refuses to credit others with Christlike graces. It will be only when we acknowledge readily the sincerity and wisdom of those who differ with us that we shall fulfill whatever destiny God has for our particular group to work out.

It must be apparent that I am hopeful. The Church of Christ is historically a very young group, still in the adolescent stage of growth. I say this despite the sweeping assertion that this particular group dates itself from Pentecost. The truth is that our traditions have evolved from the Campbell-Stone movement on the western frontier in the early nineteenth century, and this makes us young. I realize that nothing quite so angers an adolescent as being reminded that he is one, but sober analysis supports my analogy.

Like the adolescent, we have been quite unaware of our past and of our debt to those who went before us. Like the adolescent, we have been unaware of those around us. An adolescent tends to be all wrapped up in himself, knowing little of what others do or think. The church I grew up in was like this. My friends and I cared nothing of what other religious groups did, because we were self-sufficient and self-contained in our own little world of religious exclusivism. Once or twice we ventured out, but so thoroughly trained had we been that we merely ridiculed what we saw.

But there is no cause for dismay about adolescence. It passes at length into maturity. Many of the religious groups in America today which pride themselves on their maturity were once just like this. Religious groups are really much like humans in their growth. They begin by being born into a big world which cares little for them, and takes scant notice of them. Consequently, they huddle closely together and formulate their "group language" and get acquainted with a set of group beliefs. This gives them a sense of security, and is pleasant.

By and by, as adolescents, they pass through the feelings and attitudes I have just described. But eventually, such groups mature. This is happening now to my own people. It is painful. We have "growing pains." But the general rise in levels of formal education, and a wider knowledge of different religious parties, is slowly but surely changing us. We are growing up. Nothing can stop it. And adolescents may think that nothing is better than childhood, but no really mature person would trade what he has for the tyranny of adolescence again.

Thousands in the Churches of Christ are profoundly disturbed already by the aridity which authoritarianism produces. They are apathetic when their preachers speak to them only the time-honored platitudes and party clichés. The time is ripe for the beginning of a slow, massive turnover. I have no doubt that it is underway. I am glad to see it begin because I so deeply value my heritage in the Church of Christ. Friendships beyond assessing have come to me through my association with these people. I have no intention of leaving them so long as one of their churches is free enough to hear such compassionate strictures as fill the pages of this book. I join my voice to that of every writer here in pleading for that better spirit which is not only possible, but which is already in existence

in many places among our people. I echo their plea
that we shall learn how to differ from others in mutual
love and respect and that God will lead us, together
with *all* Christians, into fields of greater Christian
service than we have yet known.